WOMEN AND RESISTANCE IN THE EARLY RASTAFARI MOVEMENT

WOMEN AND
RESISTANCE
IN THE EARLY
RASTAFARI
MOVEMENT

D. A. DUNKLEY

LOUISIANA STATE UNIVERSITY PRESS
BATON ROUGE

Published by Louisiana State University Press
www.lsupress.org

Designer: Mandy McDonald Scallan
Typeface: MillerText

Cover image: *Unshackled*, by Irica R. Dunkley, 2020. All rights reserved.

Library of Congress Cataloging-in-Publication Data

Names: Dunkley, Daive A., author.
Title: Women and resistance in the early Rastafari movement / D.A. Dunkley.
Description: Baton Rouge : Louisiana State University Press, [2021] |
    Includes bibliographical references and index.
Identifiers: LCCN 2021004089 (print) | LCCN 2021004090 (ebook) | ISBN
    978-0-8071-7569-9 (cloth) | ISBN 978-0-8071-7627-6 (pdf) | ISBN 978-0-8071-
7628-3 (epub)
Subjects: LCSH: Women in the Rastafari movement—Jamaica. | Rastafari
    movement—Jamaica—History—20th century.
Classification: LCC BL2532.R37 D86 2021 (print) | LCC BL2532.R37 (ebook)
    | DDC 299.6/76082097292—dc23
LC record available at https://lccn.loc.gov/2021004089
LC ebook record available at https://lccn.loc.gov/2021004090

FOR IRICA AND THOMAS

CONTENTS

ILLUSTRATIONS

ACKNOWLEDGMENTS

Writing a scholarly book is never entirely an individual achievement. The process normally involves the support of people inside and outside academia. This was certainly the case with the research and writing for *Women and Resistance in the Early Rastafari Movement*. A diverse community of people, including colleagues, friends, and family, gave invaluable insight, advice, and inspiration that proved essential to the development of this book.

While there were moments when I thought the project would perish because of the difficulty locating sources that directly addressed women who joined Rastafari during its first three decades in the 1930s through 1960s, insight and advice from colleagues and friends, for example, helped me to find alternatives, such as primary sources that involved these women in some way that was meaningful to the project. Documentation at the archives in Jamaica, Britain, and the United States on Rastafari interactions with the British colonial state in Jamaica and on Rastafari's community of Pinnacle and African Reform Church in the 1940s and 1950s were a significant part of my close reading for information that pertained to women.

I am grateful to the diligent staff of the Jamaica Archives, the National Library of Jamaica, the British National Archives, and the Smithsonian Institution's Museum Support Center in Suitland, Maryland, for their assistance with finding primary and secondary information in the colonial government records, newspapers, and anthropological research on the 1930s through 1960s. The anthropology section of the Smithsonian's Support Center, led by Jake Homiak, an avid anthropologist and collector of Rastafari artifacts, provided me access to Carole Yawney's voluminous uncataloged papers, among other items in the Smithsonian's impressive collection. Yawney herself was a Canadian anthropologist whose work on gender issues in Rastafari marked one of the significant turning points in the scholarship on the movement in the early 1980s. I also found email correspondence between Yawney and Barry Chevannes in the 1990s, which brought back fond memories of my work with Chevannes as his undergraduate research assistant. As is well known, Chevannes, a Jamaican anthropologist, wrote one of the most prominent scholarly books on the Rastafari movement. The Smithsonian's Support Center also gave me access to the raw footage of interviews with early Rastafari women done in the late 1970s and early 1980s, interviews conducted by anthropologists Renee Romano and Elliott Leib, among others. Leib also kindly consented to my use of the unedited footage of the interviews.

An interdisciplinary group of scholars from the University of Missouri, the University of the West Indies, and the University College London also helped to improve the structure and clarity of my arguments and bolster my knowledge of secondary sources related not only to Rastafari, but to women and gender studies, Black resistance, Black nationalism, Black socialism, and Black religions. I must thank my colleagues who were particularly generous with their time in reading the chapters. Wilma King and Flore Zephir were the earliest readers of the chapter on Tenet Bent. I had also presented early iterations of this chapter at the 2015 conferences of the Caribbean Studies Association, held in New Orleans, and the National Council for Black Studies, held in Los Angeles, and received helpful feedback from audience members, including Caribbean theologian Delroy A. Reid-Salmon and Caribbean historian Ula Y. Taylor.

At the same time, I am grateful to Martha Kelly, David Schenker, David Amponsah, Mamadou Badienne, Christopher A. D. Charles, Raymond Ramcharitar, and Wilton Lodge, who read and provided me with invaluable feedback on different chapters. I am very grateful to the Department of Black Studies and Research Council of the University of Missouri for their generous start-up funds and grant, respectively, that enabled my research trips to Miami, Jamaica, and Britain over the course of 2014 through 2018. I did interviews in all three places, in addition to examining archival documentation in the latter two. I thank Jenny Keegan of the Louisiana State University Press for her interest in this book and especially for recognizing that Caribbean history expresses much of the integrated history of the Atlantic world.

I am also grateful to the anonymous reviewers for suggestions that strengthened the book.

I appreciate the help from the many people outside of academia who directed me to private documentation and provided interviews for this book. These individuals include members of the early Howellite organization and the International Peacemakers Association, formerly the African Reform Church of God in Christ, which were both formed before Jamaica achieved its national independence in 1962. Montinol Howell, Audrey Lewis, Florence Stewart, and Yvonne McLean provided interviews and helped me to locate other early women and men of the Howellites, who I interviewed about women and the early development of the Rastafari movement. Other interviewees who helped to make the book possible include Alphonso Gallimore, Delrieta Simpson, Gerald Lloyd Downer, Canute Swaby, Geraldine E. Fong, Adassa Campbell, Besentie Montague, Stanley Haughton, Douglas McKay, Burnett Hall, and Jonathan Reid.

Karl "Dippy" Vernon accompanied me to conduct several interviews in Sandy Bay in Clarendon, Jamaica, several of which he also efficiently transcribed. Besentie Montague gave me a warm welcome to the Peacemakers Association compound at Green Bottom in Sandy Bay. She also allowed me to survey records of the organization, including its financial documents. Their preservation of so many documents and photographs that had originated in the 1950s and 1960s is truly commendable. The material was helpful in understanding the colonial and Jamaican government records I had examined at the archives in Jamaica, Britain, and the United States. Montague further facilitated my research with an invitation to attend their church services and the opportunity to speak at the podium on one such occasion. I spoke on the value of maintaining their archive.

I would also like to thank my mother, Miss Joy, who showed me the agency of a poor Jamaican woman from a tender age. Underestimated from youth, she was, nonetheless, able to navigate abuse and poverty and invest in my education. She recognized that education was indeed one of the surest routes out of the persistent poverty of most of the citizens of postcolonial Jamaica.

Finally, the most important contributor to the materialization of this book is my wife, Irica, who unconditionally encouraged and supported me throughout the journey of writing it. She carefully read every chapter and made many invaluable suggestions, in addition to creating the painting used on the cover of the book, while navigating the challenges of having a young child and teaching social studies at the middle-school level. Needless to say, she knows more about women than I will ever be able to know, and it helped a great deal that her mother, Miss Cutie, was a Rastafari practitioner and a Jamaican. I dedicate this book to Irica and our jovial and affable son Thomas, who lifted my spirits during much of the research and writing process that produced this book.

WOMEN AND RESISTANCE IN THE EARLY RASTAFARI MOVEMENT

Introduction

Resistance and Early Rastafari Women

In August 1934, Delrosa Francis, a Rastafari woman of Seaforth district in the parish of St. Thomas, Jamaica, was charged by Robert Powers, a district constable, for assaulting a policeman and disturbing the peace of the public. The charges resulted in a trial, with Francis organizing a total of seven witnesses, including four women, Rachel Patterson, Francella McNish, Gertrude Nathan, and Amelia Gordon—all of whom vigorously supported Francis's attempts to defend her rights to justice and fairness. Francis, they asserted, was innocent and should be treated fairly instead of being treated as an "outcast" of society because of her Rastafari identity.[1] The witnesses argued that Powers infringed on Francis's rights to freedom of speech and worship. In their account, Powers was the one who was guilty of assault and disturbing the peace. In September 1934, Francis and her seven witnesses would submit written petitions for "fair justice" to Sir Arthur Jelf, the interim governor of Jamaica.[2] They maintained that Francis's case was unfairly adjudicated, as it was presided over by justices of the peace—locals of the community who were not only known to Powers but also colluded with him to have Francis and her supporters imprisoned. Francis and her witnesses wanted the resident magistrate, a professional judge, to try the case because they believed that he would be objective. They also claimed that after the trial Powers arrested the witnesses because of their support of Francis. Essentially, the petitions implicated agents of the British colonial government in injustices against poor Black people and asserted that the petitioners expected redress and would not relinquish their rights under Jamaican law.

Francis's case is just one of the examples of the resistance or the actions, including the assertion of human and civil rights, taken by early Rastafari women to protest injustice and oppression caused by discrimination against their Rastafari identity. However, the absence of empirical research on these women, especially those who were a part of or influenced by the Howellite understandings and who developed and promoted their own understandings of Rastafari as well, has unfortunately helped to maintain the impression that they were docile and submissive to men within and outside of the Rastafari movement. The Howellites, named after Leonard Howell, had the largest number of followers, whether men or women, of the original Rastafari movement, which originated in Jamaica in the early 1930s. As recently as 2012, an article in the *Jamaica Observer,* one of the island's main newspapers, asserted that in the early years of the Rastafari movement, the 1930s through 1950s, "the profile of the Rasta woman was in general very low-keyed."[3] Such understanding of early Rastafari women not only persisted for more than a decade after the Jamaican independence in 1962; it helped to perpetuate the distortion of the history of the early women, resulting in the "obscurity" that historian Lucille Mathurin-Mair identified as affecting mostly subaltern women in Caribbean history.[4]

In light of this obscurity, later historians, such as Verene Shepherd, have sought to recover the agency of these subaltern women. But as Shepherd herself has noted, it is an "ongoing archaeological project."[5] This book is a contribution to this project. It is a contribution that was realized through a close examination of the available historical documentation and oral sources on early Rastafari women. While government documents and newspaper reports from the colonial period aided this study, interviews of early Rastafari women and other members of the movement form a critical part of its basis as they are essential to understanding early Rastafari women and their agency. As noted by Maureen Rowe in 1980, a dire need existed for "further research" on early women of the movement, which must entail identifying "the specific factors which brought these daughters to RastafarI" using not only archival documentation, such as government and police reports, church records, and newspaper reports, but also oral history sources featuring the voices of early women.[6] Similarly, Makeda Silvera, in writing in an "An Open Letter to Rastafarian Sistren" published in 1983, also indicated the need for Rastafari women's inclusion in scholarship: "We are rarely called upon to articulate our position and worldview."[7] These were valid points that represented longstanding views of both early and younger generations of Rastafari women who encountered marginalization and male domination. Early women, however, were unfortunately peripheral to the growing body of scholarship on women in the movement that started in the late 1970s.

Understandably, much of the documentation created about early women proved elusive for scholars as most of these records were either destroyed or suppressed by the colonial government. Many of the early women also valued oral history; a preference influenced by tradition as well as inaccessibility to formal education. Some women also believed that the history of the movement should be kept private or internal. Pearl Stanigar, for example, who lived at the Rastafari's Pinnacle community in the 1940s through 1950s and subsequently migrated to Florida, unfortunately refused to be interviewed. Very few people who could provide firsthand information on the women who entered the movement of the 1930s and 1940s, that is, the focus group of this book, were still alive when the research for this study began in 2014. This situation was not only a reminder that historical records on any subject matter, especially those that involve controversy, are never presented on a platter. It was a reminder that there are various approaches that can help to bridge the gap in historical knowledge.

In view of this, the biographical method and an interdisciplinary approach based on critical theory were incorporated into the historical perspective used to understand the multiple dimensions of early Rastafari women's resistance to patriarchy and colonialism. Early Rastafari women challenged colonialism, racism, and capitalism, but they also countered patriarchal issues inside and outside the Rastafari movement through both overt and covert means. The women's acts of resistance showed a sense of the intersectionality of Black oppression with patriarchy often seen by them as the main means through which colonial domination, racism, and capitalism were used to stifle their development and independence as women and Black people. Thus, the interconnectedness of women's resistance was not only due to their Rastafari identity but also to the fact that they were women in a male-dominated movement and society.

Ula Taylor's concept of "community feminism" and Katie G. Cannon's "womanist theology" are a part of the interdisciplinary approach in this book used to analyze the women's negotiations of patriarchy, their commitments to community-building as part of pursuing Black sovereignty, and their views on the role of the Rastafari religion itself in deconstructing patriarchy as part of the Black liberation struggle.[8] On the other hand, Marxist theory, which was essential to the development of critical theory in the 1920s and 1930s, informs the discussions of colonialism as the main context of domination for the development of the resistance of early Rastafari women. Marxist theory informs the framework, for instance, in which the "totalizing" tendencies of the colonial system are used in the discussions, as these "attempted to penetrate every area of life from self-constitution to interpersonal relations to education."[9] The discussions center women's resistance to colonial "domination" or the attempts to generate "differences in power—or possibilities in a wide sense."[10] The concept of symbolic interactionism, which was developed for psychology, is also used to explore women's resistance in an environment that shaped their activities, women who conceptualized their resistance through negotiating their contextual constraints. The women engaged in various acts of resistance that also help us to interrogate the documentation in the colonial archives and press, with resistance stimulating what is described by historians as reading "against the grain."[11] This approach to reading the colonial documentation helps to center the views of the women, views described by Monique Bedasse as part of the "Interior" or internal history of the movement, which helps to bring attention to previously ignored or silenced topics and people, such as early Rastafari women.[12]

Similarly, the biographical method is used in this study to illustrate some of the ways in which early Rastafari women attempted to shape the development of Rastafari's Black liberation struggle, including challenging patriarchy inside and outside the movement, from the early 1930s to the independence of Jamaica in 1962. In addition, the foundational importance of the individual experience in history underlines the significance of the biographical method in the reconstruction of the history of early Rastafari women. Specifically, the individual's thoughts and activities highlight some of the issues that were presented to and confronted by other members while providing context that can help us to further analyze how other persons were affected by political, economic, and cultural forces in the society. Moreover, individuals can also exert varying degrees of influence on these forces.[13]

The chapters are organized around themes that address early women's thoughts and acts of resistance and are mostly arranged in chronological order. Six of the seven chapters are based on documentation and recollections about the Howellite women. Most of the women who entered the movement in the 1930s and 1940s were members of this group, which grew into the largest of the original Rastafari organizations by 1940. Throughout the seven chapters, the colonial context that was created by Crown Colony government, introduced in response to the 1865 peasant uprising known as the Morant Bay Rebellion, is used to analyze the women's role in the rise of Rastafari mainly among the Black peasantry of the 1930s and 1940s. Also discussed are the ways in which Rastafari contested the context created by the developing creole nationalism of the local labor leaders, who dominated the pursuit of the political independence of Jamaica acquired in 1962 using the British Westminster system of government. Rastafari criticized this system as a hegemonic pretext for neocolonial capitalist exploitation of the Black majority, which they extended to include East Indians who entered the Rastafari movement. This criticism helped to stimulate women's resistance to colonialism and creole nationalism. Women's resistance to colonialism is discussed in the first two chapters through litigation and petitions to the government, respectively.

Chapter 3, however, focuses on Tenet Bent, a middle-class woman who married Leonard Howell and made herself critical to the origin of their Pinnacle community while aiming to build Rastafari's reputation as a movement for the empowerment and improvement of poor Black people within and beyond Jamaica. I go on to discuss women's development of the movement's religion through the promotion of the notion of the divinity of Empress Menen, the empress of Ethiopia and wife of Emperor Selassie I, whom Rastafari men mainly promoted as the promised return of the Messiah. Women, such as Merriam Lennox, empowered the movement's women and sought to strengthen the Rastafari's religious and political consciousness with their focus on the divinity of Empress Menen. Chapter 5 discusses cannabis and Pinnacle and focuses on the historical context of slavery to analyze women's role in developing the use of cannabis as a medicinal treatment in Rastafari. Rastafari men stood as strong and consistent advocates for the recognition of the medicinal and sacramental benefits of cannabis and its decriminalization; however, women were also a crucial and pivotal part of this advocacy. Both women and men supported cannabis as a sacrament and therapeutic plant. From the perspective of Audrey Lewis, women's involvement in the sustenance of Pinnacle, the first self-sustaining Rastafari community that aggressively pursued a Black nationalist agenda against creole nationalism, is discussed in chapter 6. Rastafari's Black nationalism pursued Jamaica's sovereignty through attachments to Africa, especially Ethiopia, while creole nationalism pursued this sovereignty through attachments to Britain and the West.

The closing chapter is based on the history of Edna Fisher, one of the two founders of another Rastafari organization known as the African Reform Church of God in Christ. This church was cofounded by Fisher and was largely influenced by the Howellites' Pinnacle community in several ways. It created an outward facing sacred and sovereign compound, one that was expected to exemplify and spread Rastafari's Black nationalism across Jamaica. Within a year, its leaders also claimed the most members of any Rastafari organization formed after the disbandment of Pinnacle by the colonial government in 1958. Similar to Pinnacle, Fisher's organization generated a large amount of the controversial government surveillance and press coverage on the early Rastafari movement. It also generated significant anxiety among the leadership of the mainstream churches and members of the public while reinvigorating academic interest in the Rastafari's Black nationalist politics and Ethiopic culture and religion. Fisher, other leaders, and members of the organization were tried on treason-felony charges in 1960, but her actions would eventually contribute to the Rastafari as a political and cultural force in Jamaica.

Overall, the oral history from and about early Rastafari women is discussed at varying lengths in the seven chapters alongside an analysis of the sources from the colonial archives and press. The women's testimonies and other acts of resistance contested their most prominent depictions in the colonial archives and press, which often suggested that they were naïve and submissive to early Rastafari men. Nevertheless, as each chapter illustrates, parts of what has been referred to as the different or diverse orientations that marked the genesis of the movement, including its "doctrinal differences" and "doctrinal individualism," were introduced by women, mainly in activities that highlighted their struggles against discrimination based on race, class, and gender.[14] Early Rastafari women's history is thus essential to understanding the resistance ethos of the early Rastafari movement. Women challenged inequality based on race, class, and gender in discussions of the doctrine and principles promoted by men, and some women integrated these concerns into the anticolonial political activities of the early movement.

I have used Black with a capital B throughout this book out of respect for what I perceive to be the historical conceptualization of Blackness as synonymous with Africa by early Rastafari women and men. I have also used it out of respect for the nondiscriminatory transnational African consciousness of Rastafari, enunciated by the conception that Africa or Blackness is the cradle of humanity, to which the early women of the movement made significant contributions through their oppositions to racism, classism, and gender inequality.

CHAPTER 1

The First Women to Testify in Court
for the Rastafari Movement

In March 1934, Leonard Howell and Robert Hinds, two of the founders of the Rastafari movement, were tried in the Morant Bay courthouse in St. Thomas for sedition, that is, creating animosity toward the British monarchy and its colonial government in Jamaica. The defendants, the *Daily Gleaner* reported, were charged with "abusing the King and the Queen, Queen Victoria, in fact everybody."[1] Although the sedition trial marked the first attempt by the colonial government to publicly suppress the Rastafari movement, it was also one of the earliest pieces of evidence that women were actively and publicly involved in the defense and development of the movement. For these women, namely, Rachel Patterson, Albertha Lalloo, Florence Jackson, and Doris Samuels, the trial was not merely about the suppression of their leaders, it was colonial litigation against the entire movement, a movement they believed could improve the social, economic, and political condition of Black people in Jamaica. But patriarchal tendencies in the movement bred perceptions of these women as submissive and naïve. Consequently, their involvement in the movement was initially peripheral to the agenda of the government and was therefore given little attention during the sedition trial. Similarly, the *Gleaner*, which provided daily coverage of the trial, treated women's involvement in its proceedings with indifference, even though they were instrumental in the fight against colonial rule, one of the main objectives of the Rastafari movement.

In his memoir on the early Rastafari, Douglas Mack, a Rastafari elder, noted that "the sisters were a tower of strength in the daily activities of the camps," activities they directed.[2] The movement, Mack stated, had relied on women to ensure that children were protected from Babylonian or colonial indoctrination, including its avarice, selfishness, and egocentrism. These women schooled children in the socialist lifestyle of Rastafari, that is, the equitable sharing of land, work, and capital, used to promote its Black nationalist ideology. Florence Stewart, also known as Sister Irone, a resident of the Pinnacle community, noted that they were "taught everything" by Tenet Bent, Howell's wife, and other women. "As children," they "all mixed" and were taught that "no one was better than the other." In the community, Stewart added, "Everyone planted and everyone had his own field or garden plot."[3] Mack also stated that the women "would teach the brothers how to cultivate crops to sell at the market." They "assisted in confronting the police when they raided the camps," and furthermore, "They knew how to use their feminine charms to persuade [police] officers to drop the charges."[4] Agency, that is, their sense of empowerment and independence, was therefore displayed by early Rastafari women in various respects.

This chapter discusses the agency of Patterson, Lalloo, Jackson, and Samuels, the early women who were directly involved in the sedition trial as witnesses for the defendants. While the sedition trial was one of the earliest pieces of evidence that women were actively and publicly involved in the defense and development of the movement, the historical records on these as well as other early women vary in length and mainly include court documents, police surveillance files, and newspaper reports created by the colonial government and the local press. This variation in the length and number of sources indicates the scarce attention that Rastafari women received during the colonial period, largely because of patriarchal perceptions. In light of the patriarchal tendencies in the early Rastafari movement, one can understand why some observers would have perceived Patterson, Lalloo, Jackson, and Samuels as submissive actors in the sedition trial in 1934. However, such a view is a conventional and simplistic generalization that stifles the historical inquiry. Indeed, the Rastafari women who testified at the sedition trial were protecting their leaders, but they also interpreted the trial as an attack against their movement. The trial provided a chance to publicly demonstrate their ability to defend the movement from its major opponents, which to them also meant defending themselves as members of the movement.

WOMEN AND THE CONTEXT OF THE TRIAL

Women decided to join the Rastafari knowing that they championed the liberation of Black people under the leadership of Emperor Haile Selassie I of Ethiopia and his wife Empress Menen. They pledged their loyalty to and supported the foundational leadership of Rastafari, thereby increasing the growth of the emergent movement. This growth, numbering hundreds from around the island, induced the suppression of the movement by the colonial government. On December 23, 1933, the police inspector in charge of Jamaica's easternmost parish of St. Thomas, W. C. Adams, wrote in his surveillance report that the "movement has continued to grow and develop," and in many parts of the island was "well received mostly by the lowest elements in each district."[5] Later, in the same month, Owen F. Wright, the inspector general of Jamaica, wrote to Acting Governor Arthur S. Jelf asserting his concerns over the growth of the movement and his support of its disbandment by the government. "I am satisfied with regard to the importance and seriousness of this matter at the present time," Wright stated, "and from personal conversations with men of standing from St. Thomas I am firmly of opinion that some sort of legal action should be taken," action that would stop the movement from growing any further.[6]

Although Patterson, Lalloo, Jackson, and Samuels decided to testify for the Rastafari leaders at the sedition trial, they operated within a framework based on the intersectionality of race, class, and gender that obscured their agency. The movement emerged under colonialism and the patriarchy of the Jamaican society. Creole nationalists, namely Alexander Bustamante and Norman Manley, future leaders of the Jamaican government, proposed decolonizing Jamaica within the Westminster political system adopted from Britain, while the Rastafari movement advocated a pro-Ethiopian Black nationalism through allegiance to the Ethiopian emperor and empress. Despite the growing focus on enfranchisement and political representation in the 1930s, women had no voting rights, arguably one of the most powerful tools of patriarchy in the Jamaican society. Moreover, the society perceived Rastafari women as docile based on patriarchal tendencies in the movement. In other words, the marginalization of Rastafari women was compounded by their membership in the movement. As noted by Merriam Lennox, an early Rastafari woman, the women of colonial Jamaica, in general, were "almost low rate in this country," but the treatment of Rastafari women, "such as poor unto I, Merriam and others," was worse, for "we no recognize. We just come like we are have nots people. We are forgotten people, like out of mind." The women "in society," or non-Rastafari women, experienced variable degrees of discrimination based on gender, class, and race.[7] However, the early Rastafari women contended with these kinds of discrimination as well as discrimination based on their religious identity and advocacy of Rastafari's pro-Ethiopian Black nationalism.

This was the context within which the women testified at the 1934 trial. Moreover, the government and press were key factors in shaping such a context. While the colonial government directed the social, economic, and political climate of Jamaica, the *Gleaner* newspaper, which was the only media outlet to cover the trial, highly influenced public opinion on the early Rastafari movement. In the 1930s through 1950s, the Rastafari posed a serious threat to colonial rule. But government officials emphasized the suppression of the leaders, especially the founders. Considering the patriarchy embedded in the Jamaican society itself, the government's approach was not surprising, but it would have also been beneficial to the government to create the impression that Patterson, Lalloo, Jackson, and Samuels were the victims of chauvinistic Rastafari men. Such an impression had the potential to gain support from the public, especially from non-Rastafari women, to end the movement. Nonetheless, cases of other Rastafari women challenging colonial authorities lends plausibility to the perspective that Patterson, Lalloo, Jackson, and Samuels asserted their independence at the sedition trial. Not only did early women defend the movement against non-Rastafari members, they also physically defended themselves against the police, a reality made apparent by Daisy Shaw and other women.

In October 1933, Daisy Shaw was reported to the police as "a member of the Ras Ta Fari gang," who had been "defying the British laws, saying they have their King in Africa." Shaw was also reported as a person who was "thoroughly against all ministers of the Gospel, also Churches and white men."[8] Though she was identified as a follower of Howell and Hinds, she also independently promoted the beliefs of the movement. Consequently, Shaw made enemies among churchgoers, such as Mary Gayle, a member of the Church of God in Port Morant, St. Thomas. When Hinds was arrested for "disorderly conduct" on December 16, 1933, another woman named Iris Francis was described by the police as one of "the chief ones amongst others who resisted and assault[ed] the Police to get away Hinds."[9] Francis had attended a meeting held in Trinity Ville, St. Thomas, where Hinds and other men were arrested, but Francis and other women and men absconded, leading to the issuance of warrants for their arrest. Warrants issued for the arrests of Rastafari members became public knowledge through the newspapers of the time, particularly the *Gleaner,* which also played a central role in informing the public of the government's stance toward the Rastafari movement.

Until the University College of the West Indies published the 1960 *Report on the Ras Tafari Movement in Kingston, Jamaica* to facilitate an objective understanding of the movement, the *Gleaner's* reports on the movement remained focused on the government's suppression of Rastafari men.[10] The newspaper's accounts of the Rastafari began in 1932 with Howell's return from the United States. "Messrs. Leonard Howell and Alvin Lindo," the *Gleaner* published, "arrived in the Sixaola, having been deported from America by the United States Emigration Department on the ground that they overstayed their time."[11] During the sedition trial, held two years later, the *Gleaner* recorded and published the proceedings but regurgitated the government's understanding that women were inconsequential to the operation of the movement. It reported a great deal on the testimonies of Howell and Hinds and the questioning and criticisms by the prosecution led by H. M. Radcliffe, the Crown prosecutor, who was assisted by M. V. Camacho, the deputy attorney general of Jamaica. The newspaper highlighted the appointment of Robert William Lyall-Grant, the chief justice of Jamaica, to preside over the trial.

Even more interesting, it provided a discussion of Miss Maud Wray's testimony for the prosecution, which Patterson had disputed in her denouncement of the class discrimination against the movement. Wray was not a Rastafari and served as a key witness for the prosecution. Her testimony was significant to the trial as were the testimonies of the Rastafari women. But the *Gleaner* merely identified the Rastafari women as residents of the district of Seaforth, St. Thomas, and supporters of the defendants and provided less than a summary of all the testimonies under the grammatically incorrect subtitle of "WOMAN'S STATEMENT."[12] Some of these women had even presented their accounts of events leading up to the trial, but their accounts did not make publication in the newspaper. Essentially, the *Gleaner's* reproduction of the government's patriarchal stance in its reports on the Rastafari movement benefited the impression that Rastafari women were unimportant in the society. Furthermore, it benefited the impression that they were merely pawns of the male leaders and male members of the movement.

ON THE WITNESS STAND

At a glance, it would seem that the women at the sedition trial were merely loyal to the leaders of the movement; however, they negotiated their involvement in the trial by using the court as a platform to discredit the government and as an opportunity to show their commitment to the dismantling of British rule. Patterson was the first woman to testify. In fact, this was just one public record of her attempts to defend the movement by contesting the government's discrimination against fellow Rastafari members. Six months later, she defended Delrosa Francis, another Rastafari woman in Seaforth. Patterson complained that the colonial judges discriminated against poor Black people such as herself and Francis and refused to admit their evidence in court. "These Majestrate[s] [*sic*] would not allowed a word of statement nor accept a word of evidence from your petitioner's witnesses," Patterson asserted, and accused the judges of "hurriedly" imposing penalties on them, especially imprisonment.[13]

Rastafari members were highly susceptible to imprisonment. Their relationship with the legal system has been discussed by several scholars, such as William Lewis, who argued that the experiences of Rastafari with the legal system highlights the absence of "legal pluralism" in western bureaucratic societies.[14] Legal pluralism refers to making exceptions for cultural diversity as a means to protecting persons from spurious prosecutions under the law. In place of legal pluralism, money can be used to procure good legal defense allowing even guilty persons with money to buy justice. The primacy of money in procuring good legal defense also helps to maintain the susceptibility of the poor to court prosecutions for noncriminal offenses, which do not harm other people. The lack of pluralism meant that Rastafari members had very little hope of getting justice from the courts when their religious beliefs were deemed as conflicting with the law. Their beliefs were barred from use as evidence to defend activities such as holding public meetings to venerate the emperor and empress of Ethiopia as the true rulers of Black people and the world, and since they were not officially recognized as a religion, they were not privy to any of the law's special exceptions on religious grounds. Patterson and other women recognized their vulnerability to those constraints due to the absence of legal pluralism. Yet these women contested the government's prosecution of the movement in the courts knowing that there were very few prospects of success.

Patterson's testimony provided her with an opportunity to publicly denounce class discrimination against Rastafari members, as well as to denounce the legal system. She diverted from the defendants' religious claims in supporting themselves. To prove their innocence, the defendants used the right to freedom of worship to counteract the Seditious Meetings Act, passed in 1836. The act stipulated that anyone could be charged for sedition once the authorities deemed their meetings as "exciting any person or persons to commit any act of insurrection or insubordination, or to obtain otherwise than by lawful means any alteration or change in the constitution or government."[15] But in the defendants' view, not only had they "not done so," they were being punished for rejecting what they viewed as "the 'worship of idolatry.'"[16] On the other hand, Patterson emphasized that classism underpinned the litigation aimed at suppressing the Rastafari movement, which comprised mainly peasants. She asserted that Ebenezer Brooks and Enos Gayle, the two main policemen who testified for the prosecution, were in collusion with members of the middle class and upper class of St. Thomas and other parishes, who were committed to the suppression of the Rastafari movement. Although Brooks and Gayle testified that they recorded the proceedings of a meeting that rendered the defendants' arrests, Patterson insisted that they were in the "drawing room" of Maud Wray during the meeting in question, and "were not taking notes of Howell's speech as they said."[17] While testifying for the prosecution, Wray confirmed that Brooks and Gayle were under the influence of alcohol while in her drawing room for a period of time during the meeting. Wray's drawing room, a feature of houses that symbolized bourgeois status, was used for receiving and entertaining guests. Though Wray's racial identity is unknown, her testimony supported the petitions to the government from middle-class and upper-class residents asking for the suppression of the Rastafari movement.

The socioeconomic circumstances of most Rastafari members clashed with those of Wray and other middle-class and upper-class residents of Seaforth, a small rural community located near the center of St. Thomas and close to Font Hill and Trinity Ville. These were areas where the Rastafari members had their strongest presence during the 1930s. The movement was well received among the Black population of St. Thomas, which constituted approximately 87 percent of the parish.[18] The Black population was mainly composed of members of the peasantry, and St. Thomas was also where the most recent uprising of the Black peasantry, the Morant Bay Rebellion, had occurred in 1865, a rebellion that was caused mainly by the government's land tax.[19] This uprising included "a large body, about 800, chiefly women," who were caught "in the act of demolishing the house of Mr. Duffus," a local white business owner.[20] Further, the killing of the parish's custos or official guardian, "Baron von Ketelhodt and others," was attributed to "the atrocities perpetrated by the women," and in the town of Bath, St. Thomas, it was reported that "women, as usual on such occasions, were even more brutal and barbarous than the men."[21]

Years later, fears of a Rastafari uprising could be seen in the complaints about the movement from the white and colored population of St. Thomas. The people described as colored were persons of mixed white and Black ancestry. Along with whites, they were generally upset about the strong presence of the Rastafari in the parish and petitioned the government to take serious action to end the movement. In 1933, one such complaint was submitted by Rohan Robison, a white planter and justice of the peace, who warned that due to the influence of the Rastafari, "one of these days, the people working on his Wharf carrying bananas, may strike, and then hampers him."[22] During the same time, Constable Smith was prompted to investigate the complaints from "one Mrs. Samms," which stated that Rastafari "followers congregate (people of the baser Sort) and talks about Ras taffa Ri as Lord of Lords and King of Kings" on premises she owned.[23] Complaints about congregating on public lands also provided an opportunity to encourage the police to arrest Rastafari members. In 1937, for example, a complaint stated that the Rastafari "attempted to establish a village on some waste ground" owned by the Kingston and Saint Andrew Corporation, a public body, and were "ejected."[24]

Mrs. Albertha Lalloo, the second woman to testify at the sedition trial in 1934, provided information that was unknown to the defendants before the trial and further alleged misconduct by the policemen. Lalloo had decided to testify at the trial based on information that only she knew about the police, information that she used to defend the movement and its leaders. She decided to reveal a personal conversation that she had had with Constable Gayle, one of the policemen at the Rastafari meeting held in Seaforth on December 10, 1933. She knew that the conversation could help to confirm what she described as the biased and distorted investigative practices used by the police force. Gayle, as Lalloo related to the court, had disclosed to her that the charges against the Rastafari leaders were unjustified. Shortly after the meeting held on December 10, 1933, Howell and Hinds were arrested on the basis of warrants issued on January 1, 1934.[25] But in her testimony, Lalloo said that Gayle told her "that the charges against Howell with reference to Port Morant was weak, but the other, the present one, which had to do with the meeting at Seaforth was strong, and that it was the Inspector who had caused Brooks and himself to make the case."[26] Neither Howell nor Hinds had knowledge of the alleged conversation between Gayle and Lalloo. Considering her revelations, Howell requested that Gayle be recalled for additional questioning.

As reported by the *Gleaner*, "Gayle was re-called at the request of the accused," who then indicated that "the conversation" with Lalloo "had not been suggested to him in cross-examination" of the policeman. Gayle denied "the allegation" that he had disclosed any information about the investigation when he spoke with "Mrs. Lalloo" and had previously testified that he had only spoken to the defendant about the postcards that the latter sold with the image of Emperor Haile Selassie for one shilling per copy (about £3.58 in 2020).[27]

It is possible that Howell and Hinds were trying to manipulate the court into thinking that they were unaware of Lalloo's conversation with the policeman, but Lalloo could have kept the conversation to herself. Moreover, Lalloo's story bore similarity to the records of the policemen that were collected during their investigation of the Rastafari over the course of 1933. Adams, the inspector of police for St. Thomas, was previously instructed by both the Crown solicitor and attorney general to collect stronger evidence and warned that Howell himself "appears to be a ranter who would revel in the advertisement of a prosecution."[28] Both the Crown solicitor and attorney general suggested that better evidence would be needed to pursue sedition charges and told Owen Wright, the inspector general, to instruct Adams to submit such reports. Wright subsequently directed Adams to pursue sedition charges but also insisted that stronger evidence should be collected.[29] Lalloo was not privy to this information, but Howell was aware that the police had been attending his meetings and taking notes. In July 1933, R. C. Waters, a detective inspector of the police division in Kingston, the island's capital, reported that Howell visited their office to complain "that the Police attended his meetings and made notes," and was told "that this is one of the duties of the Police and he should make no complaint at all."[30]

Florence Jackson, the third witness to testify, was unwavering in her protestation that the defendants were innocent. She testified that the police were present at the meeting on December 10, 1933, but she did not see them taking any notes. As Jackson stated, "she did not see the Policemen making notes," and similar to what the other women had said, "denied that Howell made at the meeting the seditious utterances with which he is charged."[31] Jackson asserted that whatever notes the policemen collected did not correspond with what Howell or Hinds told the people at the meeting. The notes were collected either before or after the meeting, rendering these notes mostly the personal opinions of the policemen, who were known to be biased against the Rastafari movement. One clear implication of Jackson's testimony was that it could corroborate Patterson's claims that the policemen took their notes before coming to the meeting or while in the drawing room of Maud Wray. Jackson clearly indicated that Howell and Hinds began addressing the people only after the policemen had left Wray's residence. One of the main questions Jackson's testimony raised was if the notes of the policemen were not based on what they heard from the speeches of the defendants, then what was the basis of the information in the notes that the policemen submitted to the court? Howell used the testimonies of both Jackson and Lalloo to question "the perfectly carved writing" in the policeman's notes, and then "put Gayle under a diction test" that was "subsequently submitted" by Howell "to the Court for the purpose of comparison with the reproduction of the witness" at the meeting held on December 10, 1933. However, the chief justice dismissed his test. Howell asked, "Was the Court satisfied with the results of the Constable's 'test'?" and the chief justice responded, "You can't ask the Court that."[32]

Doris Samuels, who closed the testimonies of the women, was the youngest of the women who testified. Samuels asserted that Howell "was not arrested there [in St. Thomas] on a warrant by Detective Scott, as Scott said."[33] Samuels was arguably the most threatening to the prosecution's case, as she disputed that Howell was arrested on a warrant. The law stipulated that a warrant was needed to execute an arrest. If the prosecution indeed made the arrest without a warrant, it would have nullified the case. The *Gleaner* described Samuels as a "girl."[34] It is not known what age she was, but children were not allowed to testify in court unless authorized by a judge, and there were no reports of such authorization or suggestion by the prosecution that she was a child. One can understand the courage it must have taken to sit on the witness stand and testify against colonial officials, especially the police. This would not have been an easy task for a young Black woman who was also poor, much less a minor. However, Samuels translated any possible apprehension into courage to defend the Rastafari movement. Lyall-Grant, the chief justice, reckoned with the force of Samuels's testimony, but he knew that her testimony provided grounds for a mistrial. The chief justice's response was to prohibit both Howell and Hinds from calling any other witnesses.

VESTED INTERESTS

Testifying at the trial was just one of the ways in which women indicated their vested interests in the Rastafari, a movement they believed would relieve them of their social and economic deprivation through radical political change in the Jamaican society. But they had to contend with patriarchal impressions about the movement, one of which included the assumption that they were coerced into defending their leaders at the trial. Indeed, one can understand that these women would have been willing to oblige, since the defendants helped to form the movement. However, the nature of the charge of sedition did not necessitate coercion. The charge of sedition was used to indicate the encouragement or enunciations of antigovernment sentiments, which were found to be expressed in the anticolonial rhetoric of the Rastafari movement. It would be absurd to believe that the women were being forced to testify for a movement that promoted their liberation from injustice and poverty due to colonialism, which were among the main reasons they had joined the movement.

Even while the Rastafari faced backlash from the government and other individuals in the society, women decided to join and remain as members. This continued even after the sedition trial, which ended with the convictions of the leaders. After taking "approximately fifteen minutes" to deliberate, the six-member, all-male jurors, tax paying property-owners in the parish of St. Thomas, returned with guilty verdicts, and the chief justice sentenced Howell to two years in prison at hard labor and Hinds to one year at hard labor, as he was deemed to have been led by Howell.[35] Regardless, the Rastafari movement expanded following the trial.[36] The Howellites also expanded and created the Ethiopian Salvation Society, registered in Jamaica in 1939, followed by the purchasing of land in St. Catherine's Parish for the establishment of the Pinnacle community in 1940. This was the first self-sufficient Rastafari community, where hundreds of women resided among an estimated 700 residents who joined the relocation to the community in November 1940, and whose number continued to grow following the inception of the community.[37] One resident, Gertrude Campbell, claimed that the number of residents grew to over a thousand people even before the end of 1940.[38]

Commenting on the women who joined the community in 1940, Florence Stewart related that "some of them come through them man and some of them come through them own choice," and part of what encouraged women to join the community was because "In those days, man used to a beat woman, but none of that could happen up in Pinnacle." Stewart also stated that while her father facilitated their relocation to Pinnacle, her mother was steadfast in her decision to be a Rastafari member. Explaining this decision, Stewart noted that her mother "never turned a Rasta. When you turn something, you turn and turn back," but her mother was certain that she wanted to be a Rastafari woman and emphasized that her mother "was a Rasta same like my father" when they met, thus indicating her belief that both of her parents were equally interested in and committed to the movement.[39] A similar interest in the movement resulted in Sister Elvie, the mother of Lennox—whose religious beliefs are discussed in chapter 4—joining the early Rastafari movement in the 1930s, followed by her relocation to Pinnacle in 1941. Alphonso Gallimore, another resident of Pinnacle, stated that Sister Elvie did not have a spouse.[40]

Although the number of women who joined the early movement as single women and single parents is unknown, there is evidence to show that such women were part of the movement. Similarly, there is evidence to show that women represented a notable portion of the early movement in the 1930s. Women were noted in the police reports on the public meetings of the movement, including the one that was held in Seaforth on December 10, 1933, which attracted an estimated 200–300 followers.[41] It was after this meeting that the leaders were also arrested on sedition charges, and women were among the persons who later went to court to protest the actions of the police and colonial elites. They used their testimonies to shield the movement from suppression by the government, despite knowing that the prospect of obtaining exoneration for the defendants was low. A similar case is examined in the next chapter, in which women defended themselves against policemen and judges. This case unfolded six months after the sedition trial. By that time, the police had clearly taken note of the women's testimonies at the sedition trial and had begun to take women's participation in the Rastafari movement more seriously. Incarcerating only men would not disband the Rastafari movement, or the incarceration of men largely did not deter women from continuing the movement.

CHAPTER 2

Petitioning Government
Women and the Colonial Justice System

In the 1930s, freedom of expression was one of the main issues that was being discussed by women in the colonies of Great Britain. The suffragists forced men to recognize that every woman had the right to participate in national politics. These women advocated universal adult suffrage, which became law in Great Britain in 1928 and inspired women in the colonies.[1] As such, Black women in Jamaica were organizing to assert their independence and political perspectives. Increasingly, they expressed strong interest in matters such as voting rights, racial discrimination, gender bias, and economic development. On March 20, 1934, the *Gleaner* reported that a meeting was held in the Queen Street Baptist Church, Kingston, to mark the sixth anniversary of the Lloydon Branch of the Baptist Women's Federation, formed in 1928. The Federation was "started through the enthusiastic energy of one woman, Mrs. Garland Hall, known to them all as 'Mama' Hall." Based on annual pledges, members could contribute "a penny a week," and the newspaper observed that "these littles have a wonderful way of mounting up into a respectable sum." Women of the organization spoke to large audiences about women's solidarity and independence in the home and society at large. They discussed how the notion of "Sisterhood" could help them in the struggle to be recognized as men's equals in both the private and public domains.[2]

Increasingly, Jamaican women had been expecting their voices would be heard in national as well as international politics. In 1935, Beryl DeLeon, a feminist writer and pan-Africanist, writing in the *Gleaner*, asked, "What are the women of Jamaica going to do about the war in Abyssinia [Ethiopia]?" In reminding her readers of women's accomplishments, DeLeon also stated that "Perhaps the women of

Jamaica do not realize that they are, though only indirectly at present, represented in Geneva in the activities of a body of organized women who through the sheer power of united numbers is making the moral force of their desperate opinion felt?"[3] DeLeon anticipated a strong response from the Black women of Jamaica against the Italian invasion and occupation of Ethiopia, which started in 1935. In 1944, with the granting of universal adult suffrage in Jamaica, women asserted their role in managing the political and economic affairs of the country. The Women's Federation of Jamaica, established in 1944, encouraged women to band together to protect and advocate for their civil rights and "become members of Parochial Boards and members of the House of Representatives," the legislative arm of the government.[4]

Unfortunately, early Rastafari women were never privy to the solidarity and protections offered by the Baptist organizations or even the more inclusive, all-island Women's Federation. Among the obstacles that prevented the admission of Rastafari women to these organizations were the religious and class prejudices of upper-class and middle-class women. In observing these prejudices, Rhoda Reddock commented that it was unfortunate that "in terms of class relations, some of the middle-class feminists" basically "saw their relationship to working-class women more as one of charity than solidarity, although issues related to the working conditions of working-class women were raised."[5] Middle-class women saw their relationships with women of the working class and peasantry as a way to advance and maintain their status. As a result, their concern about the socioeconomic challenges of poor women did not include empowering these women to pursue upward social mobility. The self-help programs assisted women of the working class and peasantry in becoming more proficient in low-income work, thereby maintaining their low-income status.

Even though they were among the vocal opponents of the Italian occupation of Ethiopia, Rastafari women were members of a movement whose followers were widely viewed as a "Dangerous Cult" causing "Harm" to the society.[6] The colonial government also effectively designated the Rastafari as a serious threat to the status quo. These were among the main reasons why the Rastafari founders had been

convicted of sedition in 1934. Nevertheless, Rastafari women continued to insist on their rights to freedom of worship and expression
and contested agents of the state, including policemen and judges,
whom they perceived as oppressive. This chapter examines the case
of Delrosa Francis, a Rastafari woman who defended her right to freedom of expression against a district constable, Robert Powers. Francis's
story shows how early Rastafari women challenged the colonial justice
system while also challenging patriarchy in the 1930s. While other
women had expressed their sense of agency through their defense of
the movement's leaders in court, Francis used her understanding of her
civil rights, particularly the right to freedom of expression and political
consciousness, to pursue justice for herself and her supporters through
petitions that were sent to Acting Governor Arthur S. Jelf.[7] Francis's
case, however, was another indication that women were instrumental in defending their Rastafari identity against colonial suppression.

THE VALUE OF PETITIONS

While it may have been difficult for Francis and her counterparts
to attain legal counsel, they recognized the value of petitions. Petitions have been critical to stimulating major changes in society. In
the 1830s, for example, they were used in the campaign to abolish the
British system of slavery in the Caribbean. As historians have noted,
a significant challenge to slavery came from persons who signed petitions submitted to Parliament and the Crown, most notably, "British
women." In 1833, women also submitted the "greatest single petition"
of the abolition era, one "loaded with more than 180,000 names."
Thus, women petitioners might have outnumbered "men as combined
signers of petitions to Parliament and Addresses to the monarch."[8] In
Jamaica, poor Black women used petitions because they had limited
access to other means of addressing their concerns to the government.
Many also had to commission scribes to write these petitions to voice
their grievances, as even basic or elementary education was largely
determined by race, ethnicity, and economic status during the colonial period. In 1943, for example, the illiteracy rate showed that Black
Jamaicans lagged significantly behind other racial groups in the soci-

Race, National Origin, and Literacy in Jamaica
(Seven Years of Age and Older), 1943

RACE	LITERATE (%)	ILLITERATE (%)
Black	71.9	28.1
White	96.8	3.2
Mixed (Black & White)	86.2	13.8
British Isles Races	98.7	1.3
European Race	91.6	8.4
Chinese & Chinese Mixed	86.1	13.9
East Indian & East Indian Mixed	51.4	48.6
Syrian & Syrian Mixed	94.4	5.6
Other (Race Unspecified)	79.3	20.7

Source: Government of Jamaica, *Eighth Census of Jamaica and Its Dependencies, 1943: Population, Housing and Agriculture* (Kingston: Central Bureau of Statistics, formerly Census Office, 1945), LVIII.

ety, except for East Indians (see table). Many Indians could read and write in their own languages, such as Telegu, Hindi, Bengali, and Urdu, but not in English, the language of instruction in Jamaican schools. Among English speakers, African or Black Jamaicans had the highest rate of illiteracy, an estimated 28 percent. The illiteracy rate among the mixed-race population was 14 percent and was the second highest among English speakers in Jamaica.[9]

Although it seemed that many people from low-income backgrounds did not do much writing, petitions can bridge the gap left by the absence of records in their own handwriting. In addition, petitions contained ample evidence of women's agency by offering information on various aspects of their lived experiences, including conjugal relations, parenting, employment status, altruism, religious affiliation, economic condition, political consciousness, and social justice activism. Petitions can also shed light on women's counteractions of patriarchy. A close examination of the use of petitions by early Rastafari women has provided access to their perceptions of the social, economic, and political context of the 1930s and their social justice activism as members of their movement. Essentially, these petitions indicated the antihegemonic struggles of women that emerged as a result of their interactions with agents of the state. Some of these petitions were sent to high-ranking officials in the executive and legislative branches of the government. The suppressive tactics of the colonial system and its failures to represent the interests of the Black majority were often suggested in the petitions submitted by Rastafari women. Francis and her supporters used their petitions as a form of legal representation.

The case involved seven handwritten petitions that were between two and four pages long from five women and three men and dated September 1 and September 3, 1934. They all maintained that Francis's case was handled unfairly by the resident magistrate and justices of the peace in the parish of St. Thomas. Francis and her supporters were disgruntled at the decision made by the resident magistrate to have the case presided over by justices of the peace. Justices of the peace, also known as local magistrates, were middle-class and upper-class residents of the community who could be mixed race, white, Black, East Indian, or Syrian. The petitioners accused them of colluding with District Constable Powers to have Francis and her witnesses illegally fined and imprisoned.

THE RASTAFARI AND JAMAICAN IDENTITY

The petitions submitted by Francis and her supporters are the only known records about the case. Perhaps, the case would have simply disappeared had it not been for her agency in pursuing the matter. Francis was charged with assault and disturbance of the peace on Saturday, August 4, 1934, by Powers, who also charged her supporters for the same infractions. Francis, however, accused Powers of starting the altercation when he interrupted a conversation she was having with her friend, Francella McNish, another Rastafari woman. Following her trial in the Resident Magistrate Court of St. Thomas, Francis, along with her supporters, most of them eyewitnesses, submitted the petitions calling for "fair justice," which they believed "every British Subject ought to have."[10] Francis herself did not want to be judged based on her Rastafari identity and therefore did not explicitly state this identity in her petition. In addition, Francis and her supporters indicated that they were "loyal and dutiful" subjects of the British monarchy.[11] While this phrase is suggestive of formality and respect of authority, it was also a reminder to the colonial government that every British subject of Jamaica deserved to be treated fairly, the main principle upon which the petitions were submitted. After reading the petitions, Acting Governor Jelf decided to send them to his second-in-command, Bertie H. M. Easter, formerly the director of education, but who "had been discharging the duties of Colonial Secretary" for some "several months," until October 1934.[12]

Since Francis and her supporters only alluded to an affiliation with the Rastafari movement, government officials who viewed the petitions found it difficult to use her Rastafari identity to dismiss the claims, even though they saw the movement as an affront to the society. The petitioners indicated that Powers identified Francis as a Rastafari practitioner to justify his charges against her. Powers, they contended, was prejudicial and was being supported by the justices of the peace in St. Thomas. It was these local magistrates who had found them guilty of assaulting Powers and disturbing the peace on statements provided only by Powers himself. In deliberating the accusations of prejudice, Easter seemed mainly concerned about how the executive branch of the government could circumvent becoming implicated in such a potentially harmful case.

Though many Jamaicans viewed the Rastafari as an "Ethiopian menace" to the society, one that was disturbing the peace and safety of especially the "White and high coloured folk" of Jamaica, Easter knew that he could not use such views against the petitioners.[13] The letter describing the movement as an Ethiopian menace was addressed to John Maffey, the colonial secretary in London, by an anonymous writer, who believed that the government of Jamaica was not able or perhaps slow to take a decisive stance against the Rastafari movement. However, Easter adhered to the petitioners' deflection from the religious elements of the movement because mentioning those elements would have amounted to evidence of his own biases against their religious beliefs. Thus, Easter was impelled to address the petitioners' claims of colonial injustice. Francis forced the government officials away from discussions about her religious faith or the anticolonial politics of Rastafari and into discussions about government misconduct and insufficiencies. In this way, her petition was indicative of a critical element in the resistance of Rastafari women, the defense of their civil rights.

Essentially, Francis made a strategic decision not to identify herself as a Rastafari member. Women of the movement felt empowered by their religion but often interacted with the society through nonreligious discussions. They chose to focus on their civil rights and circumvent the criticisms of religious zealotry that could serve as a means of deflecting from their complaints against discrimination in the society. They dealt with patriarchy in the movement without interference from outsiders. As Horace Campbell has observed, Rastafari women addressed the movement's patriarchy on their own while they engaged in antihegemonic struggles against the wider society. In public, these women were silent on the movement's ideas about the "vestiges" of African and Jamaican patriarchy that they believed could be used to subdue their own civic advocacy as members of the movement.[14] Such silence in public about their struggles against patriarchy in the movement allowed the women who identified as both Rastafari and Jamaican to focus on their rights as members of the society. Fueled by these "claims of belonging" to Great Britain by virtue of colonial citizenship in Jamaica, many poor and middle-class Jamaicans volunteered to fight in the wars fought by Great Britain.[15] After World War II, Jamaican and other Caribbean people's claims of belonging to the British empire helped to counteract the notion of Britishness as exclusively white or Anglo-Saxon. Rastafari women, such as Francis, helped to further complicate the meaning of belonging to Britain with their strong political and cultural ties to the Ethiopian monarchy. For them, fairness and justice should be universal, regardless of political or cultural affiliation. The women recognized their rights to justice and fairness as British subjects, but they pledged loyalty to the emperor and empress of Ethiopia as their rightful rulers. In this sense, British rule was considered an imposition that was temporary but one that should guarantee that Black people were also treated impartially and had fair access to justice.

It would have been easy for Francis to accept the ruling by the local magistrates, in light of her limited access to formal education and the disadvantages caused by a repressive colonial society that censured her Rastafari identity. However, neither the condemnation of her Rastafari identity nor her educational deficiency resulted in her inability to understand or acquire knowledge. She sought to obtain justice by petitioning the colonial government, which she knew was averse to the Rastafari movement. Francis and some of her supporters had their petitions written by scribes and signed them with an "X" between their first names and surnames.[16] A total of five of her fellow petitioners also declared their willingness to testify for her in court. The petitioners included Francella McNish, Gertrude Nathan, Rachel Patterson, Amelia Gordon, Augustus B. Gordon, James Findley, and Denvil Price. They also asserted that Powers had treated them unjustly because of their connections to Francis. The petitions all highlighted corruption in the justice system of colonial Jamaica that had severely diminished the integrity of the due process of law. Most notably, the petitions showed how Francis challenged the power relations that suppressed Rastafari women and discredited the view that they depended on their male counterparts.

In her petition, Francis asserted that her actions during the verbal altercation and fight with Powers were not a rejection of his authority but a rejection of the abuse of his authority. Powers, she noted, initiated a fight between him and her because of a conversation she was having with McNish. The two women were discussing the poor socialization and disrespectful behavior of young people on the evening of August 4 when Powers approached them asserting that he "have a wife and children that cannot misbehave themselves."[17] He then became upset and started uttering violent threats after Francis told him that he was unmarried, and she was not "speaking" to him. Powers started "pointing his finger into my face," Francis stated, to indicate that she should be mindful of him.[18] But Powers threatened to arrest her as she continued to assert her views. It was not apparent whether Powers knew Francis or McNish. However, his intervention in their conversation suggested that he prided himself on being domineering. Francis indicated that after she insisted that her arrest was unwarranted because she was "not misbehaving," Powers declared that "he will arrest me because he is out for every dam[n] Rasta-people in Seaforth," thereby indicating antipathic sentiments toward the Rastafari movement.[19]

Powers's aggression toward Francis was not only driven by his stereotypical views of women but also his aversion to the Rastafari movement. As suggested by Patterson, one of Francis's supporters who was a Rastafari woman, antipathy toward Rastafari members was common within the Jamaica constabulary. The police had previously arrested the most prominent Rastafari founders, resulting in their imprisonment at hard labor. In January 1934, after more than twelve months of police surveillance, the St. Thomas police charged the founders with sedition. Further, in February 1934, the inspector general of the force, writing to Jelf, reported that Howell, the principal defendant, who was still under police surveillance, "still continues his activities at his Tabernacle at Port Morant," St. Thomas.[20] Despite the surveillance and prosecution, the Rastafari movement was committed to the abolition of British rule, and both women and men were involved in this anticolonial struggle.

Francis's refusal of Powers's demand to take her to the police station can be construed as defiance to obey a law enforcement officer; however, it should be noted that she also invoked the law to justify such action in the petition. Francis believed that Powers had violated her right to freedom of expression, whereas both the resident and local magistrates had violated her right to a fair trial. After being taken into custody by another policeman, Constable Taylor of Seaforth district, Francis "was confined for the night and obtained bail Sunday evening, and was summoned to appear in court on the instant," that is, on Wednesday, August 8, 1934. But on that day, her trial, without any explanation, was "differed to the 22nd inst. [instant] when it was ordered to be tried by local Majestrates [sic] down stairs [sic]." Powers did not have any witnesses, and the local magistrates and resident magistrate did not allow any of Francis's witnesses to testify. Furthermore, Francis charged the local magistrates with concluding the trial abruptly and said that they then "impose a fine of £2.15.6 [an estimated £198.50 in 2020] or (therty) thirty day imprisonment in

the G.P. [General Penitentiary] Kingston."[21] Located at Tower Street
in Kingston, the General Penitentiary was the largest prison on the
island and was over thirty miles away from Seaforth. Common tickets
for entry to this prison were grand larceny, murder, rape, arson, sedition, and treason. Francis's witnesses had been fined forty shillings
each, roughly £143 in 2020, and the alternative was the same extreme
thirty days at the General Penitentiary. One of the petitioners alleged
that their "thirty days imprisonment" was to be served at the St. Catherine District Prison.[22] Similar to the General Penitentiary, St. Catherine District Prison housed individuals convicted of major crimes.

The local magistrates were often unwilling to serve poor working-class and peasant Jamaicans, who had little or no economic means
to trade for justice. These magistrates, who were not professional
judges, saw their appointments as a means through which financial
gains and power could be realized. As recently as 2018, a letter to the
editor of the *Jamaica Observer* accused justices of the peace or local
magistrates of taking payments "for services rendered and the sale of
government documents, such as passport application forms," deemed
as "yet another breach which will only bring the office of justice of
the peace into question."[23] Since the Rastafari movement was also an
enemy of the state, local magistrates were even more inclined to rule
against Francis, a Rastafari woman of the lowest class in the society,
the peasantry. Local magistrates helped the colonial system to control
individuals from the peasantry and working class. In addition to highlighting that the ruling against her was biased, Francis stated that the
Resident Magistrate Court did not have cause to discharge her case to
the local magistrates. Each parish of Jamaica was expected to have at
least one Resident Magistrate Court, as stipulated by the Judicature
Act of 1928, which should try cases in the parish unless overburdened
by the number of cases.[24] Francis argued that she was denied a hearing
by the resident magistrate because she was accused of being a member
of the Rastafari movement and because of her social class.

The petition of McNish expressed solidarity with Francis's cries for
a fair trial. It also indicated that Francis did not request any assistance
from her partner, James Findley, in defending herself against Powers
and his son-in-law, Cyril Grant. Findley simply told Francis to ignore

Powers and walk away and only removed Powers from on top of her after he attacked her. Throughout the ordeal, Francis defended herself with virtually no help from Findley. Powers made several attempts to subdue Francis, but she did not even summon her "paramour" for assistance. As McNish explained, Powers followed the "poor half stunted girl" after she stepped "into the said gold smith shop seeking refuge," at which point he renewed "the attack."[25] Powers, on the other hand, was assisted by Grant, who held down Francis so that his father-in-law could execute her arrest.

Many people would agree that some Jamaican men would have used the Jamaican Creole language and their masculinity to address Powers's and Grant's aggression toward Francis; however, it is apparent that Findley was not this type of man. "Knowing that the law will protect the girl, I keep down my temper," Findley explained in his petition, "and tried not to be angry, but quietly went and lifted off Powers from the struggling girl while Nathan Cordrington lifted off Cyril Grant from her." Even after Francis went into the "gold smith shop" for refuge and was attacked again by Powers, Findley kept his composure.[26] Francis, on the other hand, maintained that she was innocent and defended herself against Powers's and Grant's physical assaults.

Contrary to the perception that Rastafari women were dependent on their male counterparts, Francis was an entrepreneur, as Nathan indicated in her petition. Francis rented rooms in her house to persons who needed a place to live. It seemed she preferred renting to single Rastafari women, and the circumstances under which such rural women were renters varied. Elisa Sobo discovered that these circumstances included the wish to avoid "casual" relationships with men.[27] According to Edith Clarke, some rural low-income women who were economically independent also believed that they should only be in relationships with men who could "support" their economic development.[28] Benjamin Schlesinger also reported that such relationships were "expected to bring the woman a change of life," including a formal marriage, which these women saw as helping "to transform" their status "from a common woman to a lady."[29] Francis alluded to her own high regard for marriage when she told Powers that he did not "have a wife," and so she was "not speaking to him."[30] Like middle-class women, rural low-income women, such as Francis, created "a wide domestic network" as part of maintaining their financial independence. Many such women, therefore, did not require the financial "support" of men.[31] For some early Rastafari women, maintaining financial independence was part of protecting themselves from physically abusive men. Stewart, a resident of Rastafari's Pinnacle community in the 1940s, reported that no physical abuse of women "could happen up in Pinnacle."[32] Women relocated there to cultivate their own land. In addition, many women moved into Pinnacle to escape abusive relationships with men.

COMMUNAL SUPPORT AND SOCIAL IDENTITIES

A prevailing notion in the African diaspora in the West is that the "'community is family.'"[33] Early Rastafari women used the help of fellow Rastafari members as well as non-Rastafari people in counteracting colonial oppression. It is therefore not surprising that the owners of the "gold smith shop," Amelia Gordon, who was "a member of the Union Baptist Church," and her son, Augustus Gordon, submitted a joint petition that not only argued that Powers's charges against them were unjustified, but was resolute in defending Francis.[34] Amelia's religious affiliation as a member of Union Baptist Church served to validate their story, but it can also help to explain why she was one of Francis's strongest supporters. Several women in the Baptist church joined the early Rastafari movement. Could Amelia have been both a Rastafari and a Baptist? In 1936, Pastor V. R. Cameron of the Church of God at Font Hill, near Trinity Ville, St. Thomas, wrote to Edward Denham, the governor of Jamaica, condemning the verbal assaults of "a certain Baptist Minister who was once pastor of theirs (not all)," but who "got against them and told the Leaders of this group that he will use his influence to see that this group movement is brought to nothing."[35] By 1943, approximately 52 percent of Baptists were women and many maintained a "dual affiliation" with the church and the Rastafari movement.[36]

The sense of the community as family was stronger in the petitions of the women than in those of the men. Price, for example, pleaded to Jelf to overrule Frances's trial, which he believed was unfair, but spent much more time on requesting the removal of the charges against himself. Price stated that it was "quite a mystery" that he was charged with and found guilty of "beating Constable Powers," since "on the said night of the said charges" he "was at his home at Old Valley Road shelling his own corn until after midnight."[37] On the other hand, Nathan included in her petition that she "rented a room from Miss Delrosa Francis" and was being punished for being acquainted with her. As Nathan explained, "on the night of the said occurrence," she "was sick in bed and [k]new nothing about what had happen," but was interested in learning about what had happened to Francis. "Your petitioner followed her to court just to hear the nature of her trial," Nathan stated, but "they attached my name as one of the persons that was disordered in the street on the said night of the occurrence."[38]

Patterson's petition can also help us understand how Francis, as well as Patterson herself, used aspects of what Taylor described as "community feminism" to obtain justice for fellow Rastafari members and other poor Black people in their community.[39] Taylor used this concept to discuss the African consciousness and political activities of diasporic Black women who were single women, spouses, and mothers, in addition to being politically conscious and active: women who focused on their home lives, such as caring for spouses, children, siblings, and friends, as well as instigating, leading, or partaking in the struggles for racial and communal uplift. Their activism challenged patriarchal notions aimed at undermining the agency of women. Patterson's claims made it apparent that Powers had been surveilling the Rastafari movement and showed his contempt for its members. In her petition in support of Francis, Patterson asserted that Powers went into a Chinese liquor store where he sought the help of some young men by telling them he wanted "to play hell in Seaforth tonight with the Rasta-people," and then ordered them "to make songs upon the people who attached to the Rasta-Farie religion."[40] The men, Patterson further stated, consumed the drinks before leaving the store and stood in front of it playing musical instruments while singing derogatory songs about Rastafari members living in Seaforth. Among the persons named by Powers and the group of young men was Albertha Lalloo, who had testified at the sedition trial of the founders, along with Patterson herself. A Mrs. Murray was also named, but her husband, Gabriel, was the only one the police eventually arrested. Gabriel was arrested in 1941, with sixty-nine other male Rastafari members, which the police believed would disband the movement.[41] Powers, Patterson also stated, declared he was "the master of Belleview-property and the King of Seaforth."[42] Bellevue was a mental hospital in Kingston, where Powers believed Rastafari members should be confined.

As mentioned earlier, Powers had no witnesses at the trial, but Patterson pointed out that he had sought to obtain her support to lend credence to his accusations against Francis and her witnesses. His effort, however, proved futile, as she refused to offer the testimony and told him that "if I should go with you, I will have to speak the truth, and that will be against you." In response, Powers decided to prosecute all the witnesses who went to the trial with Francis to give evidence to support her case, and hoped that "by so doing there evidences will not be taken by the judge."[43] Before Powers started to declare his intention to charge the witnesses, Patterson had also secretly asked Esta McFarlane to take note of his expressions. It is not known whether McFarlane was a Rastafari member. She also did not submit a petition, as she did not witness the altercation between Francis and Powers. But McFarlane's camaraderie and willingness to help Francis was implicit in Patterson's petition.

THE OFFICIAL RESPONSE

Francis's case highlighted Rastafari women's contributions to the movement's denouncements of the colonial government. On September 6, 1934, within five days of receiving the petitions, Easter, the acting colonial secretary, notified the petitioners that their complaints would be dealt with by the government. Jelf, the acting governor, had ordered Easter to dispose of the matter quickly. The impending arrival of Denham, the permanent governor, who arrived on October 24, 1934, also made Jelf eager to dispose of the matter. Jelf wanted to demit office as an effective interim governor who had assured his permanent replacement, Denham, that the Rastafari was merely a deluded cult of escapists his government had taken swift action to put under control. Therefore, there was no need for Denham to be alarmed about the movement. Denham's initial thoughts on the Rastafari reflected Jelf's assurances that the movement was unimportant and only made up of a few religious fanatics and escapists who were poor, deluded, unkempt, and merely spent their time praying for repatriation to Africa and smoking cannabis. Writing on November 6, 1934, Denham stated, "Ras Tafari or Rasta people—a sect in St. Thomas—round Morant Bay. Wears beards and believe the Lord will return for them in Abyssinia," and specified their belief that ships would be sent for them to return to Africa and "*ganja smoking* amongst the sect."⁴⁴ It downplayed the political and cultural importance of the movement as an anticolonial force and was regrettably Denham's only diary entry on the Rastafari movement, given that he died unexpectedly from a heart attack in 1938.

However, prior to Denham's arrival, headlines in the local press showed the continued influence of the Rastafari movement on the masses of the people, which included fears of its resuscitation of a peasant uprising in St. Thomas through the movement's continued encouragement of denouncement of the colonial government.⁴⁵ An editorial in the *Gleaner*, published on August 6, 1934, under the alarmist headline, "Fooling the Masses," showed that the press was fearful of the Rastafari spreading political dissension in the society and advised further action by the police to suppress the movement. The editorial specified, "We hope the police of St. Thomas will render it impossible for these specious characters, some of whom wax fat upon the ignorance of their less intelligent fellowmen, to continue their tricks in that parish." It also stated that "The best advice that can be given the masses is to live by the sweat of their brow, and leave Ras Tafari and other cults alone."⁴⁶

Easter officially addressed the petitioners' claims in Francis's case in two identical letters dated September 14, 1934.⁴⁷ These were dispatched eleven days after his initial response to the petitions that had simply stated that the government would investigate the matter. Although the petitions presented serious accusations against the police and judges, Easter did not recommend an official inquiry into the matter. His unwillingness to consider an inquiry had serious repercussions for the government. It was therefore important that the government did not infuriate the petitioners in its responses. As Barry Chevannes has observed, the peasantry could act in unison, though some of them owned land and were economically better off than their peers, which "should not be taken to mean that those owning any but the smallest tracts of land were guaranteed even a measure of prosperity."[48] The peasantry, as Ken Post also noted, included members of the working class who took up residence in depressed communities near the city center of Kingston.[49] The prospect of peasant solidarity and unrest that could include St. Thomas as well as Kingston, the island's capital, helped to ensure that Francis and her supporters were taken seriously by the government. The final letters Easter sent in response to the petitions simply stated, "I am directed to inform you that the Officer Administering the Government has no power to interfere in matters which have been submitted to and adjudicated upon in a Court of Law and is unable to take any action in regard to your representations."[50]

The letters alluded to the possibility of a court appeal, but Easter knew that the petitioners would have realized that filing such an appeal was a lengthy process, one that could also be compromised by the same elements of corruption in the judicial system that inspired the complaints of the petitioners. As the petitioners indicated, low-income people in Jamaica were highly susceptible to the miscarriage of justice. A Rastafari identity increased such susceptibility. Therefore, a strong possibility existed that Francis and her supporters would see the pursuit of an appeal in the courts as a futile exercise.

Reading the letters from Easter, it might be difficult to see that he alluded to an appeal to protect the government and disarm Francis and her supporters. However, a "Confidential Minute Paper" from Easter's office will remove this difficulty. The advice from Camacho, the attorney general, stated that Easter should "Reply in each case that M.S. [the Majesty's Service] has no power to intervene in matters which have been submitted to and adjudicated upon in a court of law and is not prepared to take any action in respect to their representations."[51] In addition, the Minute Paper comprised a handwritten memo noting that "the representations & requests in all the letters is the same stating that the witnesses are innocent of the charge on which they were convicted & a claim is made verdict by the RM [Resident Magistrate] is misguided."[52] The Minute Paper further indicated the precarious position that the government would be in if it were to explicitly inform Francis and her supporters of an appeal: "If these people are dissatisfied with the J.P.'s [Justices of the Peace] findings and deliveries in these cases they have the right to appeal. They know this perfectly well and their only reason for not appealing is that they know or have been advised that they have not got a hope in the appeal court."[53]

Francis and her supporters might have approached the resident magistrate or one or more of the local magistrates in the parish, who held the Rastafari movement in contempt and therefore suggested to them that it would be futile to take their claims to the appeal court. In addition, Francis was a woman, which further diminished the prospects for success in the appeal court. As a woman, she had to contend with patriarchy, and the Rastafari movement was denounced by the government. It was also unlikely that other officials in St. Thomas would support an appeal by Francis and her supporters. Appeals were financed by the government and required the support of legislators of the parishes. However, some of these legislators, including R. Ehrenstein, the representative for St. Thomas in the Legislative Council of Jamaica, opposed the allocation of public funds for appeals. In May 1934, Ehrenstein along with other members of the Council voted against the Appeal Court Bill on the basis that it required "£700 to provide a half year's salary for the Judge," and another "£50 for Legal Assistance for Appellants."[54] Later, in April 1935, Ehrenstein alone argued that three judges of the Supreme Court should continue to try appeal cases.[55] Prior to this recommendation, Lyall-Grant, the chief justice of Jamaica, writing in January 1935, had also proposed granting a Supreme Court judge the power to summarily dismiss appeal cases without a hearing or should the "Judge see no reason to interfere with the conviction or sentence." This judge, he further stated, could "dismiss the appeal without calling on the appellant."[56] Lyall-Grant also proposed granting the judge the power to increase the sentences in both civil and criminal cases and was confident that this would greatly diminish the number of appeals.

Unfortunately, the records do not show the decision that was made by Francis or the other petitioners after they received the letters from

Easter. Even if they did not pursue an appeal, Francis had defended herself and she had also defended the Rastafari movement. She defended herself against Powers and challenged the decisions of the judges of St. Thomas. Such actions indicated her independence and sense of empowerment. Although Francis was a Rastafari member, she recognized the value of solidarity with other poor people in the parish, both Rastafari and non-Rastafari members who felt strongly about being disadvantaged by the colonial justice system, in fighting oppression. Francis's struggle against the authorities revealed the injustices that the Jamaican poor encountered because of the actions of government agencies. Both the petitions and Minute Paper of the government highlighted an effort to keep Francis and her supporters from pursuing and obtaining justice, but Francis's ordeal showed her refusal to be subservient, even to high-ranking officials. The petitions in her case bear testimony to the active involvement of Rastafari women in the struggles against colonial injustice and discrimination.

CHAPTER 3

The Middle-Class Woman
Reshaping the Rastafari Family and Community

Since its inception in the early 1930s, the Rastafari movement has experienced notable changes in its class structure. It has transcended the shores of Jamaica to include people of different social and economic backgrounds in countries all over the world, which has inspired scholars to characterize the movement as "inherently transnational in character, outlook, and composition."[1] Estimates put the total number of members worldwide at 700,000 in 1988, and 3–8 million members by the end of the twentieth century.[2] The latter figures might be an exaggeration; nonetheless, there is noticeable diversity in the movement. This diversity can be attributed to various factors, such as women's counteraction of patriarchal assumptions within the movement and their subversions of the class divisions in society. Class, it should be noted, is used here as "the economic conditions which shape" this identity, or defined "through the medium of economic values, profits, wages, investments, etc."[3] In other words, class is largely determined by relationships to the means of production, principally land and capital, and the social status or influence in society that one derives from these relationships.

Contrary to popular views, middle-class women started to join the Rastafari movement in the early stages of its development. From this perspective, we can gain a sound understanding of how women influenced the class dynamics of the early movement within the class structure of Jamaica. Here, Walter Rodney bears much relevance, as the notion of class solidarity through an association with Blackness formed the basis of diversification of the movement beyond its mostly Black peasant following while maintaining its African consciousness.[4] This chapter explores the class implications of Tenet Bent's involvement in the early Rastafari, despite operating in a patriarchal movement and society.

Bent was one of the first women to have engaged in diversifying the class composition of Rastafari in the Jamaican context. She was a middle-class woman who decided to marry Leonard Howell, recognized as a founder of the movement.[5] Bent's light-skinned complexion indicated that she also challenged the racial divisions in the society, one where "the traditional light-skinned elite and upwardly mobile black families" remained "keen for their children to 'marry light.'"[6] Further, she had broken off a previous engagement to marry a man whose family was both wealthy and considered as white. While Bent herself was also considered as "white," she chose to marry a dark-complexioned man.[7] For many middle-class Jamaicans, Bent's decision symbolized a betrayal of her class background. She was supposed to be among what Herbert Duffus, a Jamaican judge, described as the "persons with a proper home background," a statement he made when he was handing down the sentences of Rastafari individuals at the treason-felony trials in 1960.[8] Edna Fisher, the only woman among the convicted individuals, was born poor but had joined the middle class when she was adopted by an aunt and subsequently became a successful businessperson, employer, and landowner in Kingston and St. Andrew, where she built a house that formed the basis of the Rastafari church she cofounded in 1959. Fisher is discussed further in chapter 7. Judge Duffus's view represented a hierarchical society, one in which class took precedence in directing the social order, and it was also a testimony of the values and norms of the colonial context in Jamaica that Rastafari struggled to change based on its "socialistic" notions of social and economic equality.[9]

A CLASSLESS MARRIAGE: PERSPECTIVES OF THE JAMAICAN COMMUNITY

Bent was born on March 7, 1912, and within the context of Jamaica's social strata, she was considered a person from a middle-class family. Her parents, Ellen Ebanks-Bent and Edward Bent, were the owners of approximately one hundred acres of land in Southfield, St. Elizabeth, where she and her six siblings were born and raised.[10] Hélène Lee described the Bents as an "upper-class" family with "Irish, Scottish, German, and Jewish blood," in addition to African blood.[11] They were probably seen as upper class in rural St. Elizabeth, but in the wider Jamaican society, they were middle class given the amount of land they owned and the "tripartite racial" hierarchy, which was used by the colonial system to divide the population of the island.[12] This hierarchy placed mainly whites on top, browns or mixed-race people, such as the Bents, in the middle, and Black people at the bottom. Bent attended Mayfield Primary School in Southfield, St. Elizabeth, which was considered a prestigious school in the parish.[13] At age twelve, she was enrolled into the Hampton High School for Girls, another prestigious school in St. Elizabeth.[14] The Bents were also prominent members of St. Mark's Anglican Church in Southfield. The Anglican church was not only the church of the state; during slavery, it was considered as the "planters' church" and widely viewed as elitist.[15] Essentially, Bent's upbringing was more representative of European understandings, which conflicted with the Rastafari movement that opposed the colonial order of Jamaica. In 1935, Howell, for example, dubbed the colonial system as "Our SLAVE MASTER," that is, an organ of the white planter class, which accumulated its wealth from enslaving Black people.[16]

Bent was perhaps the first middle-class person to become a Rastafari member, though other persons of racially mixed ancestry joined the early movement. The Rastafari founder, Henry Archibald Dunkley, for instance, was mixed race but not middle class. Bent also decided to marry the most widely known Rastafari and founder of the movement, thereby declaring her entry into what many Jamaicans at that time considered a classless marriage or disgraceful union. Leonard Barrett has observed that many new Rastafari members in the 1960s came from the middle class, whereas previously, "the membership" of the movement "was essentially lower class."[17] Thus, Bent's marriage fueled even more fears of an attempt to strengthen the movement beyond "the illiterate classes" in the 1930s.[18] Bent was married to Howell in Kingston on January 31, 1937.[19] Prior to meeting Howell, she had been living in Kingston and shared a friendship with a woman known as Miss Powell, the owner of a guesthouse and restaurant in the city center. Powell was mystified by Bent's decision to marry Howell, and her decision to abandon her engagement to marry a son of the wealthy Machado family. As a result, their friendship ended.[20]

Bent's assertion of her sense of freedom started from before she met Howell. She had left idyllic Southfield against the orders of her parents. A younger sister named Louise had joined her in Kingston for a while but was unsuccessful in convincing her to return home to Southfield. Their father Edward drove his lorry on a seventy-mile journey into Kingston to sell the products from his farm to wholesalers and market retailers, known as higglers, and visited Bent, but he also could not convince her to return to Southfield. In the 1930s, fewer than 300 people lived in Southfield, and it was known for its pristine natural environment, tranquility, and safety.[21] Southfield's mostly peasant poverty was hardly analogous to the squalid living conditions of the poor in Kingston, which was beset by high unemployment rates that created "growing areas of poverty and squalor." Such places afflicted the city through their "abysmally poor filthy housing, starvation, petty crime, prostitution, disease and death."[22] Despite living mostly on her own in the city center, where she was close to its realities stemming from the growing areas of squalid poverty, Bent remained steadfast in her decision to maintain her freedom and independence from her parents. This sense of independence and freedom was also visible in her decision to abandon the engagement to a wealthy Machado, a family also considered as "white."[23]

THE CHOICE OF CLASS

The Machado family owned the B. & J. B. Machado Tobacco Company, established in Kingston in 1875. Bent began working there as a "receptionist" after leaving "secretarial school" around 1936.[24] Shortly thereafter, she was engaged to one of the Machado sons, which would have further elevated her social status. But while the Machado family supported Jamaica's mainstream or creole nationalism, before it even showed signs of succeeding in the early 1940s, their business enjoyed preferential treatment on the British market, which contributed to its profitability even during the decade-long Great Depression of 1929–39. The Machados had also emigrated from Cuba at the start of a revolution which is said to have had a "powerful rhetoric of antiracism," one that "became much more dominant in the years between the legal end of slavery in 1886 and the outbreak of the third and final war in 1895."[25] While in Jamaica, the Machados became wealthy business people who employed a mostly low-paid Black labor force, which Bent later joined, though in a relatively elevated role at the receptionist desk.[26]

The low wages and poor industrial relations in big businesses in late colonial Jamaica could hardly be ignored by any employee living in the 1930s. By 1938, the island's working people embarked on a massive strike action that spread to many sections of the island. Among the main "causes of working class unrest and dissatisfaction," wrote Richard Hart, were "low wages," and the "arrogant racist attitudes of colonial administrators and employers."[27] A royal commission of inquiry, known as the Moyne Commission, was convened to investigate the causes of the strikes, which erupted in several other British colonies in the Caribbean. Among the commission's recommendations was the 1944 enfranchisement of the adult population of Jamaica so that they could elect persons to represent their group interests. It was during these events that Bent chose entry into the Rastafari movement, which promoted a Black nationalist ideology for the future Jamaica and advocated a socialist vision of this future, one that conflicted with the corporate interests of families such as the Machados, who owned and had significant holdings in big business ventures. Following Jamaica's independence from Britain in 1962, the Machados transitioned into upper-class status, a status realized through their wealth and the continued influence of the racial legacies of British colonialism, which placed "phenotypically white" families at the top of the Jamaican social hierarchy.[28]

Though Bent's decision indicated the rejection of financial ease, the man she eventually married was not struggling financially, but he had to contend with the independence that Bent had already established for herself from before they met. While Howell himself may have been "an attractive man, a dressed man, a pleasable man that went around with a nice briefcase filled with attractive documents, a man with the word of God in his mouth," he was also a business owner, and by virtue of his financial status, could qualify as a member of the bourgeoisie.[29] The *Gleaner* reported that by 1940, he "owned a bakery in Kingston," bought a van used to deliver its products, and owned "dozens of handcarts on the streets."[30] But as a member of the working class in Kingston, Bent also had a personal stake in the plight of workers in the city, an interest that she extended to the plight of the peasantry after learning of the Rastafari movement through Howell. She grew up around the peasantry of Southfield but was shielded from its realities by her parents' affluence. Her consciousness of the realities of Jamaican poverty developed after leaving Southfield for Kingston. The concentrated pockets of poverty all over the city of Kingston made this poverty more detestable and often worse.

In Kingston, Bent was also surrounded by social unrest of the working class and unemployed poor accompanied by protest rallies, including those addressed by Amy Jacques Garvey, who protested the 1935 invasion of Ethiopia by fascist Italy. These rallies were held at Ward Theatre, which was only a mile away from the cigar factory at Park Lodge where Bent worked.[31] While there is no record stating how Bent felt about Jacques Garvey, their similarities seem striking. Both were light-complexioned middle-class women who married dark-skinned men who were leaders of sociopolitical movements promoting African consciousness. Bent's commitment to her family and Rastafari community also stood as signs of the "community feminism" that Taylor has applied to Jacques Garvey's commitment to her marriage, family life, and the Black struggle.[32] Among the principal motivations of such women was keeping the family together to ensure the well-being of its members, including "the woman herself."[33]

In 1941, in an interview done by Len S. Nembhard, a local reporter, Bent expressed the interest she had developed in protecting the fellow Rastafari people from starvation. "Our people," Bent asserted, "are starving, but they are afraid to go in the roads for anything" because of the police, who had raided their community, Pinnacle. She also asserted her belief "in God" as the ultimate source of her strength and was explicit about her conviction that with God's help, their community would survive, even during her husband's imprisonment.[34] In these statements, she announced her ability and willingness to take up the mantle of leadership at Pinnacle, as Jacques Garvey also did with respect to the Universal Negro Improvement Association and African

Communities League after her husband, Marcus Garvey, was convicted and subsequently incarcerated in the United States in 1924. Bent's parents initially entertained the view that Howell "dictated her every move," but abandoned this view when the couple visited Southfield, their only visit to the Bents' family house. Bent's parents realized that she was not the person they once knew, or had affectionately referred to as "little Teeny," but someone who was increasingly enigmatic and self-assured. Ultimately, her parents became "perplexed by her superior complex behavior."[35] Not only did she not subscribe to the class rules of the society they cherished; she had developed her own understanding of how to approach one's choices in life.

MARRIAGE AND FAMILY

The family that Bent created from the marriage bears resemblance to other middle-class families in Jamaica at the time. What had upset and blinded Bent's parents, for example, was the fact that she had married a Rastafari man. The Rastafari religion simply conflicted with her parents' Christianity, especially since they raised their children in the Church of England, or the Anglican church. Nonetheless, Bent's marriage showed signs of the empowered condition of middle-class wives, based on Bent's actions and testimony, and the scholarly statements on such families from the late colonial period in Jamaica. No systematic study of middle-class family life exists for the period of the 1930s and 1940s, but in the 1950s through 1970s, anthropologists, such as F. M. Henriques, Raymond T. Smith, Madeline Kerr, and Jack Alexander, asserted middle-class women's maneuvering to exercise authority over their husbands and decision-making for the family.[36] Thus, middle-class families showed significant signs of having the same matrifocality that the anthropologists identified among peasant and working-class families. In 1957, Smith observed, for example, that "The lack of authority of the husband-father may be marked" in the middle-class family, "particularly in a situation where it is common for men to validate their occupational status by marrying lighter coloured women, and where they may have to keep incrementing their occupational status in order to prevent the centre of status interest from swinging back onto the wife-mother."[37] In 1977, Alexander observed a similar paradoxical reality about the middle-class husband-father. Alexander pointed out that "it may be precisely the greater indispensability of the middle class male that can help to account for the image of him as marginal, for if he is perceived as deflecting his activities from the family that perception will be threatening to the functioning of the family."[38]

Bent was one of these lighter-colored women who had married a darker-colored man, and although she found out about the children Howell fathered during the marriage, she used this knowledge as part of maintaining her marriage and family. Rumors that Howell had as many as "thirteen wives" fueled the opinion that Bent was being led by him.[39] Lee has also suggested that the rumors of Howell's infidelity might have resulted in Bent having a nervous breakdown in 1943.[40] However, no records of a medical diagnosis of a nervous breakdown or institutionalization as a result of such condition were found. In dealing with the children Howell fathered with others during his marriage to her, Bent opened her home to these children and through a magnanimous sense of morality, swung the pendulum of moral authority and status interests in her direction. One of these children, Anell, wrote fondly of Bent during his "boyhood days," while citing "the fun" he remembered he "use to have" at the house in Pinnacle, which Bent lived in with Howell and their sons.[41] Montinol, the older of their sons, stated that he had some memory of that period, even though he was four, and remembered that his mother allowed Anell to visit the house.[42] Many middle-class married women opted out of employment after they were married and used the politics of status-interests to tie their husbands' assumptions about being the head of the family to insisting on their husbands' adequate performance of their responsibilities to the family, including maintaining the marriage and financing the standard of living expected by their wives. Bent herself even declared that, "No matter what happens he has always been a good husband."[43]

The politics of status-interests, in other words, gave middle-class women, such as Bent, opportunities to perform what were deemed to be "men's jobs," through an arrangement that empowered them to assume control over the children, family decisions, finances of the family and its standard of living, especially in cases where "the man is not sufficiently committed to the family," based on standards sustained by these women.[44] The fact that infidelity still occurred in these marriages should not distract from the insistence on men's commitment to maintaining the marriage, insistence identified by anthropologists as within the women's sphere of influence and largely resulting from the prospect of fully returning the family to the matrifocal model. Such insistence included providing for the family's financial and emotional well-being, and the insistence of the women that these should not be jeopardized by infidelity.

As a married woman, Bent saw herself in the same light as many other married middle-class women of her time who helped their husbands succeed in their occupations, as this assisted maintaining the social status and stability of their family. Soon after marrying Howell, Bent would encounter the challenge of navigating Howell's arrest and confinement. On February 15, 1938, Howell was "certified insane and sent to the Mental Hospital" by the colonial government and was not released until December 20, 1938.[45] Within weeks of this confinement, Bent relocated to a new residence at No. 6 Sea Breeze Avenue in Bournemouth Gardens on Windward Road, Kingston, which was nearer to Bellevue, the mental hospital. She visited Howell daily and provided him with meals and emotional support and insisted that he be treated fairly. She also used her secretarial training to ensure that he stayed in contact with the Ethiopian World Federation (EWF), headquartered in New York, and the International African Service Bureau (IASB) in London. The EWF coordinated activities in the African diaspora to assist in the Ethiopian resistance to fascist Italy's occupation of Ethiopia from 1935 to 1941.[46] The IASB was an anticolonial organization with Marxist underpinnings founded by Trinidad-born George Padmore and C. L. R. James, Guyana-born T. R. Makonnen, Sierra Leone's I. T. A. Wallace-Johnson, and Jamaica's Amy Ashwood Garvey—Marcus Garvey's first wife.[47] Bent's "correspondence" with these organizations would even provoke close surveillance of her by the Jamaican police.[48]

Owen Wright, the inspector general of police, received regular updates on Bent's visits to Howell and the letters that she wrote and received on his behalf. The letters Bent sent bore Howell's signature, but the grammar of these letters, intercepted by the police, were not Howell's, as they stood in stark contrast to his only known piece of writing, *The Promised Key*, which had many grammatical deficiencies.[49] Bent also managed the purchase of 375 copies of *The Voice of Ethiopia*, delivered in December 1938. This was the "journal" of the EWF, which was distributed to Howell's followers.[50] "Literature" expected from Padmore was delayed, causing Bent to also "worry," but the police reported that Howell assured her that he would look into it upon "his release from the Asylum."[51] The literature in question was Padmore's 1938 publication, "Hands Off the Colonies!," published by the Socialist Party of America, which finally arrived in the early part of 1939.[52] In Bent's anxiety over the package from Padmore, we not only see her interest in maintaining the Rastafari movement, but also elements of what anthropologists called "the greater indispensability of the middle-class male that can help to account for the image of him as marginal, for if he is perceived as deflecting his activities from the family that perception will be threatening to the functioning of the family."[53] In other words, Bent recognized that maintaining a functional family was tied to Rastafari's success. Her protection of her family materialized in helping to manage correspondence essential to the movement's development. But Bent was also invested in purchasing the Pinnacle property.

BUILDING THE PINNACLE COMMUNITY

Both patriarchy and Bent's class background obscured her contribution to the creation of Pinnacle, the Rastafari's first self-sustained community. But this was not a new development. Dunkley, a Rastafari founder, also complained that even he had to contend with class prejudices in the movement that tried to connect him to the haute bourgeoisie based on his light or brown complexion. These prejudices came to light in 1937, he stated, and were from fellow founders Hinds and Joseph N. Hibbert, among other leaders, such as Altamont Reid and Cecil Gordon, who told him, "'brown man' can't lead them go anywhere, 'brown man' can't lead them to Africa, and Africa don't want no 'brown man.'"[54] Some individuals in the wider Jamaican society, including other women, such as Feany Howell, Sybill Windall, and Miss M. Falconer, who contributed in significant ways to the building of Pinnacle, also had their efforts shrouded by patriarchal and classist assumptions. However, Bent was determined to help build Pinnacle not only for the benefit of her family but for that of other members in the community.

Developing the Rastafari movement was a significant challenge, but through her generosity and resourcefulness, Bent helped to materialize the Pinnacle community. Her support of the initiative to purchase Pinnacle was not explicitly stated in the records, but according to Gerald Downer and other members of the community in the 1940s, Howell combined what he had with Bent so that they could buy the property.[55] She contributed financially to its establishment partly through the sale of valuable personal items, including her pearls. In August 1938, an intruder broke into her residence at Sea Breeze Avenue in the middle of the night to look at boxes of "receipts" at the premises. Except for a "wristwatch," all of Bent's valuables were left behind, including her pearls, and the story was published in the *Gleaner* under a headline stating, "Robber Leaves Pearls Behind: Lucky Woman Still Has Jewellery Valued £100" (about £6,432 in 2020). The "boxes" of "receipts" were placed at the front of the house in public view.[56] The receipts described transactions which the public could interpret as lavishness or the accumulation of assets. Whatever the reason for the intruder's exposure of the receipts, they potentially painted Bent in an unfavorable light to the public. Nonetheless, the letter to Padmore dated 1939, inquiring about the publication that Bent had started "to worry" about has also made it apparent that the pearls were used as part of the fundraising for the establishment of Pinnacle.[57] Howell had expressed the wish to sell her pearls in London, where he assumed the prices would be better than in Jamaica. The following year, April 1940, Pinnacle was purchased from Albert Chang, a Chinese businessman, who was the owner of the property, known as "Palmetto Cottage and The Pinnacle," located in the hills of the parish of St. Catherine.[58] Bent was the one with "contacts" in the mainstream of Jamaican society, including Chang, whom she knew well enough to negotiate favorable terms for the purchase of Pinnacle.[59] Various estimates have been provided for the size of the property, estimates that range from 153 acres to as large as 1,300 acres.[60] Chang agreed to sell the land for a total of £1,200 (approximately £66,010 in 2020), but to receive payment in installments, starting with a down payment of £800 (roughly £44,010 in 2020).[61]

Other women involved in the accumulation of the financial resources that enabled the purchase of Pinnacle, including Feany Howell, Windall, and Falconer, were members of the executive board of the Ethiopian Salvation Society (ESS), established by the Howellites in January 1939 as a "Christian" benevolent association and charity.[62] The Society was headquartered in New York, but a branch was formed in Jamaica, where its aims and objectives stated that "They had no race prejudice and the Society was formed for the benefit and advancement of the masses."[63] Feany Howell served as secretary of the ESS, and Windall and Falconer were assistant secretaries. These roles made them members of the governing board. The board members were also described as business partners in Leonard Howell's multiple ventures, including ownership of the van and bakery in Kingston, and were "not badly off."[64]

The board members of the ESS were guided by a constitution, and Bent played a role in its creation, as she was not only a board member but a central figure in the operation of the organization as its first secretary.[65] This constitution supported women with children, providing grants ranging from £1 to £4, some £55 to £220 in 2020, for sick and deceased children up to the age of sixteen.[66] In April 1939, the ESS held a two-day Jubilee for Rastafari members at the Garvey movement's Liberty Hall, Kingston, attended by "hundreds of members from different parishes," and the *Gleaner* report noted the "orderliness" of the people.[67] In addition to its constitution, Bent's influence could be seen in the fund that was started by the ESS for victims of the drought in St. Elizabeth in July 1939. The first area identified for the distribution of "funds and gifts to the people" was Bent's hometown, Southfield, followed by Flaguman and Round Hill.[68] The purchasing of Pinnacle in April 1940, however, was the biggest venture of the ESS. In November 1940, hundreds of women joined the exodus to the Pinnacle community, a total "of over 700" people.[69] Fearful of moving there so early after the birth of Montinol, born on December 2, 1939, Bent would arrive at Pinnacle in January 1941. Within a year of moving to the community, she gave birth to a second child, William, born on January 28, 1942.[70]

Bent not only cared for her children but extended this care to the entire community. Lee notes that Bent "rounded all the houses where small children were living, making sure they were fed."[71] She also prioritized educating the children, motivated in part by her dream of becoming "a teacher" at an earlier stage in life.[72] She helped her husband establish a school at Pinnacle, housed in the "community mess hall" where the more than 700 reported residents of the community also ate together and gathered for fellowship on Sundays.[73] Though pressed for time given many other roles at Pinnacle, Bent was occasionally one of the teachers of the children at Pinnacle, children taught at arguably the most critical stage of their development, the early childhood years. Children attending the Pinnacle school were later sent to nearby colonial schools, at around age "eight or nine," including "Mount Moreland Primary School," which enrolled students between ages "six and fourteen."[74] In explaining the education of these children, Chevannes observed that "Pinnacle was not an isolated community. After leaving the community's infant school, Howellite children pursued their education in the schools of nearby villages."[75] These children were prepared to take on colonial teaching after receiving their Rastafari schooling from Bent and their other teachers. Downer, who grew up at Pinnacle, also stated that the community was enriched by Bent, known as "the mother" of Pinnacle, who made the members of the community feel as though they were "living as a family."[76] Downer and his mother relocated to Pinnacle in 1940.

Within seven months of moving to Pinnacle, Bent found her life in the community suddenly upended by a police raid on July 14, 1941. The police came armed with two warrants for the arrest of Howell and a wanted man named James Nelson, whom the police had reasons to believe was hiding at Pinnacle with Howell's permission. Howell "evaded arrest" during the raid, and remained hidden "for nearly a fortnight."[77] Several policemen interrogated Bent about Howell's

SHE WAS LEFT
— B E H I N D —

Mrs. Howell, the former Miss
Bent of St. Elizabeth.

FIGURE 1.
Tenet Bent, described as "left behind" by her husband Leonard Howell during the police raid on July 19, 1941. Courtesy of the National Library of Jamaica.

whereabouts, but she refused to disclose any information that could have helped them. Her decision to remain loyal to Howell clearly made an impression on the police, which a *Jamaica Times* reporter, Nembhard, realized when he visited the community four days after the raid. The police maintained their presence in the community for two weeks, and during his visit, Nembhard observed that "a Police Officer indicated a fair and frail woman sitting near the door of the deposed Chieftain's home," and also mentioned hearing the policeman assert, "That's Howell's wife over there," and "he has also left her behind" (fig. 1).[78] The description of Bent that Nembhard himself gave, however, was not one of a frail or damaged woman who felt abandoned or betrayed by her husband. Instead, Nembhard wrote that Bent's "features were those of a stern woman. Perhaps not a cruel one, but a woman who could issue orders to many a man and see them carried through."[79]

Those orders included withholding information about Howell's whereabouts, the movement, or any information that would implicate the community members in criminal activities. Bent maintained the same cautiousness during the interview with Nembhard. She "said nothing until I spoke," he stated, "and even then replied to my query with great reluctancy." He tried pressing her about Howell but stated that she "had been similarly interrogated so many times before, that she didn't worry to question my authority, she just gave me the stereotypical line: 'I don't know,'" and was convincing too. As he stated, "I believed her. Not that I just took her word for it, but you would too, if you had heard the way she said it."[80] Howell turned himself in to the police about two weeks later and was tried and sentenced to another two years at hard labor while Bent took care of the community. Even though some members of the community referred to her as "white," her dedication and service to the people of Pinnacle helped to reduce the negative effects of such perception. Mostly, the people referred to her as an "intelligent" person, who was "the first Martyr at Pinnacle."[81] The details on Bent's activities at Pinnacle during the two years Howell was imprisoned have been elusive. However, the people of Pinnacle remembered her loyalty to the community, her commitment to her family, her generosity with her time, and her role as a teacher and midwife, as well as her attentiveness to feeding the people, especially other women with babies. One must also note that these roles were being performed while she was pregnant with a second child, whom she nursed.

A part of the reason there is no further information on Bent, even circumstantial, is her untimely death in December 1943. However, the vile condition in which her remains were discovered at the bottom of a ravine, "partly decomposed and crow ravaged," indicated to the police that she did not die by accident or suicide but was murdered with exceptional brutality and her body severed and cast into the ravine.[82] The condition of her remains indicated that her murder was perhaps intended as a statement. Geraldine Fong, Bent's niece, recalled that hardly anything was left for them to identify, mostly "her bones," and the police were so guarded about the whole "inquiry" that the news of it "did not reach them until months later" when her "Uncle Arthur was summoned to Spanish Town to identify" the remains, and they were only told at that time that her remains were found "by a farmer who was looking for his donkey."[83] Howell was suspected of her murder and imprisoned for a while based on the accusation.[84]

By focusing on Howell, did the police miss the chance to find Bent's killer or killers? Whatever the answer to this question, clearly the residents of Pinnacle thought very highly of Bent, especially after the police raid, which left her to manage the community. They believed that she "lost her life for the struggle, the first major loss of life in the battle for Rastafari."[85] On April 4, 1944, Arthur Lewey, the attorney general of Jamaica, issued a statement advising the police that even though he had "no alternative but to enter a nolle" in the case of Bent's murder, "so long as Howell's followers observe the law, they are entitled to continue to live unmolested in whatever way they please."[86] Implicit in Lewey's advice is that Bent's death was such a terrible loss that perhaps the community would disintegrate on its own without the need for further police intervention. This wish, however, would not materialize. The community continued and experienced several other police raids, which are discussed in chapters 5 and 6.

The more important implication of Lewey's statement is the admiration that residents of Pinnacle had for Bent, sentiments that they have continued to express for her over the years. Despite her middle-class background, as well as the suspicions of some Rastafari about the involvement of light-complexioned Jamaicans in the early movement, Bent earned the respect and admiration of many of Pinnacle's residents. Downer recalled that she was considered the mother of the community, and in this role, Bent extended her conception of motherhood to include the community as a family. While such conceptions were embodied by peasant women, Bent used her prominent position as a leader's wife to strengthen their promotion. Bent also used her skills in secretarial work and writing to help the movement maintain its connections to the African diaspora world through correspondence with the EWF headquarters in New York and the IASB in London. Bent's work was obscured in much the same way that women's work in the home have been overshadowed by patriarchal assumptions that have designated women as dutiful wives or servants. Nonetheless, Bent worked diligently, keeping her family together, navigating police interventions and a state hostile to Rastafari, while helping to build a community for mostly poor people seeking a better life.

How differently might the early movement look if there was ample accessible documentation and enough oral knowledge of early women, especially women who did not or could no longer fit the characterization of a peasant condition? This is not meant to imply that the early movement had numerous middle-class women or even middle-class men. But we should consider that the reach of Rastafari in the 1930s and 1940s extended beyond persons of low-income status, and this reach, as indicated by Bent's case, was maintained by a rejection of colonial class attitudes and norms in order to embrace an African consciousness. This African consciousness was inclusive of the features of diversity, such as multiple class, ethnic, and racial profiles, that have been identified as inherent to the Rastafari movement based on its current composition. The extent of the class diversity of the early movement has the potential to modify the narrative of the genesis of Rastafari at a critical moment in the anticolonial struggle in Jamaica. This struggle has been discussed primarily through the lens of a class division composed of the leadership of the creole nationalist movement on the one hand and the radical nationalism that Rastafari's leadership represented on the other. But what if the middle-class leadership included involvement in the Rastafari? How does this change the way we currently understand the leadership of the nationalist struggle based on class divisions?

Bent, a middle-class woman, provides us with evidence to at least begin to consider the leadership of the nationalist movement as including elements of solidarity between radical peasant and middle-class leadership. The middle-class Jamaican Marxists of the 1950s, including a woman named Ivy Harris, would attempt to foment this kind of solidarity by capitalizing on the Rastafari movement. Harris was profiled in the police surveillance of Rastafari in 1959–60, which will be noted later. In the earlier case visible through Bent's experiences, the solidarity came from within Rastafari, or from members of the movement with middle-class upbringings and those who acquired capital, land, and business interests to qualify for bourgeois status, who gave their skills and knowledge to the movement's development. Bent's contributions involved helping the movement to develop its potential through its pursuits of economic, social, and spiritual development of its people. Her middle-class orientations were used to maintain the focus on community development. Still she also recognized the utility of class solidarity to communal uplift, which is akin to the cohesion of Africans and East Indians discussed by Rodney, a solidarity formed in response to the common experiences with the racial as well as cultural and economic contempt of Europeans. The middle-class dimension, which may be more accessible by looking closer at women, shows a Rastafari movement that was central to the anticolonial struggle of a wider cross-section of the population. This discussion of the impact of Rastafari on the middle class modifies the image of the early Rastafari as mainly associated with the peasantry. The next chapter discusses the thrust toward more inclusion in the early movement by considering a woman's interpretations of its doctrine.

CHAPTER 4

The Rastafari Religion

A Womanist Perspective

At seventy-three years old, Merriam Lennox was still preaching the Rastafari religion. She started preaching in her midtwenties to educate the people of colonial Jamaica about Rastafari and the Black liberation struggle in Africa and the African diaspora. Religion was, and still is, critical to Rastafari's Black liberation ideology, which has guided the movement since its inception in the 1930s. In fact, many, perhaps most, persons would concur that Christianity is the backbone of Rastafari. Furthermore, a large body of scholarship on Rastafari has been produced through Christian lenses.[1] Rastafari emerged from Black liberation resistance to racism, classism, and colonialism in Jamaica. However, its anticolonial doctrine is intertwined with Ethiopianism, a pan-Africanist ideology based on biblical doctrine as its validation that developed among Black churches in southern Africa in the late nineteenth century. Principally, Ethiopianism was premised on the prophesy of Psalm 68:31, which states, in part, that "Ethiopia shall soon stretch out her hands unto God."[2]

Since its establishment, Rastafari has experienced notable changes that have resulted from a myriad of interpretations of the connection between its doctrine and Christianity. Such interpretations led to the development of different missionary organs or mansions within the movement, such as the Howellites, Nyahbinghi, and Bobo Shanti, which developed independently of each other.[3] Most notably here, however, are the early Rastafari women such as Lennox, who interpreted Christianity to empower themselves. Lennox's reasoning on women, especially Empress Menen of Ethiopia, was essentially guided by the Bible. In 1930, Wayzäro Mänän was crowned Empress Menen of Ethiopia alongside her husband, who was crowned Emperor

Haile Selassie I.[4] Lennox used her biblical interpretation of the role of Empress Menen that she preached both within and outside of the Rastafari community to stimulate doctrinal change that helped to reduce patriarchy in the movement.

As previously mentioned, the documentation generated by and about women in the early Rastafari is scarce; however, Lennox is one of the few women on record who offers much insight into women's thoughts and experiences, including how women's interpretation of Christianity in the early movement challenged the patriarchal nature and structures of the religion of Rastafari. Lennox saw herself as a spokesperson for early women whose voices are largely absent from the archives. Rastafari members have relied on each other for their understandings and interpretations of the movement's religious conceptions, and they have done this mainly through their reasoning sessions with much liberty. Lennox and the researchers who observed her activities noted her interactions with mainly women in such reasoning sessions, as well as her preaching of the views she developed from them and her own understanding of the movement's doctrine. Lennox used these views to spread the Rastafari message of equality and unification as critical to achieving Black liberation and universal human progress.

In interviews with anthropologists Renee Romano and Elliott Leib in 1979 and 1983, Lennox asserted that women and men are equal, or "from he made himself a part of a woman then it is himself" (fig. 2).[5] To put it simply, Lennox believed that women and men are equal partners in a codependent arrangement that will mentally and culturally prepare them to improve their ability to overcome deprivation and resist oppression. In the 1930s, the Rastafari founders and other early leaders established a doctrine that advocated the dominance of men in the movement through the divinity of Emperor Selassie. However, by the 1940s women, such as Lennox, were engaged in activities to promote the empowerment of themselves in the movement, activities that can be associated with womanist theology, a branch of Black feminism, in which Black women saw themselves as bestowed with divine authority to act as God's mediators. As scholars have observed, "the

FIGURE 2.
Merriam Lennox, Kingston,
Jamaica, 1983.
Courtesy of Jake Homiak.
International Rastafari
Archives Project, National
Anthropological Archives,
Smithsonian Institution.

Bible is the highest source of authority for most Black women" in the Americas.[6] Among the principal characteristics of womanist theology is its use of the women in the Bible as holding "on to life in the face of formidable oppression."[7] Womanist theology has promoted the liberation of all women from patriarchy, racism, class discrimination, colonialism, and neocolonialism.

Though early Rastafari women did not use the term womanist to describe themselves, they exuded the characteristics of womanism. That womanism remains a developing tradition also indicates its likely presence from before the term was coined during the mid-1980s by Black women writers in the United States, namely Alice Walker, who used it as part of the struggle to extend the Black liberation movement to include Black women's resistance to the intersected oppressions of sexism, racism, classism, and neocolonialism.[8] Described as

Black feminism by Walker and several scholars, womanism was largely intended to differentiate Black and Afrocentric feminists from white and Eurocentric feminists, who neglected the intersections of patriarchy, racism, poverty, and neocolonialism. Another important element of womanism was its designation of Black women as agents of political and cultural uplift within their movements. "For Rastafari women," Ella Maria Ray has observed, "the womanist perspective privileges the internal self, the sacred, and the spiritual. It highlights what it means to be a Rastafari woman and how as such, she and her co-religionists are the source of validation."[9] Walker also referred to the communal spirit of womanism, noting that except where women had to separate themselves from men for their health, safety, and well-being, womanism was committed to the "survival and wholeness" of all women, men, and children.[10] Womanist theology specified Black women's right to criticize theological knowledge and interpret the holy scriptures through their African-oriented lenses. In other words, its focus on women's "voices and experiences of the Christian faith," rather "than anything said or decided by men," promoted Black and African-centered women's "freedom of will and mature intellect."[11]

Lennox used her theology to empower herself and other Rastafari women. She went beyond Rastafari men's critical reading of the Bible as part of her personal quest for a God she could call her own. While Rastafari men used the same quest for individual divinity to empower themselves, women such as Lennox expressed their views on their own divinity to improve or customize the understandings of divinity developed by men.[12] In this way, Lennox contributed to the development of the Rastafari's "I and I consciousness," which, as Noel Erskine writes, was developed from their literal reading of "'I said ye are Gods,'" a biblical quote from John 10:34.[13] Lennox used this notion of human divinity to argue for the equality of the sexes, or for a consciousness that was meant to serve the needs of the whole community based on a womanist understanding, an understanding that women were made equal to men in God's image and likeness and were bestowed with the freedom of will and mature intellect to interpret God's intentions for humanity based on their reading of the scriptures.

LENNOX AND THE CONVERSION OF RASTAFARI WOMEN

In 1933, at eighteen years old, Lennox was baptized into Christianity but became a Rastafari member in 1941 after her mother, Sister Elvie, moved from the St. Catherine lowlands to Pinnacle in the hills of the same parish. "I was baptized in the name of Jehsus Christ," Lennox related to Romano and Leib, but in the Christian church, "Jehsus Christ" was the one "who the people call Jesus Christ." A voracious reader of the Bible, Lennox believed that Christ, under the name of Jehsus, foretold his return and was "in no other person save His Imperial Majesty, the Emperor Haile Selassie I," the return of "the ancient king of Israel."[14] At the same time, Howell, the main founder of the Pinnacle community, which socialized Lennox into a Rastafari woman, was seen as a prophet, healer, leader, and governor, who acted as a spiritual guide and philosopher to protect the communal spirit and the recognition of Emperor Selassie's divinity. Howell's leadership, however, did not inhibit Lennox's reworking of Rastafari to facilitate the empowerment of women. Established in November 1940, Pinnacle was still in its infancy when Sister Elvie and Lennox joined the community. Each adult or each family had to work out how they would interact with or accommodate the community's principal commitments of promoting the self-reliance and self-determination of its people. Lennox's testimonies are more revealing of her views and work on the doctrine of Rastafari, but through such testimonies, and those of others who knew her and her family, we can gain insight on the formative years of her life as a Rastafari member, which were shaped by her years at Pinnacle.

While at Pinnacle, Lennox saw her mother, Sister Elvie, working among other Rastafari women as they tried to sustain their families through the fight against colonial poverty. Many of these women, including Sister Elvie, were single parents, despite the popular belief that early Rastafari women were lured into the movement by their male spouses. This belief helped to bury women's voices in the early movement and popularize the view that they were merely the Rasta-man women. In an interview in 2018, Kassa Hynes, a young Rastafari woman, asserted, "My generation slaughtered that concept" of the

Rastafari woman as merely the Rastaman woman. The generation Hynes referred to was composed of women who entered the movement in the 1990s onward, and by "slaughtered" she meant they were the ones who exposed the notion of the Rastaman woman as merely a remnant of the patriarchy in the movement.[15] But anthropologist Carole Yawney had published on the notion of the "Rastaman woman" in 1983.[16] Rastafari women of the 1930s and 1940s also joined the movement without men and resisted the patriarchal tendencies of both Rastafari and non-Rastafari men.

Alphonso Gallimore, a Rastafari man who lived at Pinnacle, indicated that Lennox's father "never" visited Sister Elvie and Lennox after they moved to Pinnacle.[17] It is even possible that Lennox's father had no knowledge of their whereabouts or had to surrender the relationship with Sister Elvie and their daughter due to Sister Elvie's departure to Pinnacle. Many women at Pinnacle were the sole custodians of children and breadwinners of their households. As these women were from the Jamaican peasantry, they were accustomed to being matriarchs or heads of their households, even while living with men. Findings based on research done in the 1950s by anthropologists, such as Clarke and Smith, showed the popularity of matrifocality among the peasant family in the rural Caribbean. Both attribute the dominance of women in these families to poverty. Clarke, who studied Jamaica, attributed the dominance of women to the economic "conditions which make it impossible for men to perform the roles of father and husband as these roles are defined in the society to which they belong."[18] Much of these conditions were due to the often racist policies of the colonial government, which restricted access to land used by the peasantry, mostly Black, to improve their standard of living, and maintained an exploitative labor market through low wages. Smith, researching British Guiana, attributed the matrifocality to men's inability to find jobs or self-employment that paid enough to sustain the practices of male dominance.[19]

The matrifocal arrangements at Pinnacle were also attributed to the women's sense of empowerment and self-reliance, notions mentioned by both Stewart and Canute Swaby, who also lived at Pinnacle. In her account of her experiences, Stewart stated that the treatment of women was "very respectful," meaning men did not mistreat women like they did in the wider society, a sentiment echoed by Swaby.[20] "All the women" residing in Pinnacle, Swaby stated, were "Rasta," and as such, they saw themselves as men's "equals," and although they saw men as "kings," they were also seen as "queens." The "men didn't rule women," he asserted. The women would accompany the men to the fields, if they wished, to "weed grass, clean it up properly." Women were "hard worker[s]," and this was even more apparent "when the man them did gone to prison and leave the woman them. The woman them did have to work hard to mine the pickney [children] them" on their own.[21] Much of Swaby's recollection is reflective of Ray's womanist view that the women are empowered through the sense of coreligionism of the Rastafari women and men. Further, Swaby's recollection is also reminiscent of Lennox's understanding that women should assert their equality with men, equality which is divinely ordained.

Lennox learned about the value of self-reliance from her mother, Sister Elvie, and other women at Pinnacle. Sister Elvie herself was a dressmaker and subsistence farmer. The lessons Lennox learned from the self-reliance of Sister Elvie and other women helped to shape her reasoning about women in the movement. Self-reliance is a principle of the Rastafari movement, a movement built on the struggle for economic independence. But it also resulted from an understanding of history that was visible in Lennox's story. Women's self-reliance during the period of slavery in Jamaica included examples such as the enslaved woman caricatured in the early nineteenth-century character known as "Quasheba," who was depicted as showing "no signs of subjection" and demonstrating "great pride in her economic independence.'" In addition, wrote Mimi Sheller, the "formerly enslaved women themselves capitalized on their special position as care-givers and working family heads to challenge ongoing exploitation and protect their customary rights during the transition from slavery to freedom."[22] These rights were also developed on the basis of African traditions, retained during slavery, including the position as working family heads. During the period of transition from slavery to freedom, known as apprenticeship, 1834–38, four formerly enslaved women named Diana Hall, Eliza Hall, Elenor Hall, and Frances Thomas absconded from their work in the cane fields for two weeks, and defended their actions by asserting "that they had many children," whom they needed to feed.[23] Women who were never enslaved, such as Nanny of the Maroons, placed high value on the sustenance and protection of their families and communities. These values were transmitted to the women of the peasantry, including those who became Rastafari women. The women at Pinnacle worked with the men in the fields, burned charcoal, worked in its bakery alongside men, and collected bat manure in the caves in providing incomes for their family, incomes which sustained and uplifted their community.

Although women were self-reliant and respected in the Pinnacle community, they also had to contend with the patriarchal values and tendencies of men. Howell himself, the leader of the community, wrote that Empress Menen was always obedient to the emperor: "When He speaks to her, she obeys His Royal Voice," Howell asserted in *The Promised Key*.[24] Lennox reworked these notions that conflicted with the lessons she learned from Sister Elvie and other women at Pinnacle. Anthropologist Jake Homiak, who interacted with Lennox in her later years, indicated that these elder women decided to exercise freedom in directing their life in Rastafari, even though it was patriarchal. "Merriam," Homiak related, "was like most Rastafari women of her generation," who "found whatever place in the movement that suited them, and while it may have been patriarchal, they kind of made peace with that and figured out their place within it."[25] Lennox decided that her place in the movement was to become a Rastafari practitioner, as this was the means she believed that she could use to empower other women.

In addition to the lessons Lennox learned about women's agency at Pinnacle, she developed her notions about gender equality from the knowledge she acquired from outside of Pinnacle during the 1940s after she began exploring other groups of Rastafari in the island's capital of Kingston. Homiak stated that Lennox frequently visited the Rastafari communities of Trench Town and Jones Town in Kingston during the 1940s. This was while selling her ground provisions, vegetables, and seasoning in the Coronation Market, located in the city center. With visiting several groups of the early Rastafari, she widened her network and built her influence on women within the Rastafari movement. Around 1947, she encountered Ras Dermonite, one "of the Pioneer Nyahbinghi Ancients," who was previously a dock worker in Colón, Panama.[26] After returning to Jamaica, Dermonite became an associate of Joseph Myers, known as Bongo Myers, who led a group of Trench Town Rastafari, starting around 1938. Lennox also visited Myers's group at Ninth Street in Trench Town, and it is possible that she met Dermonite through Myers's group as she was visiting several Rastafari groups in Kingston.

Essentially, Lennox pursued her religious interests while sustaining herself and family at Pinnacle. In 1954, she would move to Central Village, St. Catherine, when the police started to disband Pinnacle, but she continued to spread her message about Rastafari while taking care of her three children, a girl and two boys. The father of the girl is unknown, but she had the two boys with Carter Weezy, also known as Brother Little, whom she had met at Pinnacle and continued a relationship with in Central Village. Although Lennox had three children, she also thought of herself as a mother to all children, especially young women who encountered men who believed in having multiple sex partners. "You the daughter is the head of his house," Lennox asserted. "Those daughters that save and come up a fi you [is your] daughter them," and if it is "your king man that seven daughters will run to say save me," it is "you" who will "have to be the head of the house and seated in to save her."[27] Years later, from 1985 through 1987, Lennox resided at a Rasta Yard that housed a Haile Selassie restaurant in Port Maria, St. Mary, but was expelled from the compound due to a disagreement she had with Rita Marley. Homiak recalled hearing that the expulsion stemmed from comments Lennox made about Rita.[28] That Lennox disagreed with the wife of Bob Marley, who had risen to become the most famous and richest Rastafari, was another sign of her agency and womanist ideas about the right treatment of women.

EARLY RASTAFARI WOMANISM

Although notions of the equality of the sexes figured into the scholarship on Rastafari womanism in the postindependence period, such as studies by Ray and Tricia Hepner and Randal Hepner, in 1998 and 2001, respectively, Lennox's religious work has shown that womanism had manifested in the early years of the movement. Women who joined the movement after the 1962 political independence of Jamaica had inherited the views of the older generation of women who, on many occasions, were overt in challenging patriarchy and sexism in the movement. The later Rastafari women who demonstrated "highly variable views of gender," as the Hepners have written, were similar to Lennox in the sense that they also stimulated conversations about gender inequality in the movement. Like many of these later women, Lennox was in her twenties when she began to "move toward a prowoman consciousness," which essentially referred "to those sentiments shared by women who continue to struggle for their equal rights as women, though not at the expense of their relationships with men or the fulfillment they derive from motherhood."[29] Lennox's views on women, as Yawney indicated, must not be construed as unique because other early Rastafari women also insisted on "speaking about themselves."[30] Lennox herself also recognized the same spirit in non-Rastafari women, such as Sylvia Pankhurst, the British suffragist and communist, whose newspaper she read and used in showing how misguided some men had become. As Amy Bailey, a Garveyite and feminist, wrote in 1940, men insisted that women "must follow" them.[31] Similar to many Rastafari men, non-Rastafari men used the Bible to justify this view.

However, Lennox asserted, men had failed to heed the message of the Messiah in the form of the emperor of Ethiopia, who had also chosen women, including Pankhurst, to deliver God's message to the people. The fulfillment of the Messiah's love of the people transcended notions of class, race, and gender bias. According to Lennox, despite being "a white Anglo-Saxon girl," Pankhurst was at "work in the King's palace, but because of such and such she was discharge. Yet, when she was discharge from his palace, she had pronounced the words throughout the universal that it come down to us in pamphlets."[32] These pamphlets Lennox referred to included Pankhurst's weekly newspaper, the *New Times and Ethiopia News for Liberty, International Justice and Democracy,* founded in 1936. Its availability to Rastafari women and men in Jamaica was mentioned by Francis Kerr-Jarrett, one of the

largest landowners in St. James and the custos or official guardian of
the parish, in 1956, when he expressed that he was "concerned about
the number of publications and documents about Ethiopia which reach
the Rastafaris." He "pressed" Governor Hugh Foot "to communicate
with those who issue these publications and to explain to them the evil
practices and influence of the sect in Jamaica."[33]

Nonetheless, Lennox noted that Pankhurst "send the message
through the white world, white and black and pink and everyone,"
because "from the beginning woman was a messenger."[34] Pankhurst
herself "considered" the campaign for "the defense of Ethiopia" as her
"most important political activity."[35] Writing about the Italian occupation of Ethiopia in 1935–41, for example, she asserted that "it had
been left to Ethiopia alone to lead the struggle for justice" around the
world, and not only was this a struggle "for the brothers of Eritrea
and Ethiopia," but for Africa as a whole. The Ethiopian sovereign was
"among the first publicly to proclaim" an end to colonialism globally,
starting with Africa.[36] Indeed, some early Rastafari women chose to
simply abide by the rules set by men in the struggle to end colonialism, but Lennox and other women committed themselves to the task
of introducing women's ideas about the doctrinal direction of the
movement and their expectations. What was critical for these women
was developing their knowledge of the Bible and use of it for guidance.

Lennox pointed out that her own journey as a person of faith had
started in the church, but added that she "live to see and understand
that the message of King James [the Bible] was written in I and I, for
the half has never been told." With this, she enunciated the womanist
assertion of women's right to independently read, interpret, and cite
the scriptures. When she says "the half that has never been told," she
means that herself and other women knew a lot more, including differences in interpretation or understanding, of the Bible than what men
had professed.[37] Lennox and other early women also created social
groups to help them to balance the status quo of male leadership in the
movement. As Homiak recounted, "Merriam didn't become someone
in my circle until probably the mid-1980s, but I remember distinctly
Merriam was with a large group of elder Rastafari women," including
"Sister Daphne, Ma Ashanti," and others, but "Sister Merriam was the

oldest of the bunch," and "all of those were all at the stage where they were important sisters." Part of this prominence came from the fact that they "could actually be connected with several" of the foundational leaders.[38] But Lennox and the other women used their associations with these founders to boost their morale and their authority on knowledge of the doctrine and history of the movement.

Though it cannot be discounted that Lennox's age, or the fact that she was a "postmenopausal woman," played an important role in producing her prominence in the 1980s, she started to build her knowledge and influence on Rastafari from an early age. She was respected for what she had to say about the history and doctrine of Rastafari. Lennox was one of the women "called upon to speak in the Tabernacle," which was unprecedented for women in the Nyahbinghi. Most notably, the men of this group insisted on the separation of women and men during menstruation. But Lennox, as Homiak observed, "probably had the most respect of anyone" in "the Binghi House," and could even "smoke the chalice in the Tabernacle."[39] In 1979, Lennox was featured leading a group of early women in singing the lines, "come together sister, brother," "time is gliding on," and "hear the voice of Ethiopia, everyone," in a documentary film entitled, "Rastafari Voices." Later in this film, there was another woman who insisted that the "daughters would have to be fully committed to Rastafari to overcome the power of Babylon." The "Daughters," she asserted, "don't realize themselves, they are really brainwashed by Babylon. They don't see themselves as Ethiopians." Another woman also added, the "Daughters are filled with the bad wine, the bad doctrine," and "so when I and I daughters are free from the Babylonian system, they will come to know themselves."[40] These women encouraged other women to join them in opposing domination by Babylon, or what Rex Nettleford has called the machinations of the "exploiter class."[41] This class represented the mostly white elite that had benefited from the British system of slavery and colonialism, who enriched themselves and gained power by exploiting a mostly unfree African labor force and later added East Indian and Chinese indentured laborers to working conditions that bore many similarities to slavery. Such conditions included poor wages that prompted even some colonial administrators, including Joseph Beaumont, the chief justice of British Guiana from 1863 to 1868, to classify indentureship as "a monstrous rotten system rooted upon slavery."[42]

Rastafari members attached various meanings to Babylon, but in sum, it was meant to represent any oppressive system that was contrived as part of keeping Black people in bondage, whether through slavery or capitalism, and in the case of womanists, such as Lennox, it also included the oppressions of patriarchy.[43] With such mindset, Lennox and other women became vocal members of the early movement and among its most recognizable figures from the preindependence period of its development. Lennox herself had garnered enough respect to also motivate her to continue as a Rastafari and eventually saw herself as a mother of the entire Rastafari community, who "never" believed that "Rasta had forsaken her."[44]

CONFRONTING LEADERSHIP NOTIONS

Throughout her life, Lennox was committed to reworking the Rastafari religion using the Bible. However, she had to contend with notions of the Rastafari doctrine that were established by men who were leaders or key figures in the movement, such as Howell, Samuel Elisha Brown, Emmanuel Charles Edwards (also known as Prince Emmanuel I), and John Africa. These men had written guides for Rastafari's doctrine, which also reflected their patriarchal inclinations in their thoughts on women and gender relations in the movement. Howell outlined his thoughts on such issues in *The Promised Key,* published in 1935, and Brown did the same in his "Treatise on the Rastafarian Movement," published in 1966. Edwards, the founder of the Bobo Shanti (also known as Bobo Ashtani or the Ethiopia Africa Black International Congress), published a 1979 pamphlet entitled, "Love in Black Supremacy Internationally," and John Africa published a magazine article, "Black Woman," in 1979. Indeed, there were men in the movement who recognized that women were critical to the development of Rastafari. However, those publications helped to entrench patriarchy in the movement by ignoring the agency of Rastafari women.

In 1934, the *Gleaner* reported that Howell told his followers that "in 1914 there was a war in 'Jago' [World War I] which proved the coming back of Jesus Christ on earth to reign as a righteous king and set up righteous laws." Howell speculated that it was not until "November 6, 1918, a man was seen at the River Jordan, and some said He was Christ Himself."[45] Contrary to Howell's reasoning, Lennox asserted that the Messiah was seen earlier, and this took place in Africa, on the banks of the River Nile, which runs through Ethiopia, the kingdom of Queen Sheba. The first sighting of the Messiah, she also indicated, was at the beginning and not the ending of the First World War. To substantiate her claim, she referred to her reading of publications by authors, including Judge Joseph Rutherford, one of the first persons she believed to have told "the nations" of the world about the revelation of the Messiah's return in 1914 or just before the First World War.[46] Rutherford, a Missouri judge, was also the second president of the Jehovah's Witnesses. Having read his 1925 article, "Birth of the Nation," Lennox concluded that the return of the Messiah occurred in Ethiopia, not anywhere else.[47] Rutherford was considered a racist by Ethiopianist Rev. Fitz Balintine Pettersburgh and simply dismissed as "Judge Lucifer The Devil."[48] Howell adopted many of Pettersburgh's conclusions in *The Promised Key*. Lennox rejected Rutherford's racism but used aspects of his writings to argue that the Messiah had returned in Ethiopia and was Black.

While Howell claimed that the emperor had been crowned at the same time that Empress Menen was, he asserted it was the emperor that God had chosen as the one who was above humans and their laws. Empress Menen, he indicated, was the model of women's obedience and deference to men. In other words, she had no powers beyond what the emperor allowed her to have, and she was there to carry out his will. Howell also professed that Adam was the "tree of knowledge," and Eve was "the mother of evil." While Adam was "the leper" or the victim of evil forces, these forces were due to the misconduct of Eve, "the queen in hell."[49]

Writing later, Edwards, like Howell, did not consider Empress Menen as "the Black Monarch of the universal world," only Emperor Selassie, who ruled over "the universal world of right and Justice for all black sons and daughters," and lived "in every one sister and brother in one Royal blood." Though Edwards referred to "Black Africa" as "our

Father Mother land," he placed men as the head of the household and limited women to making mostly a gynecological contribution to the kingdom of God.[50] John Africa likewise advised women that "we could never be equal but this means we will complete each other together." A "woman has certain functions which are more natural to her," he asserted, "and the man has graces that are his alone," such as "creating and seeking a new world," with women playing a supportive role, mainly to inspire men "at no matter what cost." Women had "functions," while men had "graces."[51] Essentially, these views relegated women to a secondary role despite the significant contributions they were making to the movement's survival and development.

Similarly, Lennox contended with Brown's views on race and Rastafari's doctrine. Brown argued that white people worshiped a different God from the God worshipped by Rastafari, since "Gods are the creation of the inner consciousness of nations." In addition, he identified men as the only forbearers of Rastafari, or "the true prophets of this age, the reincarnated Moseses, Joshuas, Isaiahs, Jeremiahs who are the battle-axes and weapons of war." Ethiopia, Brown believed, was "the land of David's throne," even though the kingdom belonged to Queen Sheba, who had handed power to her son, Menelik I, born from her relationship with Solomon, son of David.[52]

Lennox rejected the notion of a different God for white people, which Brown proposed. "Whether you black, whether you pink, whether you red, whether you white," she insisted, "it is one man who is God, and it is Jah Rastafari, not another son." Further, a woman "gives birth to the Savior," and Lennox used this in discussing the women who saved their people by admonishing men anointed to assist the Messiah. Women who read their Bibles, Lennox professed, knew that God had blessed them to spread the doctrine as part of helping the people, women such as "Miriam," the eldest sibling of Aaron and Moses. God imbued Miriam with the "spirit," causing her to "develop and full up" in the same way that Rastafari women were also inspired to enter the movement.[53] In Numbers 12:1, Miriam disclosed the interracial marriage of Moses to "an Ethiopian woman," a revelation that, according to Lennox, was to be interpreted through the lens of Miriam's womanist opposition to the marriage because Moses was unprepared for the sacred union with "an Ethiopian woman."⁵⁴ The scripture stated, "Miriam and Aaron spake against Moses because of the Ethiopian woman whom he had married: for he had married an Ethiopian woman," but Lennox's argument was that her Ethiopian identity indicated that the marriage required more commitment than Moses seemed prepared to give at that moment.⁵⁵ Moses needed to develop his leadership of the people before entering the equally sacred role of marriage to an Ethiopian noble woman. Lennox argued that God ordained such women to be prophets and leaders in the same way that Empress Menen was ordained and endowed with the same powers as Emperor Selassie. God punished Miriam with leprosy because her intentions were misrepresented by Moses, who realized his error and asked for God's forgiveness. Miriam's importance as a leader herself was confirmed when she was "shut out of the camp seven days; and the people journey not till Miriam was brought in again."⁵⁶

When asked if it was "the law that say the man is both the spiritual and physical head of the woman, what does that mean," Lennox further asserted, "he's the said man in Queen Omego [Empress Menen] who manifest himself" and declared that "I am the Alpha and I am the Omego, the said woman."⁵⁷ As a result, women could fill any leadership position in the Rastafari movement, and women who entered the movement in later years benefited from such interpretations. Lennox's interpretation highlighted the inherent contradiction in the Judeo-Christian intimation of the first person of the trinity as God the father, noted within the purview of the 1980s by Imani Tafari-Ama, who wrote of each Rastafari adherent understanding themselves as King Alpha or Queen Omega.⁵⁸ For later women, becoming empresses signaled their defense of women's sovereignty beyond the "market system" or economic sustenance of themselves and families.⁵⁹ This sovereignty has been seen as fundamental to respecting women's ability to engage in the same religious reasoning as men and give doctrinal directions to the movement.

Lennox and other women of her generation recognized the importance of Empress Menen as a symbol of women's equality with men, a notion that paved the way for later women of Rastafari to adopt the title of "empress." The same year, July 18, 1983, that Ras Iration, an elder Rastafari man, told the attendees at the Rastafari Assembly in Jamaica that women and men were interdependent from the inception of the world, Lennox informed Romano and Leib that she was also the "empress."[60] Perhaps Lennox and Iration had a discussion about gender equality. Orthodox Ethiopian women also stood as models of religious devotion for Rastafari women and, at the same time, models of cultural and political resistance. They were the first to resist Ethiopia's colonization by Europeans and inspired their nation's anticolonial struggles. Walatta-Petros (1592–1642), for example, resisted Jesuit conversion, which led to the failure of one of the earliest attempts by Europeans to colonize Ethiopia. She also inspired the men of her Habasha ethnic group, who eventually "joined" her in resistance to the Jesuits.[61]

Many years later, Rastafari women who would infer that they were empresses would use the designation to guide their relationships with men. In 1979, Sister Farcia stated, "The dread is the head but men are beneath a righteous daughter and by virtue of their corruption and loss of masculinity, cannot stand our wrath. It is written in the book of Isaiah, 'In the last days, a woman, shall encompass a man.' These are the last days."[62] A younger generation of women whom Ray studied in 1998 would also insist "that men live up to the high principles of Rastafari." These women were by then "clear that creation required male and female—Alpha and Omega"—and decided "to follow the [movement's] codes of restriction as a way to be living reminders of how Rastafari men are to behave and what they expect of them as Rastafari."[63] Empress Yuajah, which means You Are Jah (God), is another one of the many examples of later Rastafari women who felt that women and men were equal but urged that women who also deferred to men should not be seen as their men's subordinates. Author of many self-published books, Yuajah has assumed the title of empress herself and has also used the title to give doctrinal and cultural directions to men. Her published works include *How to Become a Rasta: Rastafari, Rasta Beliefs, Rastafarian Culture*, in which she asserts that "a Rasta woman is only subservient to her man if it is written on her heart to do so," but it "is not a requirement of what it means to be a Rasta woman."[64] Many years before Yuajah and the women in Ray's study entered Rastafari, Lennox had argued that women and men needed each other to grow. As she stated, "It is a part of him that build her up," just as she should build him up so that they could support each other, or "so that she just hoist between the *irics*, for they [women and men] are weak fence."[65]

MATTERS ON THE BY-WALKS

Even though Lennox was not formally appointed as a Rastafari preacher, she believed that her experiences and work were of great importance to the Rastafari community and the rest of the world. In reflecting on her "life as a Rastafari woman," she stated, "It is only because reason of strength that I am not on the out-world missionary to preach this gospel to every nation and king word and tongue and to tell them of the breaking of day." In addition, she related that for the "forty-one years" she had "been taking part in this great revelation" of the Rastafari movement, she had been preaching her own version of the doctrine on the streets to whoever was willing to listen. She interpreted the scriptures and preached the Rastafari religion in the parishes of St. Catherine, Kingston, St. Andrew, and St. Mary. "In the early days," she stated, "we speech on the by-walks, but we were still interfere by some other people," who marveled at women preaching for the movement, as the assumption was that only men could be preachers.[66] Lennox, however, defied what has been described by scholars, such as Tracye Matthews, as the "masculine public identity" that was normally applied to the Black struggle. Lennox exemplified the women who "worked within" the existing "constraints to serve the interests of the entire black community."[67] The other members of the wider society denounced the actions of these women who promoted and defended the Rastafari movement. As Lennox related, her preaching resulted in insults and attempts by men and women in the wider society to suppress her.

Lennox also confronted men in the movement who believed that only they should be out on the by-walks preaching. Her belief that "woman did travel with Jesus Christ," and therefore "would be with Selassie in this time," stimulated controversy among men in the movement.[68] But growth in faith, Lennox understood, was only possible with the corporation of the sexes. Women and men not only needed each other to survive under Babylon but also to develop into faithful people who would manifest God's intentions for the perfection of humankind in their own relationships with each other. Thus Lennox and other early women assumed responsibility to teach the younger generations of Rastafari about their destiny in the movement, which included their involvement in promoting the corporation of the sexes in the process of development and fulfillment of God's wishes for the world. The notion "that the woman should be silent in the church" could not survive.[69] Lennox insisted that God had intended this silence only for the women of Corinth, as recorded in the Bible, so that they could lead the church of Corinth out of its corrupted ways.

On the by-walks, Lennox preached that women and men should be equal partners in the household, "for wisdom hath buildeth her house, which is a woman, and understanding, which is the man." Explaining this formulation, she reiterated that "Woman is a part of the man, a part of the man even himself." Further, validation of these ideas, she indicated, could be found all over the Bible, which had many examples of women who showed that "a woman was made part of the man." This simply meant that it was "his own power he manifest in the woman," to which Lennox added that the "first man that exist is God, which is man and then woman and then children, a manifesto of a multiplication."[70] This showed the complexity of God's work but also showed that God created men and women as equal sides of the same creation known as the human being. However, men had been using biological differences to make the case that men and women were not equal. Lennox insisted women and men were made to complement each other, and their physiological differences were meant only to ensure the continuation or "multiplication" of humanity.[71]

Despite her interactions with different Rastafari groups, Lennox challenged men's dominance of the Rastafari religion in the 1940s through 1990s. While she was tolerant of different mansions of Rastafari, she argued that there were overarching principles that all Rastafari should adhere to, especially the elimination of sexist, classist, racist, and xenophobic practices. Lennox stated that she was "only one of the Rasta woman that living in Old Harbor here as a dreadlocks," and although feeling isolated from other Rastafari who did not wear dread-locks to "set themselves off visually as a distinct group," she was still "travelling through."[72] In other words, she persisted in spreading her message on Rastafari. Lennox embraced what many people inside and outside the movement saw as the most radical strand of Rastafari, the dreadlocks, before it became a normative practice of the movement in the 1960s. She stated that "plenty of de old time Rastaman couldn't tek de message of de Locks-Dread Nyahman," but she embraced it in the 1950s.[73] As a woman, she realized that anxieties in the Jamaican society about her Rastafari identity were greater due to her locks, but this did not quell her spirit or preaching.

She even gained acceptance into a community where she was the only Rastafari adherent whom people could easily identify because of her dreadlocks, but noted in her later years, "I've been in the country, until I leave to this village" and "love the place," after becoming "much acquainted with the people around." Even though her neighbors were predominantly Christians, her preaching made them "love to hear the doctrine," which she promoted among even "the church people," who listened to her views on Rastafari and the Bible. But Lennox also had many heated debates with these people, especially the "Adventist people," over whether they should be Rastafari. Adventists "are people that I have most argument" with, Lennox stated, because "they know much about the King for there are book the Adventist print, it is called *The Hope of the Race*, and they know much about the King."[74] *The Hope of the Race*, by Frank Loris Peterson, was published in 1934 by the African American Adventist Church. Lennox had clearly read this book in which Peterson discussed Ethiopia as central to biblical history in the chapter titled, "Ethiopia Reaches *unto* God," and in which he asserted that God "miraculously sent a message of Himself to ancient Sheba," a reference to Ethiopia's Queen Sheba.[75]

Empress Menen and Emperor Selassie granted the Adventists permission to build churches, schools, and hospitals in Ethiopia, which Lennox interpreted as a sign of the cordial relations between the Messiah and the Adventists but was disappointed by their use of these relations. In reference to Emperor Selassie, "They know him as the King," Lennox asserted, "but they don't serve him as God." She decided to debate his identity with them rather than to "vex with them" and justified this decision by stating that "the writers say whosoever serve him as king shall get a king pay, and whosoever serve him as God shall get a God pay."[76] In the end, Lennox instructed them to decide which salvation was better, the one from a king, or the one from God. To become Rastafari, they needed to make this decision for themselves, just as Lennox herself had done many years before she met them. Lennox was born on August 18, 1915, and passed away on September 19, 1995, in Half Way Tree, Saint Andrew, Jamaica. Although registered as Miriam, she spelled her name as Merriam.[77]

Lennox's case summons us to think about ways in which other women were possibly creators of the doctrinal diversity of the early Rastafari movement. Her case also helps to provide a framework for research that is inclusive of the voices of both women and men on issues concerning gender, sexuality, race, and African history in the development of Rastafari doctrine. While it is not yet possible to provide estimates of the number of early Rastafari women who were advocates of Rastafari's doctrine from womanist perspectives, the observations of researchers, such as Homiak, have indicated that Lennox's departure from men's understanding of the doctrine of Rastafari were shared by other early Rastafari women. One of the aims of this chapter is to encourage inclusive research on the development of Rastafari by encouraging readers to think about the ways both women and men were creators of the doctrinal diversity in the early movement. Questions on issues similar to those Lennox recounted in her discussion of Rastafari doctrine can provide insightful research on women's contribution to the foundation of Rastafari doctrine.

CHAPTER 5

Women and the "Holy Herb" Dilemma

The cannabis plant, more commonly referred to as ganja, has been used as a sacrament and for medicinal, culinary, and recreational purposes by Rastafari since the inception of the movement in the early 1930s. Its adoption by the early Rastafari movement was closely connected to the African herbal traditions. In addition, the Bible played a crucial role in Rastafari's understanding of cannabis. They believe Solomon was buried under a cannabis tree, and wore clothing made from hemp, or cannabis fiber, but cannabis was erased from the Bible through its myriad translations over many centuries. Rastafari members insist that accurate knowledge of history would vindicate their use of cannabis and show that their beliefs and practices were right by biblical custom and divinely ordained. Eventually, cannabis became synonymous with Rastafari and a principal symbol of the movement's resistance to the colonial system. More important to this discussion is women's use of cannabis. Early Rastafari women used cannabis for several purposes. They smoked, cultivated, and sold cannabis as well as incorporated it into culinary practices. While it seemed that men dominated cannabis use as a sacrament, women were highly focused on its medicinal value.

Nonetheless, women's relationship with cannabis was initially ignored by the colonial authorities, mainly due to patriarchal and sexist notions. In the mid-1950s, some Rastafari women were arrested and imprisoned for possession of cannabis. But for the most part, they were still perceived as passive in its production, use, and sale. Some individuals in government and the wider society also assumed that these women were effectively barred from participating in cannabis rituals because of the patriarchal tendencies in the Rastafari movement. Others opined that Rastafari men coerced women into producing, using, and selling cannabis. But women used cannabis to exercise cultural freedom and exert their Rastafari identity inside and outside of the movement.

From the inception of the movement, women deemed cannabis as important in maintaining their resistance to colonialism and were instrumental in establishing cannabis as a cultural element of Rastafari. As noted in chapter 2, in 1934, Denham, the governor of Jamaica at the time, stated that the Rastafari movement advocated cannabis use as a critical part of its belief system. It is important to note that while Denham did not specify women's role in such advocacy, the Rastafari movement comprised both women and men. In fact, in the 1930s, Rastafari women participated in Rastafari rituals involving the use of cannabis. One of these cases involved a 1934 police raid for cannabis conducted on a Rastafari tabernacle in Port Morant, St. Thomas, which revealed that women were members of the 50–60 followers who regularly gathered there for worship. The women, including Alice Rennie, Irene Thompson, and Florence Gordon, participated in the ritual smoking of cannabis and resisted police arrest in defense of this practice. The women were held in police custody for disorderly conduct.[1] Gordon, for instance, was arrested "for inciting" her spouse "to resist arrest" and later "testified that her post of honour in Rasta's mythical kingdom was the glorified position of that of the 'Virgin Mary.'"[2] In other words, she saw herself as a mother, defender, and nurturer of the movement and its culture.

Ivy Thompson and Annie Stewart of Seaforth, St. Thomas, were women who were also arrested for defending men, such as Edward Hall, against their arrest for cannabis use in 1934.[3] Stewart even owned the premises where they were arrested. While critics of the movement have suggested that Rastafari women engaged in cannabis use because of men's influence, women, as newspaper reports in the 1930s indicated, found cannabis significant even before they joined the movement. Women of the peasantry, including Hilda Matthews, protested her arrests for cannabis because she used it as a "drinking herb."[4]

THE ORIGIN OF CANNABIS USE IN THE
RASTAFARI MOVEMENT

By the time the Pinnacle community was established in 1940, cannabis was entrenched in the culture of the Rastafari, and women were playing a critical role in this development. Before proceeding to further understanding women's use of cannabis, we should consider the origins of cannabis usage. The history of cannabis use can be traced back to 2700 BCE in China, 2000 BCE in India, and about 1320 CE near Lake Tana, Ethiopia. In Ethiopia, it was used for a range of recreational, household, and pharmacological purposes. It was smoked using "ceramic pipe bowls" and used to make hemp for the manufacturing of ropes, masts, and textiles.[5] The presence of cannabis in West Africa was not documented until the twentieth century. However, knowledge of its use had spread to West Africa and Southern Africa from North and East Africa centuries before Europe's arrival in the Americas in the late fifteenth century.[6] From around 1545, as researchers explain, cannabis became "the basis of a vast fiber industry especially in India and North America," and by the middle of the nineteenth century, cannabis and hemp were known in the West for their pharmacological properties.[7] At the time, medical treatment "was based mainly upon the use of herbs and plants," and government officials permitted the use of cannabis and hemp in "the medical treatment of illness and disease." But the rapid development of the pharmaceutical industry quickly led to the replacement of plant-based medicines by "synthetic" variations.[8]

Cannabis use around Lake Tana, Ethiopia, was used to validate Rastafari's use of cannabis. Brian Du Toit has argued that the presence of cannabis in Lake Tana suggests that it "entered Ethiopia from southern Arabia, or that it spread from the east African coast in a northerly direction from Bantu-speaking to Cushitic peoples."[9] Frequent use of the term "'Cush' or 'Kush'" for cannabis emerged within the early Rastafari movement as a reference to Rastafari's roots in Ethiopianism. This indicated, as Charles Price observed, that Black "religious thinking" prior to Rastafari included a belief "that the term 'Cush' or 'Kush,' a term of Hebrew origin, refers to Black people of Africa, especially those of Ethiopia and Egypt." Price also observed that Leonard Barrett, whose research on Rastafari started in 1946, noticed their use of "'Cush' or 'Kush'" for "Ethiopia," like its "Greek translation," which meant "'burnt' or 'black.'"[10]

Cannabis was used as "currency" and traded for livestock by the Black people of South West Africa, where it had arrived from East Africa, and from there also spread to Ethiopia in the fourteenth century.[11] Knowledge of such practices predated the arrival of the cannabis plant in West Africa, knowledge that arrived in West Africa mainly from North Africa through Muslim slave traders. This knowledge helped to facilitate the development of cannabis cultivation and its use among West Africans, which was reported around the time of the Second World War, in places such as Nigeria and Ghana. Beliefs in the sacred and healing properties of cannabis also complemented West African beliefs in the sacredness and healing properties of plants, herbs, and trees. These beliefs set the stage for the development of cannabis cultivation and its use by West Africans.

The general assumption is that cannabis was brought to Jamaica by East Indian indentured laborers, who began arriving on the island in 1843, mainly to work as contracted manual laborers on sugar plantations.[12] An estimated 36,412 East Indians arrived in Jamaica between 1845 and 1917.[13] By 1943, East Indians and mixed-race East Indians constituted a little over 2 percent of the population.[14]

After cannabis arrived in Jamaica, its usage quickly spread to the Black peasantry. This was the group from which Rastafari developed in the 1930s. Hindu customs were fused with African beliefs in the sacredness and healing characteristics of plants, herbs, and trees. The East Indian customs helped to validate and popularize the properties of cannabis, such as the features reported in the *Report of the Indian Hemp Drugs Commission, 1893–94*. This stated that worshippers of the gods Siva and Rama asserted their attainment of a high level of consciousness when they smoked or ingested cannabis.[15] Although beliefs that cannabis was a remedy for illnesses also traveled with East Indians to Jamaica, such beliefs were closely connected to the African herbal traditions of the Black Jamaican peasantry. Thus, a fusion of African and East Indian customs occurred. East Indians, mixed-race

East Indians, and African-descended persons who partnered with East Indians, such as Albertha Lalloo, would have contributed to this process in the Rastafari movement.[16]

Many similarities developed between East Indian and Rastafari beliefs around cannabis that suggested cultural cross-fertilizations that solidified the bonds of East Indian members to Rastafari. Cannabis use by East Indians gave Rastafari another opportunity to assert its biblical understanding of cannabis as divinely ordained. The use of cannabis by East Indians showed that its use extended beyond Africa, as God intended. Essentially, East Indian traditions helped Rastafari to validate its claims that cannabis was right by biblical customs and was blessed by God for use by all people for divine and healing purposes.[17] Such beliefs conflicted with views of the government, churches, and medical industry, which designated cannabis as a narcotic. Rastafari, however, built the spiritual powers of cannabis on the foundation of African beliefs in the sacredness of plants, herbs, and trees, understood to be "alive and full of ache (power)," "endowed with a soul," and to have "a particular Orisha (spirit)" that guarded them.[18] Some of these beliefs originated with Nigeria's Yoruba and the Congo Basin's Pygmies, such as the Efe, Mbuti, and Aka, groups that reported to researchers in the 1970s that cannabis use improved their "health," "strength," and "bravery."[19] Cannabis thus became a part of Rastafari's retention of African traditions and was part of "what they popularly refer to as the 'Ital' tradition, which centers on the eating of herbs, grains, fruits and vegetables."[20]

WOMEN AND THE DEVELOPMENT OF CANNABIS

Scholars have tended to agree that Rastafari men have smoked cannabis more than women.[21] However, until now, very little historical analysis on how women used cannabis in the early movement existed. Oral history and primary documentation have indicated that both early Rastafari women and men were responsible for promoting or transmitting information on the medicinal properties of the plant inside and outside the movement, thereby making a significant contribution to the sustenance of cannabis use as African heritage and its development as a widely accepted form of medicine. Stewart, an early Rastafari woman at Pinnacle, stated, "they cut our ganja, cut our cane, our corn and went home with it" while recounting the affinity to cannabis use, including general household use for medicinal and culinary purposes as well as sale by both women and men. Consequently, cannabis was planted alongside other crops, and recalling its sale by both men and women, Stewart added that "when ganja was booming, people buying cars, every weekend people went to hotels to enjoy themselves."[22]

Cannabis use is understood as an extension of the natural or organic medicinal and culinary traditions of Black Jamaicans, most of whom were descendants of enslaved Africans who used herbs, plants, and trees for medicines and cooking during slavery. These practices were stigmatized, marginalized, and suppressed by Anglican clergymen and the Nonconformist or Independent missionaries, many white doctors, and some slaveholders but nonetheless maintained largely by women. Research on slavery has shown that enslaved women used their African traditions to cater to the healthcare needs and nutritional well-being of the enslaved community. Thus, early Rastafari women, most of whom were descendants of Africans and from the Black peasantry, continued traditions that promoted the development of cannabis as a widely accepted form of medical treatment.

During slavery, women were recorded as dominant in preserving many of the African beliefs in the healing properties of the natural vegetation. As previously noted, enslaved women used this knowledge and their skills to protect and nurture their community. These women asserted their African identity to protect their community from the ravages of slavery. Sasha Turner writes that among these women were those who "dominated health occupations, taking on roles as doctresses, midwives, and nurses," women who "white doctors arriving in the island needed to displace." These "Black healers" were "most especially women," such as those reported on the estates of John Tharpe, a white planter who owned several sugar properties and managed others as their planting attorney. An estimated "thirty-four" women, compared with the "seventeen" who were men, were recognized as medical practitioners by the enslaved people on properties Tharpe owned and managed.[23] Much of the knowledge of the natural vegetation that developed within the enslaved community was preserved by women and appropriated by European doctors while only some of them admitted that the knowledge was "brought from *Africa.*"[24] Richard Shannon, an eighteenth-century English physician, for example, stated that enslaved people created cures for yaws and venereal diseases using powders made from the bark of the sandalwood tree, which originated in Central West Africa. They used the bark "sharpened with sour palm wine or citrus juice" to make the powders used for various ailments.[25] The Maroon communities also created their own medicines to help members physically and psychologically sustain the fight against enslavement.[26]

Use of the flora of Jamaica and Africa provided enslaved women with a means to exercise control over their healthcare and dietary needs and that of family members and other members of the enslaved community. African Jamaican women became carriers of these beliefs, which guided the socialization and care of children and adults. These healing and culinary practices remained critical during the postemancipation period and continued into the early twentieth century, a time of limited access to public healthcare.[27] Rastafari emerged from this pluralistic society based on racial, cultural, and economic exclusion. Early Rastafari women would use their African culture to resist the colonial system. They entered Rastafari with the African knowledge of the medicinal, culinary, and spiritual beliefs in the natural environment and used this knowledge to sustain their families and the movement.

In the formative years of the movement, women played a prominent role in the use of cannabis for medicinal and nutritional purposes. As Montinol Howell recounted, "women could spot things more easily in children who were sick," for example, and would administer remedies made with "herbs which is something that has a lot of medicinal value."[28] While he remembered only a few women smoking cannabis at Pinnacle, he recalled mostly women as the ones making and administering cannabis remedies. Although children were not allowed to smoke cannabis, they received cannabis treatment for various illnesses. Women made various cannabis concoctions to remedy a range of sicknesses, including cold, flu, and fever. Montinol's younger brother, William Howell, born at Pinnacle in 1942, recalled that "to us, ganja was a medicine" used for various illnesses, and researchers also found

Rastafari women using cannabis as a medicine during the postindependence period. William recalled, "the first time I really smoke marijuana was in the United States," and when his sister, Catherine, was in England, where "someone offered her a smoke," she retorted, "But I am not sick!"[29] As a result, a large number of Jamaican children grew up seeing or hearing about the use of cannabis as a medicinal treatment, as well as a culinary additive. Women added cannabis to drinks that they gave to infants because it was also "thought, among other things, to make them clever."[30] Obiagele Lake, writing in the 1990s, showed the survival of these cannabis practices among Rastafari women, who used it to make teas that were given to children as pain relievers and to treat several illnesses, including asthma, joint pain, and other ailments. These included mixing cannabis with cane rum or "white rum," to use for skin irritations and to relieve muscular and joint pain.[31] Women also believed that the plant's nutritional content made it suitable for culinary uses, which included seasoning for vegetarian meals, including soup.

Rastafari women also integrated cannabis into the movement in ways that tied its medicinal value to its religious significance in the movement. For them, the physical, nutritional, as well as the emotional and mental benefits of cannabis justified it as the "holy herb," or a sacrament of the movement and a source of healing.[32] It should also be noted that to persist in their use of cannabis, women, like men, ascribed various names to it, such as "wisdom weed," to also show its importance to "their doctrine, practice and worship."[33] Among the longstanding myths about Rastafari women, Lake wrote, "is that they do not smoke ganja." However, this myth was fueled by the fact that men were more commonly seen "smoking ganja in public."[34] Most of the women with whom Lake interacted smoked cannabis. Of about thirty-five women, she mentioned encountering only one woman who did not smoke.

In 1958, Rastafari's first Universal Convention, held at the Coptic Theocratic Temple in Kingston, was attended by 300 members "of both sexes from all over the island," and there were newspaper reports of rampant cannabis smoking by the attendees.[35] Smoking cannabis became a popular part of the reasoning rituals in which women participated from before the independence period. Jah Bones, an elder Rastafari man, recalled a session he had organized with five men and two women, Sister Alice and Sister Etta, in 1958, which involved smoking the chalice, or cannabis pipe. These reasoning sessions were ceremonies "of varying degrees of formality," which involved the ritualistic smoking of cannabis.[36] At the more formal sessions, known as Grounation and Nyahbinghi, women could be seen passing the cannabis pipe, also known as the "chillum pipe," to other women and men.[37] In 1975, Barrett visited the Rastafari community at Nine Miles, St. Thomas, to attend a Nyahbinghi, where he observed members of both sexes smoking cannabis rolled in paper, or "spliffs," which were made "up to seven inches long."[38] In 2002, Jeanne Christensen participated in a Nyahbinghi session where groups of women entered and left the tabernacle while smoking cannabis.[39]

For both women and men, cannabis smoking symbolized the conception of the church as an individual or, as Joseph Owens recorded, that "the true church is not a building, but the person of a believer."[40] They smoked cannabis as part of sanctifying the believer, the true church. Women joined the protest of Rastafari through cannabis smoking, described by Barrett as "the first instrument of protest" to show their "freedom from the laws of 'Babylon.'"[41] The pursuit of this freedom highlighted what social science theorists, such as Anne Cudd, have called the "concerted effort" through which resistance often stands a better chance of becoming effective.[42] Women's involvement in cannabis smoking also bolstered the retention of African culture as integral to Rastafari's spiritual practices. The use of cannabis formed part of showing that its use "was right by customary acceptance and by traditional 'mores'" from before the genesis of the movement.[43]

Women at Pinnacle, in the 1940s and 1950s, therefore, represented their sense of oneness as Rastafari members by using cannabis to aid their family and community members. However, while many men often saw cannabis as "the symbol of brotherhood, manhood and wisdom for them," women tended to promote its ability to uplift the Rastafari community through its healing powers.[44] In the 1940s and 1950s, these women at Pinnacle also made themselves part of maintaining it as a close-knit and independent community through cannabis sales. This aided in continuing the freedom of Pinnacle's residents from the exploitation of their labor power by the colonial capitalist system.

These sales enabled the residents to live by their communal principles, wherein work was done in unison and the goods shared in what the press described as a "socialist" or "communist" experiment.[45] This was confirmed by its description by the leader. A number of early Rastafari leaders would choose areas in the hills that facilitated the cultivation of cannabis in relative secrecy, such as the site of Pinnacle, situated in the hills of St. Catherine. These areas were also known for their fertility, while maintaining access to densely populated areas, such as Spanish Town, Kingston, and Bull Bay in St. Thomas, which had growing markets for cannabis. These areas presented opportunities for cannabis sales to the public through the persons who had visited Rastafari communities, such as Pinnacle, for the purpose of buying cannabis.[46] Women at Pinnacle, therefore, stored cannabis in their homes, even if they did not smoke it. Sometimes they were attacked while going to market in Spanish Town, for example, and the newspaper reports on some of these attacks specified that they were done by persons hoping to find cannabis.[47]

Women also sold cannabis outside of the Rastafari communities. Homiak recalled his encounters with Mama Bubbles, an elder Rastafari woman, as late as the 1980s. Mama Bubbles "had a son who was growing weed" at Angel's Heights in Bogwalk, St. Catherine, and where Homiak said he "made several trips."[48] Women, such as Mama Bubbles, were not shy about defending cannabis as an income earner, despite its denouncement as a narcotic and illegality in Jamaica, which began in 1913, or almost two decades before the inception of Rastafari. The high value these women placed on cannabis helped in making Rastafari the target group of the government's mission to destroy cannabis use by the population. Neither Rastafari women nor men saw cannabis use as "a criminal offense" but, rather, writes Chevannes, as part of "a religion to defend."[49] The law suppressing cannabis helped to create what Barrett also described as "a kind of survival system," one developed by early Rastafari men and women.[50] But this also ensured that cannabis provided a means for the government to suppress the movement, which was perceived as a group of outcasts by many influential members of the society. What follows is a discussion of the diverse ways in which early women initiated some elements of the survival system used in negotiating the government's suppression of the movement through cannabis.

WOMEN AND THE CANNABIS RAIDS

Medical treatments, especially those made with cannabis, were often maligned by the colonial government, the elite members of society, and the churches. The Jamaican upper and middle classes, members of the local press, and the Council of Evangelical Churches led a campaign in support of local legislation against cannabis use in any form. This legislation materialized in 1913 as Law 15, or The Opium Law. Although named for opium, the law specified, "It shall not be lawful to import into this island any prepared opium or ganja." In addition, it banned "the growing of opium and ganja in Jamaica."[51] The penalty for possession of cannabis was initially a £100 fine, roughly £9,912 in 2020, or one year in prison, with or without hard labor, if the fine was unpaid. Passage of the subsequent Dangerous Drugs Law in 1924 specified that cannabis offenders faced up to £250, approximately £14,360 in 2020, for second and subsequent offenses, and the possibility of two years imprisonment.[52] In 1941, the Dangerous Drugs Law introduced mandatory imprisonment of a year for first-time offenders.[53] Subsequent amendments to the Dangerous Drugs Law in 1948 and 1961 empowered judges to impose maximum mandatory sentences of up to five years and unlimited fines even in the case of first-time offenders.[54]

Early Rastafari women, such as Audrey Lewis, argued that the suppression of cannabis was a strategy "the government have fooling the people," one that was not only about undermining cannabis or Rastafari.[55] The criminalization of cannabis, Lewis indicated, served to manipulate the society into rejecting the African traditions of the masses as inferior to the customs and traditions of Europe. In other words, cannabis eradication became crucial to continuing the colonial domination and suppression of Black people. The emphasis on cannabis was connected to its use in improving the economic condition of the people. More important was that the government promoted the notion that cannabis was harmful and targeted Rastafari for suppression largely because the movement was becoming one of the most influential advocates of the value of African traditions. According to Lewis, this value was demonstrated by the sale of cannabis to facilitate the economic uplift of poor Black people by the 1940s.

Suppression of African traditions also existed during slavery as enslaved women used herbs to facilitate "sterility" or abortions.[56] In light of this, slaveholders suppressed African medicines to increase the population of enslaved people and deflected attention from the harsh practice and conditions of slavery that stimulated acts of sterility and abortion. Nonetheless, these conditions produced both physical and psychological hardships and helped to necessitate the retention of traditional African cultural practices. "Herbs and powders" were noted especially among women who practiced the African-derived folk religious tradition known as Obeah. The preparations were used by other women to make conscious decisions about their healthcare needs. In addition, Barbara Bush writes, African "women carried their skills with them to the New World and were valued as 'doctoresses' and midwives." Despite the attempts by some white doctors to suppress their use of "folk medicines," the skills of these women were valued on the sugar plantations. The "more perceptive Europeans" eventually "acknowledged the efficacy of many folk remedies derived from Africa."[57] But this efficacy, Lewis believed, explained why the government suppressed cannabis use by Rastafari members. "We would be a better people" if the government did not suppress cannabis, she stated, for "is only that we could find to live off a; nutting else for us to live off a."[58]

Prior to the 1954 police raid on Pinnacle, the involvement of Rastafari women in cannabis use received little attention as men were thought to be either the main or sole producers and smokers of the plant, which was designated a narcotic by the government. Between 1941 and 1953, for example, the police conducted several incursions into the Pinnacle community, but no women were reported as arrested on cannabis charges.[59] Recalling these raids, William Howell stated that they were mainly "for Ganja," though some were "plain Money Shake Down," since cannabis was sold to persons who visited the community.[60] Describing an undocumented police raid in 1951, Lewis also noted that the police pursued only the men, including her father.[61] In 1954, during a massive raid on Pinnacle, 44 percent of the 140 persons arrested were women, who were found in possession of cannabis, however, most of them received lighter sentences than men from Judge H. P. Allen of the Resident Magistrate Court of Spanish Town, St. Catherine. Together, the women were sentenced to a total of 306 months, while the sentencing of men totaled 894 months, almost three times more. Adina Manning, along with Alfred Bennett and James Bennett, for example, were accused of cultivating 5,000 cannabis plants on a three-acre lot and having an additional eighty pounds of freshly cut plants. Manning was sentenced to eighteen months, whereas the men were each sentenced to twenty-four months. Similarly, Robert Stephens, who was about eighty years old, was charged jointly with Adlyn Scott, who was about seventy years old, but Stephens was sentenced to twelve months, while the case against Scott was withdrawn.

Although court records have indicated that women received lesser sentences than men, this does not negate women's knowledge, use, or production of the cannabis plant. Moreover, some of these women sought to protect men and their children who were arrested for the possession of cannabis. They were aware of the misperceptions that the wider society had about their agency in the movement. In other words, they were aware that members of the wider society believed they did not partake of cannabis and were submissive. Thus, women used this knowledge to circumvent or reduce harsh punishment for themselves and family members. Women, Mack indicated, were usually the ones who tried "to obtain bail for a brother who was incarcerated; usually for possession of ilee (marijuana)."[62] In 1941, the *Gleaner* also reported "a large number of the women-folk" from Pinnacle "came down to see their men-folk marching into and out of the Court."[63] These men were originally arrested for cannabis but later charged with assault and larceny, which at the time carried harsher sentences for first-time offenders. In court in 1954, Mary Brown, who knew that her husband, Claudius Brown, had a previous conviction, pleaded guilty to being the sole owner of the cannabis. Mary was sentenced to nine months for the cannabis found on their premises. After hearing his wife's sentence, Claudius pleaded guilty, and told Judge Allen that "he would like to follow his wife who had been previously sentenced," and "was given a two-year term" because of his previous conviction.[64] Dorothy Bryan, jointly charged with her daughter, Alice Marriett, for two pounds of cannabis, "pleaded guilty" in exchange for Marriett's release, and the "case against Marriett was withdrawn."[65] Olive Malabre, who had two teenaged daughters, Eugenie and Winnifred, pleaded guilty so that "the case against her two daughters" could be "dropped."[66]

After the trials, women continued their various uses of cannabis in more covert ways, and this helped to fuel the suspicion that they were secondary to men with respect to cannabis use by the movement. Nonetheless, both women and men continued to challenge the illegality of cannabis by highlighting the benefits of the plant to the individual and society at large, even after the Jamaican independence from Britain in 1962. Following independence, a host of male reggae singers would advocate the religious values and healing properties of cannabis in their songs, such as Peter Tosh's "Legalize It" (1976) and Bob Marley's "Kaya" (1978).[67] Similarly, female reggae singer Rita Marley, in her song "One Draw" (1982), promoted cannabis use while noting women's importance in African consciousness and history.[68] Ultimately, women's and men's resistance to the suppression of cannabis contributed to the development of greater insight into the use of cannabis for cultural and medicinal purposes among members of the wider society. Such insight helped to facilitate the state's decision in 2011 to initiate discussions of the decriminalization of the possession of small quantities of cannabis, a total of two ounces or fifty-six grams per person, which many Jamaicans also believed marked a watershed moment in a process that will ultimately lead to the legalization of cannabis in the island.[69] Elderly women of the movement, such as Sister Ita and Sister Wood, who spoke to the National Commission on Ganja in 2001, even defended the medicinal use of cannabis by teenagers, stating that those who "use herbs are into a more sober, normal lifestyle than the downtown rush."[70] These women's views had an impact on the conclusions of the ganja commission, views deemed critical knowledge to factor into the parliamentary deliberations over the decriminalization of cannabis prior to its official decriminalization by Parliament in 2015.

Early Rastafari women helped to developed cannabis use through their knowledge and continuance of African herbal traditions. Despite the suppression of cannabis by the government and patriarchal notions, they persisted in using it primarily for medicinal purposes. Jamaica has gained a great deal of knowledge from the early Rastafari women about the use of cannabis as a medicinal treatment for various illnesses, including respiratory problems and rheumatic disorders, such as arthritis, and for the alleviation and management of pain. As of 2020, cannabis has been legalized for recreational use in fifteen states in the United States as well as two territories (Guam and Northern Mariana Islands) and Washington, DC, and thirty-four states and two territories (Puerto Rico and US Virgin Islands) allow the use of medical cannabis.[71] Persons must be twenty-one years of age to use cannabis in any US state where it is legalized or decriminalized. The usual process toward legalization involves first decriminalization, and some states have followed a pattern of legalizing medical cannabis before also making its recreational use legal. Jamaica is at the decriminalization stage but should not have to simply "sit and watch" and wait for the United States to act or hope that the legalizations at the state level in the United States will change federal policy, which controls the foreign policy of the United States.[72] Jamaica should, instead, capitalize on the developments at the state level, including challenging the US government's position on cannabis with documentation of the knowledge that has been long possessed by Rastafari women and men. This is not the same as taking a "position to defy international treaties."[73] What it means is ensuring drug policy is based on knowledge developed through experiences that started long before the criminalization of cannabis, knowledge both Rastafari women and men have developed around the medicinal as well as culinary benefits of cannabis and the best practices for its use for these purposes.

Just as Rastafari clearly benefited from women's understanding of cannabis from its early period, the future development of the cannabis industry stands to benefit from women if they are not marginalized in this industry. In addition to what women know about cannabis, women's recollections of the history of the early movement can add to understanding of the movement's diversification in the early years.

CHAPTER 6

Audrey Lewis and the History of the Early Rastafari's Development

Although Rastafari has become a major cultural force that has often been equated with Jamaican culture internationally, resistance to the heavily influenced European rules, values, and norms of the Jamaican society were a crucial part of Rastafari's development. The early movement countered British colonial domination, as well as the creole nationalism of local labor leaders who pursued political independence through the British parliamentary system. Thus far, this book has provided stories about, as well as voices of, several early Rastafari women on various aspects of resistance. However, Audrey Lewis is the only early Rastafari woman presented who discusses the historical development of the Rastafari movement against the British colonial government and creole nationalism. Lewis was also known by her married name, Audrey Whyte, but reverted to her maiden name and is therefore referred to by that name here (fig. 3). Lewis recognized that the attempts of the colonial government to suppress Rastafari had serious epistemic implications, namely the distortion of the movement's history and, by extension, its development. Therefore, past experiences stood as an important tool of resistance for the Rastafari movement, and Lewis sought to preserve and publish its story through oral history, both from the perspective of the movement and also from the perspective of women. As such, she was invested in ensuring that Rastafari remained an important part of the cultural landscape of Jamaica.

Lewis was socialized in the Rastafari movement from her childhood days and provided a largely counterintuitive account of the various experiences of women and men who entered the movement in the 1940s. In an interview conducted at her home in Salt River, Clarendon, on May 5, 2013, she gave testimony of the diverse range of

FIGURE 3.
Audrey Lewis, Hill 60, Salt
River, Clarendon, Jamaica,
1998. Lewis is seen standing on
the tomb of her late husband,
Ruppert Whyte.
Courtesy of Jake Homiak.
Papers of Carole D. Yawney,
National Anthropologi-
cal Archives, Smithsonian
Institution.

women's adversities that had resulted from the suppression they faced
during the colonial period. Her account of Rastafari history shows
that women helped to sustain the cultural life of the first Rastafari
members through their varied forms of resistance to counter the range
of suppression they faced. Moreover, women's defense of men signified, overall, their defense of the whole movement from suppression.
Lewis's account bears similarity to the narratives of enslaved people.
These slave narratives documented "evidence" of the conditions of slavery and the effort of the enslaved to resist slavery in the Caribbean, the
same region into which Lewis was born in 1932.[1]

Lewis's testimony can also be referred to as what Monique Bedasse
described as "Interior History," a history that highlights the importance
of "representation" through the "ways in which Rastafarians" themselves think.[2] This must also include a critical analysis of their often-var-

ied recollections of the history of the movement. These accounts can be evaluated using the documentation from sources such as the government and press, but they also give us an opportunity to perform the same critical analysis on the documentation. Thus, Lewis sheds further light on life in the Pinnacle community, one that challenges the colonial views on the original movement and its leadership. Incursions on Pinnacle that were conducted by the public health officials, an unknown police raid conducted in 1951, and women's agency in defending the men of the movement during this raid are factors discussed by Lewis in her discussion of the relationship between government and the Rastafari movement. This discussion has indicated that the movement gained a growing following and was also able to overcome suppression because it encouraged socioeconomic improvement and divine authentication of the African heritage of the people. After surviving the colonial period, the movement was also able to attract even more followers to become a cultural staple in and beyond Jamaica.

THE CULTURAL DIVIDE: JAMAICA AND RASTAFARI

Through its history of British colonialism and slavery, Jamaican society developed as one highly susceptible to cultural resistance, and Rastafari was formed out of such resistance. The movement remained dissatisfied with the status of the African culture in the society, even though the island's culture was viewed as plural by some scholars and creole by others. M. G. Smith's assessment of Jamaican culture using the plural society model argued that it was mainly composed of African and European norms and values developed during colonialism and slavery. The colonial government, however, subordinated African culture through a "mythology of 'progress'" that disseminated wealth and power unequally among the different racial groups making up the society. The African majority, "four-fifths" of the total population in 1961, occupied the least "structurally significant" position in this society.[3] Edward Brathwaite, on the other hand, writing in 1971, argued that the culture of Jamaica was a combination or blending predominantly of its African and European traditions to create new cultural forms. Yet the creole society was the child of pluralism since it created new cultural forms from the heterogeneous colonial past, and the structurally significant elements of these new cultural forms perpetuated European domination.[4] Pluralism was also acknowledged by creole nationalists, who used it in promoting the creation of a nation-state based on the concept of a creolized society.

While it is apparent that there was some degree of cultural fusion of African, European, and East Indian traditions in the Rastafari, Lewis indicated that the early Rastafari was not only a symbol of resistance to European cultural dominance; it explicitly challenged this dominance through the Pinnacle community established in 1940. Lee estimates that Pinnacle was established on a sizeable property of about 153 acres, but even this may be a conservative estimate.[5] As stated in chapter 3, different estimates have been provided for the size of the property. In 1946, a *Gleaner* report stated the property was composed of 1,300 acres, while a subsequent estimate provided by the island's Office of Titles at the Registrar General's Department stated that the property was about 485 acres.[6] In addition to promoting the economic welfare of its members, the community was developed to promote the African consciousness of Rastafari but met fierce resistance from Jamaica's colonial government. In her account of her experience at Pinnacle, Lewis stated that she, among other women, embraced and engaged in various African cultural activities, including singing, dancing, and celebrating Emperor Selassie and Empress Menen, the sovereigns of Ethiopia. Rastafari women made one of their most visible marks on the culture of the early movement by preserving the African folk traditions. Through the preservation of Jamaica's folk traditions, women diversified Rastafari culture by fashioning it to accommodate their own notions of their African heritage. Following her departure from Pinnacle in 1951, Lewis herself was known as the Kumina Mother or "Kumina Queen," a title attributed to other Rastafari women at Pinnacle. They ensured the preservation of Kumina. The "Kumina Queen" was essentially a spiritual and cultural "female-leader" of "the Howellites," who promoted the blending of Rastafari culture with the African-derived, religious-folk tradition known as Kumina.[7]

The role of the Kumina Queen in Rastafari signaled continuity rather than change. Women occupying the same role in Kumina were usually the persons responsible for the transmission of its religious, spiritual, and medicinal culture from the older to the younger generation. The continuity over which the Kumina Queen presided included the preservation and promotion of African religious, spiritual, medicinal culture and consciousness. Included in this Kumina cosmological and therapeutic consciousness was the practice of using the powers of ancestors to bolster the struggles of the living. This is why, as Dianne Stewart has observed, the "cross" was important in Kumina. In addition to being a "fundamental symbol of religiosity in classical BaKongo civilization, from which Kumina religious culture is derived," the cross symbolized the triumph over persecution through the resurrection or revival of the slain, vanquished, downtrodden, oppressed.[8] The integration of Kumina's culture with Rastafari culture grew the reception of Rastafari's African consciousness by helping to further legitimize this consciousness among the African-descended peasantry, who composed most of the population of Jamaica. This integration was not creolization, as it did not lead to a new practice that was a blend of Rastafari culture and Kumina. Rather, selected elements of Kumina were integrated into Rastafari to fortify its claims to being authentically African or to develop its African consciousness. This integration can be described as the "syncretizing" of Rastafari with the African-derived, religious-folk traditions already on the island, traditions that also included "Pukumina, Revival or Revival Zion."[9]

The parish of St. Thomas, where most of the Pinnacle residents came from, has been described by Olive Lewin as "the centre of Kumina," which also had "striking" similarities to the Rastafari movement, aiding the syncretizing of the two. Kumina was "one of the purest traditional African non-Christian retentions in Jamaica," which developed in the island between 1841 and 1865 with the arrival of indentured African laborers who came from mainly Central Africa.[10] Stewart, who was also at Pinnacle in the 1940s, stated she "grew to see and dance Kumina" in Pinnacle, where the "most spiritual life was when we were working with Kumina." A Kumina Queen named Sister Ina, she recounted, "used to wash feet and be filled with the spirit."[11] Clinton Hutton has asserted that "Kumina cosmology, rituals and other cultural expressions would play a significant role in the shaping of the identity of Rastafari," a role embraced and practiced by both men and women at Pinnacle, who saw no conflict between their practice of Kumina and their Rastafari beliefs and rituals.[12] Kumina, like Rastafari, was rooted in "African traditional thought," including its emphasis on "cooperation and communal camaraderie rather than the glory of the individual victor."[13] Kumina's communal spirit mirrored Rastafari's socialistic conception of the community as a family.

Women and men of the Howellites rejected the criticisms of their Kumina cosmology by other Rastafari organizations, particularly the Nyahbinghi mansion of Rastafari. Both men and women in the Howellite movement saw no conflict between Rastafari beliefs and their Kumina beliefs, including spirit possession. Such views were maintained by Howellites during the early years of the Rastafari movement when other emergent Rastafari organizations, such as the Youth Black Faith, progenitor of the Nyahbinghi, strongly rebuked Howellites for Kumina practices that incorporated Revivalist practices into its culture. Kenneth Bilby and Elliott Leib, for example, mentioned the "ambivalence" of some Rastafari toward "certain fundamental aspects of the Kumina religious experience, such as ancestral spirit possession and the emphasis placed on the continuing participation of the dead in the affairs of the living."[14] Howellites were also criticized for being "flesh eaters" because they did not adhere to the strict vegetarianism and veganism of other Rastafari mansions. In addition, some Howellite women rejected the wearing of locks. As observed by Homiak, the "combsome/dread divide" affected not only men but also women who decided whether they would wear locks.[15] As observed in chapter 4, the decision to wear or not to wear locks indicated women's sense of independence in the movement.

After Lewis departed Pinnacle in 1951, she became a Kumina Queen, a prominent cultural and spiritual leader of the Hill 60 community in Salt River.[16] In 1962, the same year as the Jamaican independence from Britain, the community was renamed "Beulah," a name derived from the Book of Isaiah 62:4–7, which partly states, "You shall no longer be termed Forsaken, Nor shall your land any more be termed Desolate."[17] The members of the newly renamed community interpreted independence as also granting them more freedom to steer Jamaican culture toward the recognition and acceptance of Rastafari's African religious culture. No longer, they reasoned, would Rastafari be forsaken or their community considered desolate or isolated from the wider society. Lewis became known as "Guyo," the cultural and religious matriarch of the Beulah community.[18]

While African folk traditions occupied a significant role in the culture of the early Rastafari, the religion was the overarching aspect of this culture. In fact, it was one of the most condemned aspects of Rastafari culture by the colonial government and wider Jamaican society during colonial rule. Christianity, Rastafari members opined, had its origin in Africa, but was appropriated by Europeans, who used it for the oppression of Black people. The Rastafari movement had its own interpretations of the Bible, and members met regularly for fellowship to pledge allegiance to Emperor Selassie and Empress Menen, whom they believed were the divine rulers of Black people and the world and would guide them to "Zion" or "the Promised Land."[19] Zion or the Promised Land indeed signified Ethiopia but were also used as religious metaphors for freedom from colonial and racial oppression in addition to social and economic prosperity in Africa or the African diaspora. As Lewis herself, among other women such as Lennox, indicated, Rastafari was responsible for enlightening the people about the return of the promised Messiah, the emperor and empress of Ethiopia, even "through the white world."[20] Further, Rastafari's *livity*, or "way of life," established Zion or the Promised Land wherever Rastafari people might be situated.[21]

Such understandings challenged European Christian notions of white dominance that Lewis and other women in the early movement also denounced. European churches, Lewis asserted, were disingenuous and suppressed Black people: the "church have nothing special for us," and "if we to follow the parson, plenty of the parsons come out of the way." The parson "tell we don't eat bread, but him a eat bread."[22] Many women joined the early Rastafari because they believed that the movement championed the rights of poor people and facilitated a better future. They felt that the leadership of the churches, namely the Anglican church, had failed to demonstrate enough regard for them as poor people and were misguided.[23] As such, Rastafari was superior to the churches because it aimed to redeem the poor, most of whom were people of African descent, from social, economic, and political repression. Rastafari also promoted among its members the "consciousness of their divine, African selves and the lifestyle that emerges from that awareness." A part of their "doctrinal individualism," this awareness was critical to their self-reliance and was used to pursue their social and economic improvement, which they also believed could be achieved through education.[24] Contrary to the perception that early Rastafari members were uninterested in education, Lewis argued that the government tried to inhibit the schooling and acquisition of knowledge by Rastafari members.

The Pinnacle community provided an elementary education with an African focus for the children in their early childhood years, and women, namely Bent, taught many of these children. As the early childhood years were a critical stage in a child's socialization, and education is an organ of culture, it was expected that they would be equipped with knowledge from the African perspective that would make them conscious of the ills of the dominant culture, that is, the British culture, by the time they were ready to attend colonial schools. In addition, it was anticipated that this knowledge would also facilitate the development of their self-awareness or self-consciousness, a critical factor of self-reliance. However, Lewis pointed out that many Rastafari children, including herself, were banned from the schools in the society. While living in the Pinnacle community, she attempted to gain access to a colonial school when she was eleven years old but was denied enrollment because of her Rastafari identity. Recounting the incident, Lewis asserted, "they would represent us in no school," so "I just remain for is there [at Pinnacle] me grow, and to leave there now, where would I go?"[25] Though it is not certain how long Lewis would have remained at Pinnacle and perhaps in the movement had she been granted access to an education in the colonial schools, it is apparent that she, as well as other children and their parents, valued education and did not see formal schooling and their membership in the Rastafari movement as mutually exclusive.

SETTING PINNACLE'S RECORD STRAIGHT

By 1940, about eight years after its inception, the early Rastafari movement, mainly the Howellites, established Pinnacle. This was, as previously stated, the first Rastafari community that sought to operate
autonomously, but it experienced several government interventions
throughout its existence. The government painted a stark picture of the
community, indicating that it was infested with criminals, malnourished women and children, and impoverished fanatics of religion.
However, the Howellites rejected the government's claims. Lewis,
who lived at Pinnacle between 1940 and 1951, and after this visited
the community until 1958, pointed out that the community was unsta-
ble because the government was intent on undermining the Rastafari
movement and used both public health officials and the police force to
stifle its social and economic development. As a woman, she believed
that Pinnacle was an equitable and just community, one built on socialist principles, and one in which women would often protect the movement from even the police personnel.

Describing her time at Pinnacle, Lewis recalled that life there was
"very nice," but this pleasure was marred by interventions of the health
department and horrific periods of raids conducted by the colonial
police, which interrupted the stability of the community. Howell's leadership of Pinnacle, Lewis asserted, also made the suppression of the
community a priority of the government. He was the most prominent
founder of the Rastafari. Officials in the government perceived him as a
despotic man who was abusing his followers in the community. Reports
in the *Gleaner* newspaper also published the government's stance that
defiant residents were tried and sometimes beaten by "special whip-
ping men," or expelled by Howell, who acted as judge and jury. One of
these reports disclosed its source for the information, a government
public health official named "Mr. A. DaCosta, Inspector of Poor for St.
Catherine."[26] News of the trials raised concerns among officials, who
also concluded that Howell was a tyrant.

However, Lewis insisted that the rules instituted by Howell were
basically the same as the ones stipulated for the wider Jamaican society. Such rules, she recounted, included "don't steal people goods" and

"do not go out by the road and give people problems," and because "all those things" came from "Mr. Howell," who had an "understanding" of their importance to building their community, his followers abided by them.[27] They felt that these rules were not only beneficial to them, but such were also important to the stability and development of their community. Gertrude Campbell, a contemporary of Lewis, who was one of Howell's secretaries in the late 1940s and 1950s, also insisted that "a lie them a tell, a them come in destroy we," when asked about the assertion that "there was a lot of violence in Pinnacle."[28] Some of the persons to whom Campbell referred were not members of the community but intruders who came there to steal their produce, especially cannabis. These were the people tried, punished, and expelled. Campbell further asserted that the population of Pinnacle, an initial 700 people, whose occupation of the community started in November 1940, climbed to over 1,000 people prior to any of the incursions by the police.[29] These people, she insisted, chose to join the community after hearing about the prospects of peaceful coexistence and expectations of economic prosperity based on a socialistic lifestyle.

Even though the movement promised a better future, Lewis indicated that poverty existed at Pinnacle because many of its residents had been the poorest people of Jamaica, especially its single women, who came there by themselves or with children. These individuals sought refuge in the community and anticipated reprieve, which was not immediately possible. Some women also came to escape from physically abusive relationships with men. Stewart herself had also confirmed Lewis's point that the women at Pinnacle were safe from abuse by men, partly because this was against the rules of the community and partly because the women banded together to protect themselves.[30]

The public health officials were dispatched to Pinnacle after cases of malnutrition were reported. However, in the report on his first visit on behalf of the Medical Board of St. Catherine, F. W. Aris observed that a "state of starvation" existed in the entire community.[31] A total of four such visits took place, three of which happened within less than a month of each other. These visits were made on November 29, 1940, December 31, 1940, January 11, 1941, and February 5, 1941,

and the reports on each visit maintained that the entire community was hopeless and destitute, circumstances deemed particularly
harsh for children and for women, seen as the primary caregivers
of the children. Writing of the living conditions, Aris reported that
the houses were "shacks" built from "plain wattle," which were "not
weather-proof," and contained "rough beds" that were "made of sticks
with no mattresses and scanty filthy bedding," and sanitation was the
worst that he had seen. He also stated that "the latrine accommoda-
tion" serving the community "was entirely inadequate," and that "water
had to be brought from some distance away."[32] After the second visit
on December 31, 1940, Aris also reported that "undernourishment
prevails," which was "especially marked amongst the children."[33] In the
absence of a field officer from the Agricultural Department of Jamaica,
the public health officer also pointed out that there was "yield from the
land" which he did not think would "be adequate to the demands of
the future."[34] Following the next visit, on January 11, 1941, eleven days
after the previous visit, Aris stated that "a state of acute starvation now
exists," and that the "symptoms are especially marked amongst the
children and young adults who are weak and emaciated."[35]

Lewis contested the severity and hopelessness of Aris's accounts,
as well as similar depictions by J. Hall, the assistant director of the
island's medical services.[36] Her description highlighted struggle,
creativity, and self-reliance. This description corresponded with a
rare photograph taken of some of the children and women at Pinnacle. Taken by a reporter for the *Jamaica Times* and published in
the newspaper on July 19, 1941, the photograph shows the children
almost uniformly dressed in clean, light-colored clothing, possibly
their school uniform, with four of the women, their guardians or
teachers, proudly standing adjacent to and behind the children. Two
men wearing dress shirts can also be seen in the photograph, as men
were usually placed at the school as guards (fig. 4). The headline
provided by the newspaper for the photograph, "The Raid Didn't Seem
to Bother These Juvenile Ras Tafarians," bears testimony to Lewis's
account of the resilience and pride of the Pinnacle residents, including the children.[37] In addition, Lewis noted that despite the absence
of piped water, a situation that also affected most of the people in

THE RAID DIDN'T SEEM TO BOTHER THESE JUVENILE RAS TAFARIANS

FIGURE 4.

A rare photograph of women and children at Pinnacle, Jamaica, July 19, 1941.
Courtesy of the National Library of Jamaica.

Jamaica, Pinnacle residents had regular access to clean water from the Rio Cobre River in St. Catherine, where they went to bathe daily and brought back some of this water for purification and household use. Bathing daily, Lewis explained, was a necessity. Later, a well was dug at Pinnacle, which also gave them regular access to water. Where food was concerned, women of Pinnacle practiced mostly small farming since most of them were members of the Jamaican peasantry. They planted a range of food crops, including red peas, gungo (pigeon) peas, callaloo, potatoes, yams, bananas, and plantains. They also reared poultry and goats, along with burning charcoal and making household and personal items, such as sandals, activities they shared with the men. They sold some of their food crops, as well as many of the items they made, at markets in Spanish Town, Sligoville, and Kingston.

Lewis even expressed delight about the quality of the sandals, adding that they sold quickly.

LEWIS AND THE 1951 POLICE RAID

While the government indicated that Pinnacle was raided for the illegal growing of cannabis, Lewis, among other Howellites and other early Rastafari members, suggested that raids were used in an effort to disband Pinnacle and ultimately end the Rastafari movement and that the government hid some of these raids from the public to protect itself. Prior to the 1948 amendment to the Dangerous Drugs Act, which made the punishments for cannabis possession even more severe, Eustace McNeill, the representative for St. Catherine on the Legislative Council of Jamaica, had telegraphed Alexander Grantham, the colonial secretary, on December 23, 1940, and reported, "I visited Poor House Spanish Town and was shown over twenty inmates of both sex," allegedly from Pinnacle, where they became malnourished, emaciated, and contracted diseases. McNeill added, "I would advise that government take immediate steps to have proper investigation as certainly this state of affairs should not be allowed to continue."[38] Grantham decided to explore McNeill's suggestion, and in January 1941, stated that "steps should be taken to dispense the misguided people of this strange cult."[39] However, subsequent admonitions from Arthur Lewey, the attorney general, on April 15, 1941, stated that no evidence of "criminal negligence" had been substantiated in any "Medical Report," and "Malnutrition" itself "might result from ignorance and not neglect."[40] Within two months of the warning from Lewey, the police in Spanish Town reported they had received a letter proving that Howell had broken the law by sheltering a wanted man named James Nelson.[41] Historian James Robertson states, "He may be the James Nelson of Duckenfield in St. Thomas, fined £50 for ganja possession in 1938."[42]

Lewis was unable to talk at length about the Nelson allegation and the resulting police raid on Pinnacle on July 14, 1941, as she was nine years old at the time. Nonetheless, she related her experience of an undocumented 1951 police raid that had devastating effects on Pinnacle. This raid, Lewis explained, occurred the same year that she had left

Pinnacle. It was also the year of Hurricane Charlie, popularly known as the '51 Storm, that had hit Jamaica and killed about 110 people and caused damages amounting to roughly £16 million sterling.[43] Additionally, this raid resulted in Lewis's father leaving Pinnacle for Salt River when she was nineteen years old. Lewis also stated that shortly before the 1951 police raid, she had decided to remain at Pinnacle and would have stayed at Pinnacle at least until the police returned to clear the community of its remaining residents in 1958, had her father not left the community to avoid arrest in 1951.

Shortly after Lewis's father left for the bushy flatlands of Salt River in Clarendon, the police went to his house at Pinnacle to enquire about him. But Lewis told them nothing and ensured that her younger brother, Alfred, who was five years old at the time, did the same. "They did not want to put my father in jail," but he fled knowing that he had knowledge about the cannabis that was cultivated in the community. It was a terrifying encounter, but Lewis remained nonchalant, keeping her fears hidden. As she explained, there was more than one police officer, and before leaving, they spat "in the copper of food" and taking "the ashes from underneath the copper" and throwing "it in the food" meant "nothing for us to eat." Despite this and similar experiences, Lewis stated, "plenty of us [women] never leave" and helped the men to escape arrest.[44]

Women also knew that the police arrested men in hopes that the women would be unable to fend for themselves and their children, thereby leading to the disbandment of the community. However, these women persisted without men and showed that the destruction of Pinnacle would continue to fail if the effort of the police remained gender specific. Referring to this gender-specific approach, Lewis pointed out that "most of the man that did leave that they never catch to carry to prison got to put on all like that lady dress, tie him head like a woman, just so that the police don't ill-treat him."[45] In other words, women helped men to avoid arrest by disguising them as women and, apparently, the women were successful, as the police thought these men were indeed women. To say that these women were under the domination of the men is therefore problematic. These were men who were desperately seeking to avoid arrest, men who at those harrowing and desperate moments had rested their fate in the hands of women, whom they were confident could help to shield them from arrest. Women, therefore, played an active role in defending not only Rastafari men but also the movement against colonial suppression.

THE POLITICAL AWARENESS OF WOMEN

Almost the entire first half of the twentieth century was characterized by neglect of the political consciousness of women in the Jamaican society. For the Rastafari woman, this neglect was coupled with the perception that they were unaware of the politics inside and outside of their movement and unable to make informed political decisions. Nevertheless, Lewis used her account of the history of the movement in the preindependence period to show that she and other early Rastafari women understood the political dynamics of Jamaica and Rastafari and disapproved of the colonial government's strategic efforts to mar Rastafari's social and economic successes. The growing influence of Rastafari, Lewis also indicated, led significant elements within the creole nationalists to also suppress the movement for political leverage. In 1962, Jamaica gained independence from Britain through the creole nationalist agenda of unifying the nation based on a national cultural identity developed through the creolization of its plural society. Nonetheless, Lewis and other Rastafari members continued to emphasize the development of the African consciousness of Jamaicans instead of the maintenance of the nation's ties to Britain. Rastafari thought the independence obtained by creole nationalists would lead to a new form of colonialism, one that would continue the social and economic inequalities of the colonial period. Rastafari's African consciousness was based on the possibility of creating an equitable society through the fair distribution of land to the people so that they could produce for themselves and family members. This project had started at the Pinnacle community but was crushed by the police raids in 1951, 1954, and 1958.

While dissecting the Howellites' encounters with creole nationalism, Lewis condemned Alexander Bustamante and the Jamaica Labor

Party's (JLP) preoccupation with suppressing the Rastafari movement and Howell in particular. Bustamante had formed the JLP to contest the first national elections in 1944. The JLP won these elections and held onto power until it lost the elections of 1955. Bustamante was thus the first chief minister, or government leader, following Jamaica's acquisition of universal adult suffrage in 1944. The JLP government shared power with the colonial authorities until the 1955 elections. Lewis deemed Bustamante "a killer [of] black," who "never like" Black people. In this description, she used the term "killer" both in its literal and metaphorical sense.[46] Not only were the police armed whenever they executed the raids on Pinnacle, Lewis also argued that imprisonment had the potential of leading to the deaths of Rastafari people. If incarcerated, they were cut off from their community while having to endure the inhumane conditions in the prisons, including the infamous St. Catherine District Prison, where the Pinnacle residents were usually sent. In addition, Lewis's condemnation went beyond the impression that Bustamante feared Howell simply because of the latter's disapproval of the trade union movement as deceiving the people with a solidarity that would not elevate their African identity or liberate them from persistent poverty. Before Bustamante was the chief minister of Jamaica, he wrote to the colonial secretary in 1939, advising that Howell was a "danger to the peace of the Community," was "the greatest danger that exists in this country today," and recommended his immediate confinement in prison or the mental hospital.[47] Lewis, in her own recollections of Bustamante, asserted that he not only condemned Howell, but he also "send in his government to us so the school never get to go on."[48]

Several such incursions occurred after Bustamante's 1944 election victory while Lewis was also in school at Pinnacle. The incursion that she remembered the most, however, occurred in 1951, as this was the one that stimulated her departure from Pinnacle. Like other Rastafari members, Lewis argued that the JLP's approach was one of aggression toward the Rastafari movement. She also argued that the aggression was inspired by the successes of the movement, such as its acquisition of land at Pinnacle and its schooling of the children at Pinnacle, rather than only the movement's criticisms of the trade unions. The main point Lewis made was that Rastafari had made itself into a viable alternative to creole nationalism, one that was gradually improving the social and economic condition of the people, one invested in their ownership of land and their education, and had even attempted to use the colonial schools. In Lewis's view, Rastafari promoted an African consciousness that counteracted the colonial education that threatened their strong sense of self-worth, resourcefulness, and independence as African descendants. These were the successes that Lewis indicated Bustamante saw and considered as the Rastafari movement's main threats to creole nationalism in continuing its influence over the masses of the people.

Lewis and other members were confident that the movement would overcome the effort to suppress it. Rastafari's triumph in this regard, she believed, was a revelation. As she explained, the politicians "know what they doing is not a part of right, but they take it for right, so don't fight them, leave them."[49] In other words, she believed that in time, Rastafari's suppressors would self-destruct, and the movement would gradually transform the society politically and economically toward African consciousness and the Rastafari's socialistic conception of the nation as a family. Like the crisis of capitalism that Marxism predicted, Lewis prophesied that Jamaica's political and economic system would continue to squeeze its marginalized majority into a fundamental state of antagonism. After all, this same situation had led to the Morant Bay Rebellion in 1865. Many members of the peasantry, acting "individually or co-operatively," opted to invest "their savings in land purchase" after emancipation from slavery in 1838, and many diversified their food crop production by shifting into cash crops, namely coffee and banana in Jamaica.[50] By 1890, they were producing these cash crops for export. Jamaica's peasant cash crop exports increased from 11 percent of the island's exports in 1850 to 23 percent in 1890.[51] However, many of the peasant landholders were ultimately deemed as "squatters" because they lacked the documentation to prove their ownership and were removed from their land by the colonial government, a process started in the 1870s.[52] Economic policy changes by the government in the 1890s, due to the rise of banana as a principal plantation crop, also led to the government's promotion of the plantation system and, consequently, the displacement of many of the peasant landholdings.[53] With this historical background, Rastafari sought to activate the process of transforming the nation into an African nationalist political condition, one that emphasized the restructuring of the nation around the building of a community through equal opportunity.

Creole nationalism remained the dominant aspect of political ideology in Jamaica, but Rastafari, as Lewis believed, indeed became a major cultural force in the country, as seen in its influence on the Jamaican language, education, food, religion, politics, music, aesthetics, herbal traditions, among other aspects that have helped to reinforce the African consciousness of the Black majority. At the same time, creole nationalists promoted independence through a national identity that represented the blending of the racial and ethnic components of the society rather than through the Rastafari's understanding that African consciousness should be the basis of unifying the nation or the foundation of its national identity. As early as 1937, Rastafari leaders had asserted that "the black or colored man as the white man, has no apology to make if he preaches racial solidarity."[54] As the colonial government and elements of the creole nationalist movement deemed Rastafari's African consciousness as alienating to other races and ethnicities that made up Jamaica and denounced the movement's religious beliefs as cultism and escapism, they were able to legitimize the attempts to suppress the Rastafari movement.

SUBALTERN VOICES

Though Lewis was not appointed a formal leader of the Howellites, she believed that it was her duty to protect Rastafari's history. She recognized the importance of transmitting this history to future generations. Indeed, her narrative is provided from her views as a Rastafari member; however, a history of Rastafari's development without the voices of both major and subaltern actors would be insufficient. Lewis is not just subaltern in the sense that she was a member of the movement, she was marginalized because of her gender status. It should also be noted that records on the early movement were created within a colonialist framework and based on the ostracism of the movement and patriarchal underpinnings of the society. Such context also accounted for Lewis's intent to provide her side of the story. Yvonne McClean, a practicing Rastafari also known as Sister Hodesh, spoke of Lewis's commitment to promoting her views of Rastafari's history and culture even in her final days: "I remember my last talk with Mama Audrey. She told me don't beat up on yourself, we are doing a lot. I used to meet with her once a week . . . talk with her on what needs to be done, and updating her on what's happening."[55] In her later years, Lewis was part of the Rastafari's struggle to wrest control of Pinnacle from private developers. She used her recollections of Pinnacle to support this struggle and was always willing to speak publicly about the colonial effort to disband Pinnacle and strip the Rastafari of any claims they could make to the land on which they built the community. She argued that the deficiencies of the early movement that the government officials had highlighted were exaggerations aimed at undermining especially the diverse and complex accomplishments of the Pinnacle community. Good sanitation, hygiene, nutrition based on organic farming methods, and independent production of a range of household and personal products formed crucial parts of their lived experiences at Pinnacle. The principal problem that these practices and accomplishments posed for the government, Lewis argued, was that they were established for the purpose of enabling the people to physically, psychologically, and materially sustain their freedom from colonial domination and resist control by the less radical creole nationalist movement. Lewis was eighty-four years old when she died at the Lionel Town Public Hospital, Clarendon, in 2016, three years after the Jamaican government finally declared one of the six central plots at Pinnacle as a protected National Heritage site.[56]

CHAPTER 7

A Prototype of Pinnacle

Edna Fisher and the African Reform Church

In January 1959, the Jamaican police reported there were only 1,640 Rastafari members on the island.[1] The previous year had seen "the last raid and dismantling" of the Pinnacle community.[2] Many of the remaining residents dispersed from the community returned to St. Thomas and Clarendon while others settled in Tredegar Park and Central Village, St. Catherine, nearer to Pinnacle. For the police, the disbandment of the community was a sign that they had diminished the Rastafari movement. In January 1959, however, the year after the last police raid and dismantling of Pinnacle, Edna E. Fisher and Rev. Claudius V. Henry launched their African Reform Church of God in Christ (ARC) and located it in St. Andrew, a parish that was normally seen as part of the island's capital of Kingston. It was clear to the Jamaican officials that the ARC, like the Howellite's organization, revered Ethiopia and promoted the implementation of the ideology of Black nationalism in Jamaica. It was also apparent that the ARC had replaced the Howellites as the most popular Rastafari organization. As noted by Judge Herbert Duffus at the trial of the ARC's leaders, who were charged with treason-felony in 1960, "a man called Leonard Howell" had "assumed exactly the same role as Henry now assumes: a self-appointed prophet to lead the people of Jamaica back to Africa."[3] Howell was tried for sedition in 1934 and sentenced to two years at hard labor.

The Rastafari movement might have become numerically smaller, but the police also reported that in 1959 it had spread to ten of the island's fourteen parishes. It was also being approached by both major and minor political parties hoping to gain the trust and support of Rastafari members.[4] Leaders in these parties realized that the movement was still influential. Approximately 300 women and men from around the island, for example, some of whom were not affiliated to any Rastafari organization, had attended the first Universal Rastafari Convention in 1958, held at the Coptic Theocratic Temple in Kingston.[5] However, central to the discussion here is that women were determined to rebuild Rastafari despite persecution from the wider Jamaican society. Paulette Sweeney, who joined the Rastafari in 1960, noted that she was raised by parents "who is well known," but people would often say that "she take herself and turn dutty [dirty] Rasta."[6] This vilification manifested in more serious ways that affected other women in the movement. One of them was Edna Fisher.

On February 26, 1970, Fisher left Green Bottom in Sandy Bay, Clarendon, and went to Rocky Point, a fishing village hub, to order her choice of catch to sell at her fish shop in Kingston on the weekend. By midday, it was eighty-two degrees Fahrenheit and showers on the eastern ridges and adjacent areas of the island had affected the day.[7] Nonetheless, Fisher was determined to get the catch of the day to supply her customers, many of them higglers or small retailers who sold at the fish markets in Kingston and St. Andrew. After securing her fish, she usually organized for Kingston, but decided to return home after reaching Free Town, three miles from Sandy Bay. While waiting for transportation to take her back to Sandy Bay, she saw a public passenger bus and quickly hailed it to stop for her. The bus stopped, but little did Fisher know that this would be the end of her eventful life. She was stabbed multiple times by a couple of men and unceremoniously dumped at the side of the road.

Fisher was one of the two Rastafari leaders, the other being Henry, who had established the ARC in Jamaica based on advocating Black nationalism and the repatriation of Black people who wanted to go to Africa. Fisher was also one of the fifteen members of the ARC who were subsequently charged with the first and still the only treason-felony crime against the Jamaican government since the enactment of the Treason Felony Law of 1869. The trial occurred on October 11–29, 1960.[8] Under Jamaican law, treason-felony was defined as planning to depose the state using violence or compelling policy changes using violence against state officials, for which the sentence could be imprisonment for life. For over thirty years, most of the Jamaica Colonial

Office files on the ARC were kept confidential or classified, but over the course of 1987–93, the public gradually received access to these files. This access sparked a variety of discussions among scholars as well as the public, discussions that made Henry the face of the ARC and the treason-felony trial in 1960. In fact, these events were deemed "the Henry-fiasco" or the "Henry Rebellion."[9]

Consequently, up to this point Fisher's role in building the ARC had never been put under a microscope. It was the norm to exclude women from the press coverage and studies of the early Rastafari movement. The women who participated in the 1934 sedition trial had a similar experience. Most of their testimonies were excluded from the press coverage of the trial. Although Fisher was marginalized in the scholarship and media reports on the ARC, she helped to transform the political and social development of Rastafari and Jamaica through her organization and direction of the ARC to spread Black nationalism. Fisher's ARC was reported by the colonial government as having the largest and most politically significant following formed after the final disbandment of the Howellites' Pinnacle community in 1958. The ARC was viewed by the government and many within the wider society as representing the reconstruction of the Howellites' struggle to establish Black nationalism in Jamaica after the fall of Pinnacle. As such, the Howellite and ARC organizations were the only ones ever charged for crimes against the government. Furthermore, it would be the controversy generated by the ARC that would mostly create the government's investment in studying Rastafari in 1960 and exploring its demands for repatriation to Africa in 1961. In many ways, Fisher was one of the two creators of a church that was to play a pivotal role in the colonial and early postcolonial attempts to both appease and suppress the Rastafari movement.

FISHER AND THE ESTABLISHMENT OF THE ARC

While Henry's relationship with the ARC has received much attention from scholars, this has not been the case with Fisher, even though she was recognized by the authorities as playing a central role in the genesis and development of the ARC. In his analysis of the press coverage of Henry's testimony at the treason-felony trial in 1960, Anthony Bogues, for example, noted "that a significant moment in the evolution of his beliefs came when he met Edna Fisher."[10] But Bogues only wrote briefly on Fisher in his study, *Black Heretics, Black Prophets: Radical Political Intellectuals.* Women have been traditionally marginalized in studies on the politics of the radical Black liberation struggle of the early Rastafari movement. Even though press reports were saturated with the government's focus on Henry as the leader of the ARC, the organization mainly originated from "a prayer circle" that was formed by Fisher.[11] Born in 1911 in Martha Brae village, a rural riverside community situated in the parish of Trelawny in northwestern Jamaica, Fisher was relocated to Kingston to live with an aunt following the death of her parents while she was still a child. She was subsequently enrolled into St. George's Primary School, a Jesuit girl's infant and primary school, located at 80 Duke Street, Kingston, which she attended up to the "second standards," around eighth grade.[12] The Jesuit missionaries had noted the resistance of Jamaican parents and children to their proselytism, citing "African inheritances" as tending to "form a considerable barrier to the practice and spread of Christianity."[13] It is not known if Fisher continued any formal education after leaving St. George's, but she could read and write very well, and was very good at accounting. As late as 2018, St. George's was still ranked among the "sought-after" primary schools in the Kingston and St. Andrew corporate area due to high performance in "Literacy and Numeracy."[14]

Fisher married in 1942, but the marriage was short-lived. Afterward, she earned a living from a fish vending business and was "regarded as strictly honest" and "very hard-working." She had "no children" or any "previous conviction," the police reported.[15] She made enough money to buy land at 78 Rosalie Avenue, located in the Waltham Park area of St. Andrew, in 1951. She also built a house on this land, where she started hosting the meetings of a prayer circle composed of thirty-five women. Many of these women were fellow members of the EWF, a pro-Ethiopian organization brought to Jamaica by the Rastafari movement, most notably Paul Earlington, who joined the movement in the 1930s and was considered the principal organizer of Local 17, the first EWF chapter in Jamaica, established in 1939. The EWF was also maintained on the island by women including a Miss Green, Iris Davis, and Carmen

Clarke.[16] Green was reported as the fourth president of Local 17, but her "appointment was a compromise between rivals," and internal divisions continued and eventually led her to "remove herself together with the Chapter of the Local."[17] Davis and Clarke joined its replacement, Local 31, established in 1942, and both women "often filled the position of secretary and wrote letters" for the Local. It is possible that these three women were also members of Fisher's prayer circle.

In addition to the EWF, Fisher had been a member of the Universal Negro Improvement Association and African Communities League (UNIA) before forming the ARC with Henry. The UNIA, established by Marcus Garvey and Amy Ashwood Garvey in Kingston in 1914, added to Fisher's network of Black nationalists, a network built through her Rastafari, EWF, and UNIA connections, as well as her fish vending business.[18] Fisher built her fish vending business in Kingston but regularly visited coastal areas in Clarendon and Manchester "to purchase fish," about thirty miles and fifty miles from Kingston, respectively. She knew people through a network of fish purchasers and suppliers that included "a depot at Beeston Street and Text Lane" in Kingston.[19] But, in 1958, Fisher would join forces with Henry to expand her prayer circle into the ARC after they met at the Palisadoes Airport in Kingston, established in 1948 and renamed the Norman Manley International Airport in 1972. Henry began preaching in Manchester, where he was born in 1903, in the town of Colleyville. Newspaper reports and subsequent scholarship have described him in detail, notably as someone prone to "visionary experiences," who began to "question the authority" of the state church, the Anglican church, from a young age.[20] He migrated to the United States in 1945, initially took up painting for a living, and later became interested in biblical studies, acquiring a preacher's license in 1950. Ordained a Baptist minister in Cleveland, Ohio, in 1953, he returned to Jamaica in December 1957.[21] Besentie Thompson, who became an ARC member in the early 1960s, stated that Henry's wife "cautioned him about returning" to Jamaica, "telling him how much they suffered there for them to return," and even gave him an "ultimatum" to "divorce him," but he left telling her that he had to "obey" God's calling.[22]

Fisher had heard about Henry's trip to Ethiopia, which he had embarked upon less than a month after he returned to Jamaica from the United States. After returning to Jamaica on December 9, 1957, he visited Ethiopia in January 1958, and again in September 1959.[23] Since Henry had visited Ethiopia and formed his own Ethiopia Coptic Church in the early part of January 1958, Fisher thought that his supporters could expand her prayer circle and that they could benefit from his knowledge of Ethiopia.[24] Rastafari members strongly embraced the connection to Ethiopia. Thus, Henry was expected to provide much insight on the leadership and principles of Emperor Selassie and Empress Menen in guiding Black people. Furthermore, Henry, like Howell, was one of the few persons who had made a convincing claim of visiting Ethiopia. Henry's knowledge of the emperor and empress was not the only important aspect of Fisher's interest in him. Fisher also decided to pursue Henry to build her own organization, which would advance Black nationalism in Jamaica.

GENDER DYNAMICS OF THE ARC

While the ARC appeared to be a male-dominated organization, Fisher saw her role as equal to, although different from, that of Henry. Henry was the religious leader and spiritual guide, and Fisher was the administrative and commercial head. As Johnathan Reid, who also joined the ARC in the 1960s, asserted, "she was a very shrewd business woman. Accountability was among her endearing characteristics." She was the one who "started the bakery at 78 Rosalie Avenue in Kingston," and the Howellite's ESS, one should note, had established a bakery in Kingston. Reid also stated that he "was afraid of her because she was so strict."[25] Furthermore, she was one of the two persons responsible for the formation of the ARC. At the same time, gender disparity in the ARC was part of the chauvinistic belief that men should oversee and provide direction for the organization. A common feature of the Black liberation struggle of the twentieth century was that the men believed "that male supremacy" was needed to fight "white supremacy."[26] On the contrary, women, even the "young girls [who] were members of the church," Fisher asserted, constantly challenged such beliefs. They believed that discipline was essential to the effective functioning of the ARC and reflected this in various forms, such as upholding the

Rastafari's ideology, which focused on biblical understandings and Black nationalism. Women would even wear uniforms, as men did, to show discipline and commitment to the ARC. Fisher herself pointed out that both women and men "dressed alike."[27]

Like the Howellites, Fisher believed that the ARC was of the same high status as her former organization, the UNIA. Howell tried to meet with Garvey, the UNIA's founder, for an "interview" in 1932, but "Garvey did not consider him of any importance to give him audience."[28] Fisher stated, however, that she felt great pride the day that "two flags were hoisted at Rosalie Avenue," one "red, black and green," the flag of the UNIA, and the other one "red, gold, and green," the flag "used in Ethiopia."[29] Douglas McKay, a member of the ARC from the 1960s, noted that "coming out of the Garvey movement," Fisher "was already grounded in her black philosophy."[30] Garveyite women created their own images of the Black woman, which did not conform to Victorian ideas, or much of "the vision of womanhood upheld by Garvey himself."[31] Adina Spencer, for example, became a feminist and socialist who wrote for *Plain Talk*, a UNIA newspaper, under the pseudonym of "Woman of the Masses."[32] The rank and file members of the UNIA's paramilitary unit, the Universal African Motor Corps, was not only composed of women, they had also volunteered hoping for "military training."[33]

Fisher's role in the ARC was also shaped by her experiences in the Coptic Church, of which she was a former associate.[34] This church was established in Jamaica by Joseph Nathaniel Hibbert, a Rastafari founder, who spent some twenty years outside of Jamaica and returned on October 12, 1931. While a member of the Coptic Church, Fisher understood that women and men were created equally and this was one of the main reasons she formed her own prayer circle and, eventually, her own church. Religion was just one of the platforms that early Rastafari women used to diversify the movement by challenging its patriarchal tendencies. In fact, Fisher's exhibition of her agency through religion could be compared to that of former Howellite Lennox, who was instrumental in interpreting and diversifying Rastafari doctrine based on gender issues. The Jamaican government knew that Fisher and other women contributed to the development and sustenance of the ARC, but the treason-felony trial later indicated that the government conformed to the narrative that these women were second-class members of the organization and pawns of Rastafari men. The government's approach had been to focus on the suppression of the men, as it had done with the sedition trial of Howell and Hinds, and subsequent arrests of predominantly men in the 1930s and 1940s. This approach also led to press reports that emphasized the role of men in the ARC, even though Fisher and other women were critical to its organization and promotion of Black nationalism to replace British rule.

THE GOVERNMENT AND THE RISE OF THE ARC

The ARC developed during one of the most critical moments in Jamaica's political history. The island was on the verge of independence from Britain, which had colonized it since 1655 and intensified the system of African enslavement, started by the former Spanish colonizers. Jamaica was a leading member of the West Indies Federation, formed in 1958, a diplomatic and economic union of British colonies, which was expected to facilitate the pursuit of self-rule by its member territories. Jamaica was also facing Cold War pressure from both Britain and the United States over the possible spread of communism to the island after the 1959 Cuban Revolution. This problem was compounded by the Rastafari movement. The creole nationalist politicians feared further growth of the Rastafari movement, which also promoted religious notions that countered those of the established churches in Jamaica. Many politicians considered the Rastafari religion as outlandish; however, they were more concerned about the movement's Black nationalist message and the fact that poor Jamaicans were in search of deliverance from colonial poverty.

Jamaicans' attachment to Africa, the Promised Land of Rastafari, had a much longer history than their associations with political parties, including the powerful JLP and the People's National Party (PNP), the two dominant parties formed in the late 1930s and early 1940s. Ethiopianism and its liberation theology helped to position Rastafari to become a powerful political force in Jamaica, one that could steer the island toward Black nationalism to accomplish its independence from Britain and western capitalism and, ultimately, facilitate the physical repatriation of those persons interested in returning to their ancestral homeland of Africa. As the ARC had assumed the position of the Pinnacle community and the Howellites' ESS, it became the new target of the government. Both the British and Jamaican governments believed that the ARC was preparing for a violent coup, one that would create a government they expected to execute their Black nationalist plans, including creating a political relationship with Ethiopia.

In March of 1959, three months after the ARC was established, there were approximately 200 followers of the church, but by June, this number had increased to an estimated 300–400 followers and included both Rastafari and non-Rastafari individuals.[35] The promotion of repatriation, it was noted, played an important role in this increase and was spread through the pamphlets the ARC started issuing in March 1959. As the ARC rose, so did the government's concern about its development. However, the government would suppress the ARC through a strategy it had previously used on Howell and other Rastafari leaders. It decided to put Fisher and Henry, as well as other key members of the ARC under police surveillance. Police surveillance remained one of the government's main strategies used to control the Rastafari movement. In 1956, for example, Hugh Foot, Jamaica's governor, wrote to the Colonial Office, London, stating that he would "ask the local Standing Intelligence Committee to see that a special eye is kept on Rastafari activities." He also stated that "there are pockets of Rastafaris in the slums of Kingston and Montego Bay which seem to be centres of various forms of crime and vice."[36] A number of the Jamaican officials believed most Rastafari members were involved in criminal activities. In April 1960, Kenneth Blackburne, the successor of Foot and the island's first Black governor, asserted that Rastafari followers, in general, were "violently anti-white," and were mainly "angry young men."[37] Amidst the government's fear of violence from Rastafari members, there was the ARC's castigation of the Jamaican and British governments for keeping Black people in colonial poverty. Furthermore, in March 1959, the ARC had issued a "Certificate of Membership" for "The Lepers Government," that is, a government representing poor Black people. "Manley and Busta," it asserted, were "just two more slave masters leading us no where."[38]

Bustamante, or Busta, founder of the JLP, and Norman Manley, a founder and leader of the PNP, headed the two political parties that dominated local politics in Jamaica at the time. Bustamante opposed and tried to suppress the Rastafari movement, as previously discussed in chapter 6. Manley, a Fabian or democratic socialist, believed that the "British constitution" was "the best in the world," as it could provide "the only good system of government."[39] In 1960, Blackburne also reported that members of Manley's cabinet described the Rastafari movement as one of those "ugly forces" intent on doing harm to "the substantial progress toward racial unity that had been made," an "attempt to put the clock back."[40] Regardless, approximately 1,200 people had attended the ARC's Emancipation Jubilee Celebration on August 1, 1959, showing that the church had assumed the status of Pinnacle in terms of having a great deal of support among the people. Similar to their relocation to Pinnacle in 1940, a number of them left their homes and even "sold their houses in the country so as to have money to take with them to Africa."[41] But a subsequent public meeting held on October 5, 1959, ended in disarray after the promise of repatriation on that day was not fulfilled by the ARC. Even the police, the government reported, were "called to restore order."[42] This event, the authorities believed, not only showed that the ARC had a large following, it also made the organization appear suspicious. Subsequently, the police began gathering more intelligence on the ARC by using informants.

Much of the intelligence the police gathered suggested that the government was concerned about the spread of communism by leaders of the ARC. Similar anxieties were expressed about Pinnacle in the 1940s, as suggested in the *Gleaner* report on the community as a "socialist colony" and conflating socialism and communism.[43] Moreover, the investigation of the ARC, led by the police, was conducted within the climate of Cold War politics, which had made both Britain and the United States fearful of the spread of communism in the Caribbean, as the July 1959 Cuban Revolution, led by Fidel Castro, was in operation, and Cuba was one of Jamaica's closest neighbors. At a meeting of the United Rases Organ (URO), held at 20 Crook Street, Jones Town, St. Andrew, on March 26, 1960, George Alphonso Williams, chairman of the URO, was reported as stating that "they also needed arms, but 'the Reverend' (Claudius Henry) was in touch with Fidel

CASTRO and although the Police would be watching him on his return he would find some means of contacting CASTRO."[44] The records do not show whether Fisher attended this meeting. However, there is evidence to suggest that Fisher made an attempt to contact Castro. At the same time, it was important for the authorities to control media reports that could potentially undermine the stability and popularity of the government. Consequently, Blackburne, in April 1960, advised that the "position so far as relates to foreign intervention is completely unreal and press reports overseas greatly exaggerate that aspect."[45]

Of greater concern to the Manley government, Blackburne asserted, were the reports indicating that the JLP and minor leftist parties, namely the People's Freedom Movement (PFM), had been trying to influence Rastafari members to vote against the PNP. Intelligence from the police "indicating that any trouble between the Rastafarians and the P.N.P. may involve also the opposition J.L.P" was seen as a more credible concern than infiltration by Cuba.[46] It was also "rumored," as anthropologist Sylvia Wynter observed in 1960, "that the Rastas turned against the Manley Government because they were encouraged to believe that if they helped, by votes and violence against the P.N.P.'s opponents, they would be assisted in their return to Africa."[47] The police report on the meeting in Jones Town, held on March 26, 1960, also stated that it was attended by Richard Hart, a PFM leader who was regarded as the most prominent Marxist of Jamaica since the 1930s.[48] In addition, Joseph O'Sullivan, an Irish-Canadian and PFM associate, was reported to have told ARC leaders he would teach them about Marxism, but the Manley government declared him a persona non grata, and he left the island on June 30, 1960, for Cuba.[49] Ivy Harris, another leading member of the PFM, was also reported to have met with leaders and followers of the ARC in St. Andrew and Clarendon, respectively.[50]

Despite Blackburne's argument that the Rastafari support of the JLP and leftist parties was a problem that required the government's focus, the threat of a coup by the ARC trumped that concern. At 5:30 a.m. on April 6, 1960, St. Andrew's Halfway Tree police raided Fisher's premises at 78 Rosalie Avenue with warrants authorized to prevent possible violence by the ARC.[51] Deputy Superintendent Wilfred McIntosh, who oversaw the raid, noted that Fisher's bedroom was the first that was searched because he knew of her involvement in the ARC and knew that she owned the house and the rest of the property. As he entered Fisher's room and read the warrants, Fisher, who "was in her night dress," exclaimed, "me want fe put on mi clothes."[52] McIntosh then began the search, as Fisher and Henry observed. Various contrabands were found inside Fisher's room as well as an unsealed enveloped in another room. Consequently, Fisher and Henry were both arrested, along with thirteen members of the church, on charges of treason-felony.

FISHER V. THE CROWN

On October 21, 1960, the tenth day of the treason-felony trial, Fisher testified against the Crown in the Halfway Tree Circuit Court. She pleaded not guilty. She denied having any knowledge of or involvement in treasonous or other criminal activities. Whether or not Fisher planned a coup with her associates to overthrow the government, both her testimony and the Crown prosecution's arguments have shown that she was instrumental in establishing and operating the ARC, an organization that assumed the work of the Howellites in building Black nationalism in Jamaica, mostly among its peasant majority. Fisher was prosecuted by Huntley Munroe and I. L. Robotham, Crown councils, and was represented by Stanley Fyfe and, later, Peter Evans, who also represented Hazel Collins, another woman in the ARC. After her arrest, Fisher spent approximately three months in jail before her case was tried before Judge Duffus and deliberated by seven jurors. She would go on the witness stand around midmorning on October 21, but her testimony lasted until the close of the proceedings at 4:00 p.m.

The prosecution began Fisher's trial by questioning her connection to the 78 Rosalie Avenue address, where they had found evidence of treason-felony. Fisher stated that "she purchased the land in 1951," and "that she resided at 78 Rosalie Avenue," where she owned a house. This house, she stated, was subsequently used to hold the meetings of her women's prayer circle, until a church, the ARC, was built next to it. In building the church, "part of the money came from Henry" and "some from her and some from the people who were interested in the church." She further stated that "a stranger who worked at the Gleaner" company on North Street, Kingston, "gave some hardwood posts" to the church, and "free labour was used in the construction of the church."[53] Supporting Fisher's connection to the property, Henry later revealed during his testimony that Fisher granted him "permission to build a Church," and her prayer circle's "35 members and himself helped to build" it. Nonetheless, he was the one, he asserted, who had "paid for the materials and [the] followers gave free help."[54]

Fisher was never seen by the government as the principal leader of the ARC, but it was important for the prosecution to show that she was actively involved in the planning of the coup of which they claimed Henry was the chief instigator. Police surveillance confirmed this claim, leading Judge Duffus to assert that "beyond any doubt," from his perspective, "the chief instigator and promoter was Claudius Henry."[55] He also likened Henry to Howell. Henry himself noted to his followers that he learned from Howell, including the mistakes made by Howell in not ensuring he kept copies of the purchase of Pinnacle. Henry told his followers that if he "never had his credentials, we'd have nothing here as well."[56]

At the treason-felony trial, the prosecution's questions were also designed to elicit responses that would implicate Henry as the leader of the coup and implicate Fisher as his conspirator. However, in describing her association to Henry, Fisher stated that she was introduced to him and then later he was brought by a friend to her prayer meeting. Henry, she stated, "was interested in His Imperial Majesty the Emperor of Ethiopia," and had "studied him in the Bible." She and her "people shared his views" and "attitude to God," as well as the view "that black people should return to Africa."[57] With mutual interest in Emperor Selassie and Black nationalism, she and Henry proceeded to build the ARC, and before long, the members increased from the thirty-five women who had composed her original prayer circle.[58] Membership quickly grew "to an average Sabbath attendance of over 200 people," and they "came from all parts of the country." Henry's message about repatriation, Fisher also pointed out, had helped to facilitate the increase in membership. As she stated, "This news went around and brought the people more," especially because "he went to Africa twice." At the same time, she elucidated her stance on Henry and the ARC, noting that she was very much interested in the movement and its doctrine, in addition to having "a very high regard for Rev. Henry."[59]

There would have been strong doubt about Fisher's involvement in the ARC and the suspected coup if the police had not raided her premises at 78 Rosalie Avenue. But the prosecution could not be convinced otherwise after what the police found at her home. The police reported that during the raid, they "seized machetes, knives and other weapons, batons, uniforms, ammunition, detonators, dynamite, ganja." They found "letters sent to Henry by his son in New York," Reynold Henry, "and letters addressed by Henry and some of his followers to Dr. Fidel Castro."[60] However, most of the evidence came from "Room A," Fisher's bedroom.[61] Deputy Superintendent McIntosh started the search in her bedroom, where he stated that he discovered "in the left side of a wardrobe in the room . . . a parcel with seven sticks of dynamite and a coil of fine wire, and a dagger." A total of "five cartons, four sealed and the other unsealed, including electric detonators were found behind the wardrobe." There was also "a brown paper parcel containing 11 sticks of dynamite," along with a crocus bag lying on the floor in which he found "a carton containing 10 packs of Du Pont-made detonators and five packets with five pins each."[62] Even more detrimental to Fisher's plea of innocence was the police's discovery of an unsealed enveloped containing a letter addressed to Castro that was signed by twelve persons, including "Edna E. Fisher, Brig."[63] Henry did not sign this letter, which was retained by the court.

The letter bearing Fisher's name and title as "Edna E. Fisher, Brig." indicated to the court that she played a prominent role in the ARC's plans to use violence against the Jamaican government (fig. 5). Nonetheless, she asserted that the members of the ARC made no plans to launch violence against the state and denied any knowledge of the materials that the police found in her room. Anyone, she argued, could have hidden them there, as there were several women who had access to the room, including Collins and Myrtle Jones. The room, Fisher pointed out, was cleaned "sometimes by Hazel Collins or Myrtle Jones or any of the other girls that may come along."[64] But how would Fisher explain the letter to Castro, of which she was a signee? She was aware that this letter was incriminating but tried to explain that she signed

FIGURE 5.
Edna E. Fisher, Sandy Bay,
Clarendon, Jamaica, ca. 1967.
Courtesy of Besentie Thompson,
International Peacemakers Association.

the letter while being unaware of its contents or that Castro would be the recipient. At the same time, she indicated that she was one of the persons in charge of the ARC when she declared that "Myrtle Jones did not do the typing," as the typing of their letters and publications was done by "another young lady whose name she did not remember."[65] Fisher's interactions with other men, including Calvert Beckford, also indicated her role in managing the ARC.

Henry, Fisher noted, had appointed men to leadership positions, namely Beckford, whom she interacted with. In one instance, she stated that she saw men with "knives" in their "waists" and they told her that Beckford gave them permission to carry them, but when she confronted Beckford, he provided a biblical excuse: "he that hath no sword, let him sell his garment and buy one," Luke 22:36.[66] Determined to have something done to stop Beckford's influence over other church members, Fisher decided to approach Henry to address the issue, since he was the one who brought Beckford into the church, and Henry gave her his assurances that he would deal with Beckford. But the prosecution could not call Beckford to the witness stand. Reynold, Albert Gabbidon, Eldred Morgan, and William Jetter were tried for treason and the murder of Gerald Scott, whose body was found "in a single grave" along with the bodies of Beckford and R. MacDonald, identified as "all Rastafarian cultists."[67] Reynold, Gabbidon, Morgan, and Jetter were found guilty on September 30, 1960, and sentenced to be hanged.

By the end of the trial involving Fisher, Judge Duffus and the jurors were convinced that she colluded with Henry to overthrow the government. Fisher had indicated that she was instrumental in the formation and operation of the ARC, but she also highlighted the importance of the leadership of Henry, whom she deemed a prophet. She was aware that Rastafari men were mainly viewed as the perpetrators of the movement by the government and the wider society. Could it be that Fisher's testimony was created by her and Henry to protect her freedom? At the end of the trial, she was sentenced to three years and Henry received ten years. Subsequently, Fisher and Henry married in 1967, a year after Henry's early release from the St. Catherine District Prison on good behavior. Fisher, released three years before Henry, reestablished a community of ARC members at Kemps Hill, Clarendon, where Henry later joined her.

FISHER'S LEGACY

Fisher was sentenced to three years at hard labor on conviction of treason-felony in 1960, but shortly after she was released from prison in 1963, she moved to Kemps Hill, where she began laying the foundations for a new initiative, a church Henry later called the New Creation International Peacemakers Association, which replaced the ARC. It was established at Kemps Hill and later relocated to a compound known as Bethel, located in Green Bottom, Sandy Bay (fig. 6). Similar to Pinnacle, the Peacemakers Association was both "a religious and entrepreneurial centre with a blockmaking factory, a bakery, a farm and several homes."[68] But Fisher's role in establishing the Peacemakers Association, as it was in the ARC, was obscured by the attention that the wider society invested in Henry's activities. Following his release from prison in 1966, he and Fisher married and together relocated the new church to Sandy Bay. "Henry claimed some 4,000 followers, of whom 1,000 were active members" by 1967–68.[69] However, Fisher was the one who had resurrected the church at Kemps Hill, and many of the young people there never met Henry until several years after the

FIGURE 6.
Bethel under construction, new compound of the International Peacemakers
Association, Sandy Bay, Clarendon, Jamaica, ca. 1968.
Courtesy of Besentie Thompson, International Peacemakers Association.

community had restarted. Thompson, a member of the ARC from the
early 1960s, for example, recalled that she herself "never knew Reverend Henry until he was released from prison in 1966."[70]

In his memoirs, Walter Rodney, the popular Marxist historian who
was banned from Jamaica by the government in 1968, noted that while
"at Kemp's [*sic*] Hill, in the middle of a most depressed area which is
the Prime Minister's (Hugh Shearer) constituency, Rev. Henry has
gathered together a number of black brothers and sisters, and they have
turned themselves into an independent black economic community."[71]
But Rodney did not know that Fisher was the one who had organized
the community and that Henry went there after his release from prison.
Rodney recalled seeing a "fish shop" that was "operated" by them "from
the outset and later they set up a bakery."[72] Both the fish shop and
bakery were established by Fisher. She also established a school, Croft's

FIGURE 7.

Headmaster (*seated front center*), teachers (*seated front right and left*), and students of the Ethiopian Peacemakers School, Sandy Bay, Clarendon, Jamaica, April 1968.

Courtesy of Besentie Thompson, International Peacemakers Association.

School, to provide the children with an African education. This school was renamed the Ethiopian Peacemakers School after the move to Sandy Bay (fig. 7). Reid, who was one of the teenagers, recounted that Fisher told him and his siblings that they "can't be going to school that far, receiving Babylon teaching and every day is a fight," and that she would "build a school," which she did "in about six months."[73] Bent, Howell's wife, also operated a school at their Pinnacle community.

The members of the Peacemakers Association considered Fisher as "the Mother, Protector, Guardian" of the community, and noted that Henry "played a miniscule role in the beginning," after being released from prison.[74] This was highly similar to the way the Howellites felt about Bent. Even afterward, Fisher "was the chief organizer." She "organized all the external and internal bonds of the movement," having also kept it "alive" while Henry "was imprisoned."[75] In 1970, she

FIGURE 8.
Edna E. Fisher's funeral, Sandy Bay, Clarendon, Jamaica, February 1970.
Courtesy of Besentie Thompson, International Peacemakers Association.

was gruesomely killed. Many members believed that her death started
the decline of the organization (fig. 8). The Howellites also saw Bent's
untimely death as a great loss to the community and believed she was
murdered. Reid asserted, "I'm not a fool. I was here when Sister Edna
died. It was widely stated and agreed that it was Miss Edna who was
primarily responsible for the upkeep of Rev. and his organization,
therefore, removing Sister Edna out of the way would sink the ship."[76]
Account books of the Peacemakers Association show several financial irregularities following Fisher's death: asset depreciations, thefts,
and numerous unexplained dismissals of personnel. Burnett Hall, a
member of the Peacemakers Association from the time it was known
as the ARC, noted that after Fisher's death, "administratively speaking,
there was a downturn," and Henry "became too trustworthy and these
brethren began stealing and undermining each other with the hope of
achieving power. There was a power struggle and the vacuum of Sister
Edna's death was being filled with undesirables."[77]

Overall, Fisher helped to create and operate the ARC and Peacemakers Association, organizations that impacted the political and social landscape of Rastafari and Jamaica in several respects, including the growth of the Black nationalist ideology and social status of Rastafari that the Howellites had started. The ARC bolstered the government's narrative that Rastafari was violent and racist, thereby inhibiting the movement's growth for a short period. But it attracted a large number of people to its meetings, and the protests that followed the arrests of Fisher, Henry, and other key members of the ARC intensified the government's fears of a possible invasion by the Rastafari movement. The protesters "spread out in the area near St. Andrew's Parish Church, the cemetery and church wall, as well as the Junior Centre," holding placards stating, "GIVE UP OUR LEADER OR ELSE PREPARE TO TAKE 20,000 OF US IN YOUR LOCK-UPS," in addition to insisting "FREEDOM, I WANT FREEDOM, SEND US BACK TO OUR MOTHER AFRICA OR ELSE DEATH."[78] Among statements reported in the press was that "unlawful marches in other parts of the island" included "intimidation of prosecution witness which had taken place by sympathisers of the defendants."[79] In addition, the "demonstrators threw large missiles at members of the Jamaica Constabulary" and had to be "dispersed by baton charges and tear gas."[80] As a result of the violence and intimidation, other Rastafari leaders distanced themselves from the ARC, including the members of the URO. It was out of this context that some of these Rastafari leaders, namely a Mr. Dabney, representing the URO, approached the then University College of the West Indies—renamed the University of the West Indies in 1962—to conduct research on the movement to facilitate better understanding by the wider Jamaican society.[81] Out of this appeal came the famous 1960 study, *The Ras Tafari Movement in Kingston, Jamaica.*[82]

Contrary to popular belief, the ARC did not object to the wearing locks or the use of cannabis. Thompson related that Henry "had nothing against ganja, but it was not permitted to smoke on the premises . . . as the government of the day would use any finding of ganja as a pretext to harass and even jail him. To prevent the worst from happening, he requested the smokers to do it outside."[83] This was to avoid the police arrests that had crippled other communities, namely

Pinnacle. However, concerned that the ARC's treason-felony trials had damaged the reputation of Rastafari, in April 1961, Filmore Alvaranga and Douglas Mack, representing the Rases of Eastern and Central Kingston, wrote to the British prime minister, Harold Macmillan, stating that "although we knew none of the Henrys, neither did they know the Rases, [and] they were not Rastafarians, yet we got the Blame, although they received the Punishments."[84] Mortimer Planno, a rising star of the Rastafari movement in the 1960s, later alluded to Henry and his associates as the "infiltrator" in a lecture he delivered at York University, Canada, in 1973.[85] Nonetheless, the ARC encouraged the Jamaican government and wider society to study the movement, a development that would help to facilitate acceptance by a wider cross-section of Jamaicans and spark the interest of persons even beyond Jamaica.

The ARC and its successor, the Peacemakers Association, not only showed the strength of Rastafari's Black nationalism that stimulated academic interest in the movement; it highlighted the involvement and importance of women as both members and leaders in the movement. Writing from Kemps Hill in April 1969, the year before Fisher's death, Henry tried to allay the fears of Black nationalism that had put Fisher and himself in prison in 1960. He issued a press release stating that "our Black Power for *Peace* movement, is not *Subversive*."[86] The appeal for understanding came soon after the Rodney protests in October 1968. Rodney was employed by the University of the West Indies when he was banned from Jamaica on suspicion of planning a Marxist Black nationalist revolution. Among the groups with which he had frequent contact was the Peacemakers Association, starting from its resurrection at Kemps Hill under Fisher, who continued to manage the organization after Henry returned from prison. Moreover, the events surrounding Fisher and the ARC impacted Rastafari women of the 1960s through 1980s, women such as Yvette Clarke, also known as Sister Nanny. Speaking in 1988, Clarke stated that "the Rastawoman has gone through I think from that time a process of really just coming forward."[87] Women such as Fisher, who were at the forefront of the early movement, paved the way for future Rastafari women to assert their equality with Rastafari men.

Conclusion

Disrupting the Status Quo

The research and discussion on early Rastafari women in this book are by no means exhaustive. Neither is the sample of women used; as Verene Shepherd pointed out, research on subaltern women in the Caribbean is an "ongoing archaeological project."[1] Nevertheless, this text has not only shown that at least some early Rastafari women challenged the status quo; it has also shown that they found various ways to resist patriarchy inside and outside of the Rastafari movement, albeit through covert means at times. It would be grossly inaccurate to suggest that early Rastafari women were low-key or docile.

This study employs an interdisciplinary framework that is critical for analyzing the primary documentation on early Rastafari women. Drawing on history, sociology, and theology, among other disciplines, this book places the recollections of women front and center in recounting aspects of the hidden past of early Rastafari women. Using data from members of the movement allows us to shed light on the views of early women that have been previously underrepresented in Rastafari studies. Discussing these data within the context of the wider society and world at the time helps illustrate challenges that women in the early movement had to counteract. A combination of epistemic and patriarchal suppression helped to create the impression that the early women were largely docile or low-key. But in reality the early women had a diverse range of connected and intersectional interpretations and experiences that aided the development of the anticolonial resistance of the Rastafari movement while also helping to shape the development of the future movement.

Women's resistance was shaped by the environment as well as their own ideas about their civil and human rights and liberation from white rule. In addition, they were playing leading roles in the early move-ment. Women were involved in protecting the movement and its lead-ers to facilitate its early growth and development. The male image and orientation of the early Rastafari were largely a consequence of the patriarchy both inside and outside of the movement. Women, however, attended the public meetings of the Rastafari, for exam-ple, despite warnings from men that they should stay away because of the threats of violence from the police and civilian opponents of the movement, meetings where men were told "to come armed with sticks and cutlasses."[2] These warnings can be described as what Taylor calls the assurances provided by patriarchy, but women could also be seen "trumping" these assurances through various "short-term lead-ership" roles and longer term household and spousal "management" strategies.[3] Such assurances or promises stood as prominent features of the gender dynamics of Black nationalist movements of the twen-tieth century.[4]

Patriarchy inside and outside of the early Rastafari gave the impres-sion that women of its different organizations were more isolated from each other than connected, but the revelations of early Rastafari women, such as Lennox, Stewart, Lewis, and Fisher, also shows that early Rastafari women, even if involved in different denominations, mansions or organizations, were more connected than isolated. They were connected by their own choices to circulate Rastafari's pro-Ethi-opian doctrine and Black nationalism. Early women embraced the doctrine and political principles of their Rastafari organizations for similar reasons that ranged from the pursuit of socioeconomic improvement and Black sovereignty to challenging racism, classism, and gender inequality.

Lennox was one of the women who represented several Rastafari organizations. Early Rastafari women also remained members of the Protestant churches, namely, the Baptist church and the Church of God. As Lewis related, women were key to syncretizing rituals of the religious-folk traditions, namely Kumina, with Rastafari practices. Lewis was even a leader of her own Kumina-inspired Rastafari orga-nization, the Beulah community, after leaving Pinnacle in the 1950s and still retained her Howellite identity. Fisher was a Garveyite and associate of the Coptic Church of Joseph Hibbert, a Rastafari founder, before creating her women's group and, later, the African Reform Church of God in Christ, which she established with the Rev. Claudius Henry. At the same time, Fisher recognized the strengths of the Howellite organization, including the activism of women of the organization and its effort to mimic the operation of the world-famous UNIA, the Garveyite's organization. Fisher pursued a partnership with Henry to grow her thirty-five-member women's group into the African Reform Church, launched in 1959. Within six months, the ARC had a reported 300–400 members regularly attending its Sunday services and was recognized by the authorities as the most influential Rastafari organization at the time. Officials in Norman Manley's government and Judge Herbert Duffus of the Half Way Tree Circuit Court had reportedly asserted that the ARC was an attempt to turn back the clock to the days of Pinnacle.

Early Rastafari women, including Fisher, also opposed creole nationalism while promoting African consciousness and Black nationalist socialism as the political ideology of independent Jamaica. In 1963, after serving three years in prison for treason-felony, Fisher, for example, rebuilt the ARC at Kemps Hill, Clarendon. It was later renamed the International Peacemakers Association, following the move to Bethel, a community built in Green Bottom, Sandy Bay, Clarendon. In the 1960s, Rodney described the Kemps Hill community and its revival at Bethel as Black Power socialist activism. Like Pinnacle, Kemps Hill and Bethel represented economic independence based on African consciousness and socialistic principles of equity. Rodney, therefore, noted that the class dynamics of the Rastafari movement aided its development into a multiracial movement by uniting the masses of the people around African consciousness and socialism.

Women such as Francis, who was a landlord, and Bent, who was employed as a secretary and came from a middle-class family, became members of the early Rastafari movement while being economically independent. Both mixed-race and middle-class women entered the early Rastafari movement. Mixed ancestry was common in the peasantry. Though the peasantry outnumbered all other groups, the upwardly mobile members used their education and business interests to aid the movement's growth while maintaining its African consciousness and Black nationalist socialism through various activities. These activities included granting members free access to land and capital to build homes and farms to make themselves self-sufficient as well as promoting the community as a family and providing education based on African consciousness to challenge racist ideas about nonwhites and their culture emanating from colonial knowledge. Essentially, these women used their social and economic status to build the anticolonial resistance of the early Rastafari movement.

Early Rastafari women who entered the Howellite movement exhibited their agency by defending their Rastafari identity as well as the movement. In 1934, Francis defended herself from an assault by a district constable in her Seaforth village. He later tried to arrest her and called on other men to assist him. But Francis's self-defense was not the most important aspect of her resistance. Her use of other Rastafari women and non-Rastafari members of the community to support her counteractions of the police and judges in the parish demonstrated the "community feminism" of early Rastafari women.[5] These women's resistance to patriarchy and colonial suppression challenged the suppression inside and outside the Rastafari movement while highlighting that women and men should be equal partners in order to protect themselves from the colonial system. Francis's community of supporters included other Rastafari women who had previously challenged the colonial authorities at the first trial of Rastafari members for crimes against the government. Only two such trials involving Rastafari members took place during the colonial period, the second of which involved Fisher's ARC. The women who testified at the first trial in 1934 were supported by other members, but they were no doubt discouraged by some members. Nonetheless, they testified against the better judgement of these members. They mainly testified against the police and members of the middle class and upper class, who had been writing to the government and newspapers to complain about the Rastafari movement. This opposition helped to encourage the women to argue against the middle-class and upper-class members of society as conspiring with the police and judiciary to malign their movement and undermine it. Though the colonial government opposed the Rastafari movement, much of this opposition was stimulated by members of the society who were outside of the government. These members of the society had vested interests in maintaining the social order from which they obtained their status and wealth.

Early Rastafari women also helped to develop the divinity attached to the cannabis plant through their use of it for ritualistic smoking, culinary purposes, and as a treatment for various illnesses. The government, nonetheless, focused on men as the chief purveyors of the movement, and, by extension, the main sources of cannabis use by the movement, and suggested that men mainly forced the women into cannabis use. The first dispersal of Pinnacle attempted through the police raid in 1941 failed largely because the police arrested only men. Pinnacle women openly defied a court-ordered eviction in 1945 by refusing to leave but were escorted from the community by armed police personnel.[6] The eviction was challenged in court and the people returned to the community before the end of the year. By the mid-1950s, however, it was clear that women were being targeted for arrests, even on cannabis charges. Women, along with children, were dispersed from Pinnacle during the police raids in 1951, 1954, and 1958 as part of the disbandment of the community, an attempt to end the Rastafari movement in general.

Despite the government's attempts to suppress the movement, women continued to spread Rastafari. Lennox, for example, assumed the role of preaching her womanist views of the doctrine within the movement and on the streets of Jamaica, and noted that she was not the only woman who was preaching "on the by-walks."[7] They also developed relationships with other such women that continued into the postindependence period. Lennox's main arguments included asserting the divinity of Empress Menen, part of highlighting the equality of women and men. She argued that this equality existed from creation with the connectedness of women and men, whose only difference that was ordained by the creator was biological, in order to facilitate, as Lennox put it, the multiplication of God's people. She also saw elder women of the early movement as having a vital role to play in the future of the movement in terms of empowering and

educating younger women. The younger women had mainly themselves, each other, and elder women to rely on for protection from the
patriarchy in the movement. As Lennox became an elder Rastafari
woman, she asserted herself as a protector of the dignity and divinity
of all women, whom she regarded as empresses. This name was used
by women from the colonial period of the movement. Women of the
early Rastafari embraced and promoted the concept of empress, a title
that has become synonymous with Rastafari women.

NOTES

Introduction: Resistance and Early Rastafari Women

1. Orlando Patterson, "Rastafari: The Cult of Outcasts," *New Society* 12 (1964): 15.

2. Delrosa Francis to the Officer Administering the Government, September 1, 1934, Jamaica Archives, Spanish Town, St. Catherine (hereafter cited as JA) 5073/34, 1.

3. Basil Walters, "The Story of the Rasta Woman," *Jamaica Observer,* March 19, 2012, http://www.jamaicaobserver.com/news/The-story-of-the-Rasta-woman_10997495.

4. Asheda Dwyer, "Left Waiting in Vain for Y/our Love: Situating the (In) Visibility of Black Women of Rastafari as Lovers, Partners and Revolutionaries in Brooklyn Babylon and One Love," *Caribbean Quarterly* 59, no. 2 (2013): 26; Lucille Mathurin-Mair, *A Historical Study of Women in Jamaica, 1655–1844,* ed. Hilary McD. Beckles and Verene A. Shepherd (Kingston: University of the West Indies Press, 2006), 318.

5. Verene A. Shepherd, *Maharani's Misery: Narratives of a Passage from India to the Caribbean* (Kingston: University of the West Indies Press, 2002), xiii.

6. Maureen Rowe, "The Woman in Rastafari," *Caribbean Quarterly* 26, no. 4 (1980): 17. Note that the capital "I" at the end of "RastafarI" is used by some Rastafari writers to emphasize the agency of the individual in the Rastafari movement. For other Rastafari practitioners, the capital "I" is also intended to show the world their belief that God or Jah is within them.

7. Makeda Silvera, "An Open Letter to Rastafarian Sistren," *Fireweed* (Spring 1983): 116.

8. Ula Y. Taylor, "'Negro Women Are Great Thinkers as well as Doers': Amy Jacques-Garvey and Community Feminism in the United States, 1924–1927," *Journal of Women's History* 12, no. 2 (2000): 105. I have also used Taylor's more recent studies which examine the operations of patriarchy as well as women's resistance in the Black liberation struggle of the Garvey movement and Nation of Islam. See Ula Y. Taylor, *The Veiled Garvey: The Life and Times of Amy Jacques Garvey* (Chapel Hill: University of North Carolina Press, 2002) and *The Promise of Patriarchy: Women and the Nation of Islam* (Chapel Hill: University of North Carolina Press, 2017). Also see Katie G. Cannon, "The Emergence of Black Feminist Consciousness," in *Feminist Interpretation of the Bible,* ed. Letty M. Russell (Philadelphia: Westminster Press, 1985), 30. For further analysis of womanist theology, see Rufus J. Burrows Jr., "Development of Womanist Theology: Some Chief Characteristics," *Ashbury Theological Journal* 54, no. 1 (1999): 53.

9. Douglas Kellner, *Critical Theory, Marxism, and Modernity* (Oxford: Polity Press, 1989), 54.

10. Boike Rehbein, "Critical Theory and Social Inequality," *Tempo Social, Revista de Sociologia da USP* 30, no. 3 (2018): 57.

11. Hannah Durkin, "Finding Last Middle Passage Survivor Sally 'Redoshi' Smith on the Page and Screen," *Slavery & Abolition* (March 26, 2019): 2, 4, https://doi.org/1 0.1080/0144039X.2019.1596397; Jon Sensbach, "Black Pearls: Writing Black Atlantic Women's Biography," in *Biography and the Black Atlantic*, ed. Lisa A. Lindsay and John Wood Sweet (Philadelphia: University of Pennsylvania Press, 2013), 99.

12. Monique A. Bedasse, *Jah Kingdom: Rastafarians, Tanzania, and Pan-Africanism in the Age of Decolonization* (Chapel Hill: University of North Carolina Press, 2017), 6.

13. Sarah Evans, *Personal Politics: The Roots of Women's Liberation in the Civil Rights Movement and the New Left* (New York: Vintage Books, 1979), 21; Linda J. Nicholson, "'The Personal Is Political': An Analysis in Retrospect," *Social Theory and Practice* 7, no. 1 (1981): 85; Christer Petley, *White Fury: A Jamaican Slaveholder and the Age of Revolution* (Oxford: Oxford University Press, 2018), 13. For other histories that use the biographical method, see Barbara Ransby, *Ella Baker and the Black Freedom Movement: A Radical Democratic Vision* (Chapel Hill: University of North Carolina Press, 2003) and Colin A. Palmer, *Eric Williams and the Making of the Modern Caribbean* (Chapel Hill: University of North Carolina Press, 2006).

14. M. G. Smith, Roy Augier, and Rex Nettleford, *Report on the Ras Tafari Movement in Kingston, Jamaica* (Kingston: Institute of Social and Economic Research, University College of the West Indies, 1960), 23–25; Ennis B. Edmonds, *Rastafari: A Very Short Introduction* (Oxford: Oxford University Press, 2012), 53.

CHAPTER 1.

The First Women to Testify in Court for the Rastafari Movement

1. "Leonard Howell Being Tried for Sedition in Saint Thomas," *Daily Gleaner*, March 14, 1934, 21.

2. Douglas Mack, *From Babylon to Rastafari: Origin and History of the Rastafarian Movement* (Kingston: Frontline Distribution International, 1999), 72.

3. Florence Stewart, interviewed by author, Tredegar Park, St. Catherine, Jamaica, July 19, 2016.

4. Mack, *From Babylon to Rastafari*, 72–73.

5. W. C. Adams to Owen F. Wright, December 23, 1933, JA 1B/5/79, 1.

6. Owen F. Wright to Arthur S. Jelf, December 28, 1933, JA 1B/5/79, 1.

7. Merriam Lennox, interviewed by Renee Romano and Elliott Leib, Old Harbour, St. Catherine, Jamaica, 1983.

8. W. E. Barclay to W. C. Adams, October 31, 1933, JA 1B/5/79, 1, 2.

9. James Martin to W. C. Adams, December 18, 1933, JA 1B/5/79, 1.

10. See M. G. Smith, Roy Augier, and Rex Nettleford, *Report on the Ras Tafari Movement in Kingston, Jamaica* (Kingston: Institute of Social and Economic Research, University College of the West Indies, 1960). Note that the version used in this book was given the now conventional writing of "Rastafari," a 1962 republication, or the same year as Jamaica's independence. The slightly revised titled was the *Report on the Rastafari Movement in Kingston, Jamaica,* published by the University of the West Indies, also previously known as the University College of the West Indies, formed during colonial rule in 1948.

11. "Sixaola in Yesterday from New York with Mails and Passengers," *Daily Gleaner,* November 18, 1932, 9. Historian Robert Hill has stated that Howell had "received a two to four-year sentence in the state prison at Ossining," and was "deported from America on November 12, 1932." See Robert A. Hill, *Dread History: Leonard P. Howell and Millenarian Visions in the Early Rastafarian Religion in Jamaica* (Kingston and Chicago, IL: Frontline Distribution International, 2001), 54–55, 55 n. 25.

12. "Leonard Howell, on Trial says Ras Tafari Is Messiah Returned to Earth," *Daily Gleaner,* March 15, 1934, 20. Emphasis in original.

13. Rachel Patterson to His Excellency, the Officer Administering the Government, September 3, 1934, JA 5073/34, 4.

14. William F. Lewis, *Soul Rebels: Rastafari* (Long Grove, IL: Waveland Press, 1993), 121.

15. Government of Jamaica, "The Seditious Meetings Act [1836]" (Kingston: Ministry of Justice, 1973), Legislation (hereafter cited as LN) 480/1973, S.2, 1.

16. "'Ras Tafari' Disciple Found Guilty of Sedition," *Daily Gleaner,* March 16, 1934, 16.

17. "Leonard Howell, on Trial says Ras Tafari Is Messiah Returned to Earth," *Daily Gleaner,* March 15, 1934, 20.

18. O. C. Francis, *The People of Modern Jamaica* (Kingston: Department of Statistics, Jamaica, 1963), 4, 5.

19. Arvel B. Erickson, "Empire of Anarchy: The Jamaica Rebellion of 1865," *Journal of Negro History* 44, no. 2 (1959): 103.

20. Brigadier-General Nelson to Major-General O'Connor, Morant Bay, October 14, 1865, *Accounts and Papers of the House of Commons, Colonies: Jamaica, Volume 51* (London: House of Commons, 1866), 30.

21. Ibid., 31; Governor Eyre to the Right Hon. Edward Cardwell, MP, October 20, 1865, *Accounts and Papers ... Volume 51,* 3.

22. Howell's Activities at Port Morant, Constable E. B. Smith, Port Morant Station, September 10, 1933, JA 1B/5/79, 1.

23. Ibid.

24. Minutes of Colonial Secretary, Charles Campbell Woolley, handwritten, February 26, 1937, JA 1B/5/79, 8.

25. Crown Solicitor to the Acting Colonial Secretary W. D. Battershill, January 2, 1934, JA 1B/5/79, 3.

26. "Leonard Howell, on Trial," 1934, 20.

27. Ibid.; "Purchasing Power of British Pounds from 1270 to Present," *Measuring-Worth*, 2020, www.measuringworth.com/ppoweruk/.

28. Crown Solicitor to the Attorney General, June 8, 1933, JA 1B/5/79. Also see Attorney General's Confidential Memo, June 27, 1933, JA 1B/5/79; and W. C. Adams to Owen F. Wright, December 23, 1933, JA 1B/5/79, 1.

29. W. C. Adams to Owen F. Wright, June 14, 1933, JA 1B/5/79.

30. Detective Inspector R. C. Waters, [Report on] Leonard Howell, Charge of Sedition in St. Thomas, July 31, 1933, JA 1B/5/79/735, 7.

31. "Leonard Howell, on Trial," 1934, 20.

32. Ibid.

33. "'Ras Tafari' Disciple Found Guilty," 1934, 16.

34. Ibid.

35. Ibid.

36. Barry Chevannes, *Rastafari: Roots and Ideology* (New York: Syracuse University Press, 1994), 127, 129.

37. John Carradine, "The Ras Tafarites Retreat to Mountain Fastness of St. Catherine," *Daily Gleaner*, November 23, 1940, 54.

38. Gertrude Campbell, interviewed by Jahlani Niaah and Ishmahil Blagrove for "Roaring Lion, The Rise of Rastafari: A Documentary," Kingston and Brampton, Frontline Productions and Knowledge Bookstore, 2001, 7.

39. Stewart, interviewed by author, 2016.

40. Alphonso Gallimore, interviewed by author, Tredegar Park, St. Catherine, Jamaica, April 24, 2011.

41. W. C. Adams to Owen F. Wright, December 23, 1933, JA 1B/5/79, 1.

CHAPTER 2.

Petitioning Government: Women and
the Colonial Justice System

1. Sophia A. van Wingerden, *The Women's Suffrage Movement in Britain, 1866-1928* (Houndmills: Palgrave Macmillan, 1999), 177.

2. "The Women's Federation of the Baptists," *Daily Gleaner*, March 20, 1934, 17.

3. Beryl DeLeon, "Are We Rearing Trained Seals in Our Schools and Homes?" *Daily Gleaner*, November 2, 1935, 26.

4. "Women's Work," *Daily Gleaner*, April 15, 1944, 6.

5. Rhoda Reddock, "Diversity, Difference and Caribbean Feminism: The Challenge of Anti-Racism," *Caribbean Review of Gender Studies* 1 (2007): 11.

6. "Dangerous Cults," *Daily Gleaner*, January 19, 1937, 9; "Harm Rastafari Advocates Are Doing in Eastern Parish," *Daily Gleaner*, May 23, 1935, 1. Also see, "St. Thomas Wars on the Ras Tafari Cult," *Daily Gleaner*, January 18, 1937, 28.

7. Papers of Edward Brandis Denham, Western Library, Oxford University (hereafter cited as WLO) MSS. Brit. Emp. S. 232–239, 1934, vol. XXI, 15, 17; Delrosa Francis to the Officer Administering the Government, September 1, 1934, JA 5073/34, 1. Note that Arthur Jelf was acting colonial secretary of Jamaica before becoming the acting governor of the island in 1934.

8. Seymour Drescher, "Civil Society and Paths to Abolition," *História (São Paulo)* 34, no. 2 (2015): 49, 35.

9. Jamaica, *Eighth Census*, LII.

10. Delrosa Francis to the Officer Administering the Government, JA, 1.

11. Ibid; Rachel Patterson to the Officer Administering the Government, September 3, 1934, JA 5073/34, 4.

12. Papers of Charles Campbell Woolley, WLO MSS. Brit. Emp. S. 276/Woolley, Box 4, Clipping from the *Daily Gleaner*, August 29, 1935, 1.

13. Anonymous letter to John Maffey, April 7, 1936, JA 68512/30/36, 1, 3.

14. Horace Campbell, *Rasta and Resistance: From Marcus Garvey to Walter Rodney* (Trenton, NJ: Africa World Press, 1994), 200.

15. Kennetta Hammond Perry, *London is the Place for Me: Black Britons, Citizenship, and the Politics of Race* (Oxford: Oxford University Press, 2015), 4.

16. Delrosa Francis to the Officer Administering the Government, JA, 3.

17. Ibid., 1.

18. Ibid.

19. Ibid., 2.

20. Owen F. Wright to Arthur S. Jelf, February 28, 1934, JA 1B/5/79, 16.

21. Delrosa Francis to the Officer Administering the Government, JA, 3; "Purchasing Power of British Pounds."

22. Amelia Gordon and Augustus B. Gordon to the Officer Administering the Government, September 3, 1934, JA 5073/34, 3; "Purchasing Power of British Pounds."

23. Errol Greene, "Report Corrupt JPs," *Jamaica Observer*, October 15, 2018, https://www.jamaicaobserver.com/editorial/report-corrupt-jps-_146914?profile=1234.

24. Government of Jamaica, "Judicature (Resident Magistrates) Act," February 22, 1928, Ministry of Justice, Government of Jamaica LN146/1999, 15.

25. Francella McNish to the Officer Administering the Government, September 1, 1934, JA 5073/34, 2.

26. James Findley to the Officer Administering the Government, September 1, 1934, JA 5073/34, 2.

27. Elisa Janine Sobo, *One Blood: The Jamaican Body* (Albany: State University of New York Press, 1993), 186.

28. Edith Clarke, *My Mother Who Fathered Me: A Study of the Families in Three Selected Communities of Jamaica* (London: George Allen and Unwin, 1957), 78.

29. Benjamin Schlesinger, "Family Patterns in Jamaica: Review and Commentary," *Journal of Marriage and Family* 30, no. 1 (1968): 138.

30. Delrosa Francis to the Officer Administering the Government, JA, 1.

31. Jack Alexander, "The Role of the Male in the Middle-Class Jamaican Family: A Comparative Perspective," *Journal of Comparative Family Studies* 8, no. 3 (1977): 371.

32. Stewart, interviewed by author, 2016.

33. Taylor, "'Negro Women,'" 107-8. Here, Taylor is quoting from historian Elsa Barkley Brown. Also see Taylor, *The Veiled Garvey*, 87.

34. James Findley to the Officer Administering the Government, JA, 2; Amelia Gordon and Augustus B. Gordon to the Officer Administering the Government, JA, 3.

35. V. R. Cameron to Edward Denham, Font Hill, Trinity Ville P.O., May 19, 1936, JA 5073/34, 2.

36. Nathaniel Samuel Murrell, *Afro-Caribbean Religions: An Introduction to Their Historical, Cultural, and Scared Traditions* (Philadelphia: Temple University Press, 2010), 257.

37. Denvil Price to the Officer Administering the Government, September 1, 1934, JA 5073/34, 1.

38. Gertrude Nathan to the Officer Administering the Government, September 1, 1934, JA 5073/34, 2.

39. Taylor, "'Negro Women,'" 105.

40. Rachel Patterson to the Officer Administering the Government, JA, 1, 2.

41. "Three Freed in Pinnacle Camp Cases," *Daily Gleaner,* July 23, 1941, 9.

42. Rachel Patterson to the Officer Administering the Government, JA, 2, 1, 2.

43. Ibid., 2, 3.

44. Papers of Edward Brandis Denham, WLO, vol. XXII, 36. Emphasis in original. Also quoted in Ken Post, *Arise Ye Starvelings: The Jamaican Labour Rebellion of 1938 and Its Aftermath* (The Hague: Nijhoff, 1978), 166.

45. Chevannes, *Rastafari,* 11-15.

46. "Fooling the Masses," *Daily Gleaner,* August 6, 1934, 6.

47. Colonial Secretary to Delrosa Francis, Rachel Patterson, and Francella McNish, September 14, 1934, JA 5073/34; Colonial Secretary to Denvil Price, Gertrude Nathan, Augustus Gordon, and James Findley, September 14, 1934, JA 5073/34.

48. Chevannes, *Rastafari,* 45.

49. Post, *Arise Ye Starvelings,* 149-50.

50. Colonial Secretary to Delrosa Francis, et al., JA; Colonial Secretary to Denvil Price, et al., JA.

51. Ras Tafari Followers, Court at Seaforth on 4.8.34 and Trial, Confidential Minute Paper, 10.9.34, JA 5073/34, 1-2. Note that Camacho, who was previously the assistant attorney general, was now serving as attorney general.

52. Ibid., 2.

53. Ibid., 1.

54. "Mr. Abendana Strongly Urges That Court of Appeal Be Not Set Up Now," *Daily Gleaner,* May 16, 1934, 8.

55. "Council Shows Concern in Respect to Audit of the Colony's Accounts," *Daily Gleaner,* April 3, 1935, 16.

56. Robert William Lyall-Grant to Edward Denham, January 4, 1935, The National Archives, Britain (hereafter cited as TNA) CO137/803/14, 3, 4.

CHAPTER 3.

The Middle-Class Woman: Reshaping the
Rastafari Family and Community

1. Katrin Hansing, *Rasta, Race and Revolution: The Emergence and Development of the Rastafari Movement in Socialist Cuba* (Berlin: Lit Verlag, 2006), 7.

2. Garry Steckles, Mark Meredith, and Nazma Muller, "The World of Rastafari," *Caribbean Beat Magazine* 31 (1998), MEP Publishers, http://caribbean-beat.com/issue-31/world-rastafari#axzz4u71DTJpf; Jahlani Niaah and Ijahnya Christian, "Introduction: What Is Rastafari," in *Rastafari: A National Museum Jamaica Exhibition,* ed. Jonathan Greenland (Kingston: Institute of Jamaica, 2013), 21.

3. Joseph A. Schumpeter, *Capitalism, Socialism, and Democracy* (New York: Harper and Row, 1975), 11, 20.

4. Walter Rodney, *The Groundings with My Brothers* (London: Bogle-L'Ouverture Publications, 1969 / Kingston: Miguel Lorne Publishers, 2001), 24.

5. Anonymous letter to John Maffey, April 7, 1936, JA 68512/30/36, 1; Leonard E. Barrett, *The Rastafarians* (Boston: Beacon Press, 1997), 1.

6. Henrice Altink, "'Marrying Light': Skin Colour, Gender and Marriage in Jamaica, c.1918–1980," *The History of the Family* (2019): 15, https://doi.org/10.1080/1081602X.2019.1582433.

7. Florence Stewart and Delrietta Simpson, interviewed by author, Tredegar Park, St. Catherine, Jamaica, August 24, 2011.

8. "Judge's Summing Up at Treason Felony Trial," *Daily Gleaner,* October 31, 1960, 9.

9. Carradine, "The Ras Tafarites Retreat," 1940, 54. Leonard Howell was the one who asserted that Rastafari symbolized the pursuit of a "socialistic life."

10. "Mr. Edward Bent Dies at 79," *Daily Gleaner,* July 18, 1950, 11. The Bent children were born in this order: Beryl, Vidalyn, Tenet, Louise, Arthur, Margaret, and Edward Jr.

11. Hélène Lee, *The First Rasta: Leonard Howell and the Rise of Rastafarianism,* trans. Lily Davis (Chicago: Lawrence Hill Books, 2003), 157.

12. Mervyn C. Alleyne, *The Construction and Representation of Race and Ethnicity in the Caribbean and the World* (Kingston: University of the West Indies Press, 2002), 193.

13. "Read Across Jamaica at Mayfield All Age," *Jamaica Observer,* June 5, 2017,

http://www.jamaicaobserver.com/news/read-across-jamaica-at-mayfield-all-age
_100895.

14. Geraldine E. Fong, personal communication, October 14, 2014; "Hampton School," Jamaica National Heritage Trust, 2011, http://www.jnht.com/site_hampton_school.php.

15. Arthur Charles Dayfoot, *The Shaping of the West Indian Church, 1492-1962* (Gainesville: University Press of Florida, 1999), 90; Bridget Brereton, "Women and Gender in Caribbean (English-speaking) Historiography: Sources and Methods," *Caribbean Review of Gender Studies* 7 (2013): 5.

16. Howell, *The Promised Key* (Kingston: Headstart Books and Craft/Frontline Distribution Int., 1995 [Orig.1935]), 4.

17. Barrett, *The Rastafarians,* 2.

18. "Ras Tafari Priest Gets Nine Months: Found Guilty of Slugging Man with Iron; Appeals," *Daily Gleaner,* December 30, 1938, 17.

19. "Cultist Sent to Prison for Assaulting Policeman," *Daily Gleaner,* January 19, 1953, 5.

20. Montinol Howell, personal communication, June 9, 2018.

21. Estimate based on the following: Jamaica, *Eighth Census,* XXXII; Gisela Eisner, *Jamaica, 1830-1930: A Study in Economic Growth* (Manchester: University of Manchester Press, 1961), 134; and G. E. Cumper, "Population Movements in Jamaica, 1830-1950," *Social and Economic Studies* 5, no. 3 (1956): 275.

22. Bryan L. Moore and Michelle A. Johnson, *"They do as they please": The Jamaican Struggle for Cultural Freedom after Morant Bay* (Kingston: University of the West Indies Press, 2011), 14.

23. Jean Stubbs, "Political Idealism and Commodity Production: Cuban Tobacco in Jamaica, 1870-1930," *Cuban Studies* 25 (1995): 61. For more information on the Machados, see Machado Tobacco Company Ltd., *The Machado Story: A Pioneer Industry in Jamaica, 1874-1962* (Kingston: B. & J. B. Machado Tobacco Company Ltd., 1962).

24. Fong, personal communication, 2014.

25. Ada Ferrer, *Insurgent Cuba: Race, Nation, and Revolution, 1868-1898* (Chapel Hill: University of North Carolina Press, 1999), 3.

26. Stubbs, "Political Idealism," 76.

27. Richard Hart, *Labour Relations of the 1930s in the British Caribbean Region Colonies* (Shrewsbury, UK: Caribbean Labour Solidarity and the Socialist History Society, 2002), 5.

28. Stubbs, "Political Idealism," 61.

29. "Judge's Summing Up," 1960, 9.

30. Carradine, "The Ras Tafarites Retreat," 1940, 54.

31. Campbell, *Rasta and Resistance,* 73, 74; Fong, personal communication, 2014.

32. Taylor, "'Negro Women,'" 105.

33. Taylor, *The Veiled Garvey,* 80.

34. Len. S. Nembhard, "Mrs. Howell Believes Only in One Man," *Jamaica Times,* July 19, 1941, 3.

35. Fong, personal communication, 2014.

36. Benjamin Schlesinger, "Family Patterns in Jamaica: Review and Commentary," *Journal of Marriage and Family* 30, no. 1 (1968): 143–44; Jack Alexander, "The Role of the Male in the Middle-Class Jamaican Family: A Comparative Perspective," *Journal of Comparative Family Studies* 8, no. 3 (1977): 369–89.

37. Raymond T. Smith "The Family in the Caribbean," in *Caribbean Studies: A Symposium,* ed. Vera Rubin (Kingston: University College of the West Indies, 1957), 72, quoted in Schlesinger, "Family Patterns in Jamaica," 147–48.

38. Alexander, "The Role of the Male," 371.

39. Barrett, *The Rastafarians,* 88.

40. Lee, *The First Rasta,* 158.

41. Anell Howell to Montinol Howell, October 12, 1993, Leonard P. Howell Foundation (hereafter cited as LPHF).

42. Montinol Howell, personal communication, November 27, 2013.

43. Nembhard, "Mrs. Howell Believes," 1941, 3.

44. Alexander, "The Role of the Male," 374, 375.

45. Draft Confidential Letter to Malcolm MacDonald, MP, April 1940, JA 1B/5/79, 63A; Owen F. Wright to Alexander W. G. H. Grantham, July 15, 1939, JA 1B/5/79, 9.

46. Giulia Bonacci, "The Ethiopian World Federation: A Pan-African Organization Among Rastafari in Jamaica," *Caribbean Quarterly* 59, no. 2 (2013): 76; Giulia Bonacci, *Exodus!: Heirs and Pioneers, Rastafari Return to Ethiopia* (Kingston: University of the West Indies Press, 2015), 160.

47. Leo Spitzer and LaRay Denzer, "I. T. A. Wallace-Johnson and the West African Youth League," *International Journal of African Historical Studies* 6, no. 3 (1973): 446. For further information on the IASB, see James R. Hooker, *Black Revolutionary: George Padmore's Path from Communism to Pan-Africanism* (New York: Praeger, 1967), 49–51.

48. Owen F. Wright to Alexander W. G. H. Grantham, November 11, 1938, JA 1B/5/79, 7/27.

49. R. A. Leevy, "Ras Tafarianism: Haile Selassie, Emperor of Abyssinia, Inspired a New Religion in Jamaica," *Public Opinion,* February 20, 1943, 3.

50. "News of the Ethiopian World Federation, Inc," *The Voice of Ethiopia,* December 31, 1938, 3; Bonacci, "The Ethiopian World Federation," 74.

51. Owen F. Wright to Alexander W. G. H. Grantham, 7, 8/27; Secret Letter to Colonel Sir V. G. W. Kell, November 11, 1938, JA 1B/5/79/735, 29.

52. L. P. Howell to George Padmore, March 21, 1939, JA 1B/5/79, C74; George Padmore, "Hands Off the Colonies!" *New Leader,* February 25, 1938, 5.

53. Alexander, "The Role of the Male," 371.

54. Henry Archibald Dunkley, interviewed by Robert Hill, Kingston, Jamaica, 1976,

10. Also published as Robert Hill and Boris Lutanie, "Le Troi-sième Homme: Interview de Henry Archibald Dunkley, par Robert Hill (1976)," *Reggae Vibes* 22 (2012): 68–73.

55. Gerald Lloyd Downer, interviewed by author, Tredegar Park, St. Catherine, Jamaica, August 24, 2011.

56. "Robber Leaves Pearls Behind: Lucky Woman Still Has Jewellery Valued £100," *Daily Gleaner,* August 27, 1938, 23; "Purchasing Power of British Pounds."

57. L. P. Howell to George Padmore, C74.

58. Carradine, "The Ras Tafarites Retreat," 1940, 54.

59. Hélène Lee, personal communication, January 4, 2021.

60. Lee, *The First Rasta,* 127; Register Book, Office of Titles, Registrar General's Department, Twinkenham Park, Jamaica, vol. 277, folio 52; "Ras Tafarites Won't Quit Famed 'Pinnacle,'" *Daily Gleaner,* August 16, 1946, 11.

61. Lee, *The First Rasta,* 128; "Purchasing Power of British Pounds."

62. Rules and Constitution of the Ethiopian Salvation Society, Friendly and Benevolent Society, Kingston, Jamaica, January 11, 1939, JA 5073/34, 1. For other mention of the Ethiopian Salvation Society, see Price, *Becoming Rasta,* 63.

63. "E.S.S. President Plans Busy Tour," *Daily Gleaner,* June 5, 1939, 4.

64. Carradine, "The Ras Tafarites Retreat," 1940, 54.

65. "E.S.S. President Plans Busy Tour," 4.

66. Rules and Constitution, 5, 8, 9; "Purchasing Power of British Pounds."

67. "Society Celebration," *Daily Gleaner,* April 4, 1939, 6.

68. "Help the Drought Stricken People of St. Elizabeth," *Daily Gleaner,* July 22, 1939, 45.

69. Carradine, "The Ras Tafarites Retreat," 1940, 54.

70. Montinol Howell, personal communication, November 27, 2013.

71. Lee, personal communication, 2021.

72. Nembhard, "Mrs. Howell Believes," 1941, 1.

73. Carradine, "The Ras Tafarites Retreat," 1940, 54; Stewart and Simpson, interviewed by author, 2011.

74. Stewart and Simpson, interviewed by author, 2011.

75. Chevannes, *Rastafari,* 123.

76. Downer, interviewed by author, 2011.

77. "Police Hold Chief of Pinnacle Ras Tafarians," *Jamaica Times,* July 26, 1941, 1.

78. Nembhard, "Mrs. Howell Believes," 1941, 1.

79. Ibid.

80. Ibid., 1, 3.

81. Stewart and Simpson, interviewed by author, 2011; "EarthLight Ises to Queen Mother of the Rastafari Movement Tenet Bent Howell," March 7, 2015, LPHF.

82. "Detained in Connection with Woman's Death," *Daily Gleaner,* December 24, 1943, 10.

83. Fong, personal communication, 2014.

84. "Howell Remanded," *Daily Gleaner,* January 14, 1944, 7.

85. "EarthLight Ises," LPHF.

86. Alexander W. G. H. Grantham, April 4, 1944, Minutes, JA 5073/34, 18.

CHAPTER 4.

The Rastafari Religion: A Womanist Perspective

1. See Joseph Owens, *Dread: The Rastafarians of Jamaica* (Kingston: Sangster, 1976); William David Spencer, *Dread Jesus* (London: Society for Promoting Christian Knowledge, 1998); Noel Leo Erskine, *From Garvey to Marley: Rastafari Theology* (Gainesville: University Press of Florida, 2004).

2. Graham A. Duncan, "Ethiopianism in Pan-African Perspective, 1880–1920," *Studia Historiae Ecclesiasticae* 41, no. 2 (2015): 199.

3. Other examples include the Ethiopian King of Kings Salvation, Youth Black Faith, the African Reform Church of God in Christ, Twelve Tribes of Israel, and the Ethiopian Zion Coptic Church.

4. The Ethiopian spelling of her name is Wayzäro Mänän, but throughout this book, I use Menen, the spelling more familiar to Western audiences.

5. Renee Romano and Elliott Leib, "Rastafari: Conversations Concerning Woman," filmed in Jamaica, Eye In I Filmworks, New Haven, Connecticut, 1983. The quotations are from the interview for this documentary film, hereafter referred to as Lennox, interviewed by Romano and Leib, 1983. All quotations from Lennox are from my transcription of the raw footage of this interview, most of which did not appear in the documentary film. This footage is stored at the Smithsonian Institution's Museum Support Center in Suitland, Maryland, which houses the collections of the National Museum of Natural History and anthropological research. Also see Renee Romano and Elliott Leib, "Rastafari Voices," filmed in Jamaica, Eye In I Filmworks, New Haven, Connecticut, 1979.

6. Katie G. Cannon, "The Emergence of Black Feminist Consciousness," in *Feminist Interpretation of the Bible,* ed. Letty M. Russell (Philadelphia: Westminster Press, 1985), 30.

7. Ibid., 40.

8. Rufus J. Burrows Jr., "Development of Womanist Theology: Some Chief Characteristics," *Ashbury Theological Journal* 54, no. 1 (1999): 53, 41.

9. Ella Maria Ray, "Standing in the Lion's Shadow: Jamaican Rastafari Women Reconstructing Their African Identity," PhD diss., Johns Hopkins University, Baltimore, MD, 1998, 19.

10. Alice Walker, *In Search of Our Mothers' Gardens: Womanist Prose* (New York: Harcourt Brace Jovanovich, 1983), xi.

11. Burrows, "Development of Womanist Theology," 45, 46.

12. Owens, *Dread*, 93.

13. Erskine, *From Garvey to Marley*, 189, xiv, xv.

14. Lennox, interviewed by Romano and Leib, 1983.

15. Diana O'Gilvie, "Tug of War: Traditional Rastafarian Women in Modern Jamaican Society," *Griots Republic*, February 6, 2018, http://www.griotsrepublic.com/tug-war-traditional-rastafarian-women-modern-jamaican-society/.

16. Carole D. Yawney, "To Grow a Daughter: Cultural Liberation and the Dynamics of Oppression in Jamaica," in *Feminism: From Pressure to Politics*, ed. A. Miller and G. Finn (Montreal: Black Rose Books, 1983), 119; Chevannes, *Rastafari*, 260.

17. Alphonso Gallimore, interviewed by author, Tredegar Park and Pinnacle, St. Catherine, Jamaica, July 20, 2016.

18. Clarke, *My Mother*, 21.

19. R. T. Smith, *The Negro Family in British Guiana* (London: Routledge and Kegan Paul, 1956), 258.

20. Florence Stewart, interviewed by author, 2016.

21. Canute Swaby, interviewed by author and Yvonne McLean, Tredegar Park, St. Catherine, Jamaica, October 22, 2015.

22. Mimi Sheller, "Quasheba, Mother, Queen: Black Women's Public Leadership and Political Protest in Postemancipation Jamaica," Department of Sociology, Lancaster University, 2003, http://www.comp.lancs.ac.uk/sociology/papers/Sheller-Quasheba-Mother-Queen.pdf, 2, 3.

23. Diana Paton, "Enslaved Women and Slavery Before and After 1807," *History in Focus* 12 (2007), https://www.history.ac.uk/ihr/Focus/Slavery/articles/paton.html.

24. Howell, *The Promised Key*, 27.

25. Jake Homiak, interviewed by author, Smithsonian Institution, Suitland, Maryland, June 23, 2015.

26. Binghi Glen Porter, "The Watch Lion Roars," unpublished communication, October 2015, 3.

27. Lennox, interviewed by Romano and Leib, 1983.

28. Homiak, interviewed by author, 2015.

29. Tricia Redeker Hepner and Randal L. Hepner, "Gender, Community, and Change among the Rastafari of New York City," in *New York Glory: Religions in the City*, ed. Tony Carnes and Anna Karpathakis (New York: New York University Press, 2001), 348.

30. Carole D. Yawney, "Review of *Women, Race and Class in a Cultural Context, Many Voices, One Chant—Black Feminist Perspectives*, and *Rastafari: Conversations Concerning Woman*," *Canadian Woman Studies* 7, nos. 1-2 (1984): 208.

31. Amy Bailey, "Our Women—Their Status," *Public Opinion*, December 28, 1940, 14.

32. Lennox, interviewed by Romano and Leib, 1983.

33. Hugh Foot to M. Phillips, September 10, 1956, TNA C01031/1958, 1.

34. Lennox, interviewed by Romano and Leib, 1983.

35. Barbara Winslow, "The First White Rastafarian: Sylvia Pankhurst, Haile Selassie, and Ethiopia," in *At Home and Abroad in the Empire: British Women Write the 1930s,* ed. Robin Hackett, Freda Hauser, and Gay Wachman (Newark: University of Delaware Press, 2009), 178.

36. Kathlyn Dodd, ed., *A Sylvia Pankhurst Reader* (Manchester: Manchester University Press, 1993), 238.

37. Lennox, interviewed by Romano and Leib, 1983.

38. Homiak, interviewed by author, 2015.

39. Ibid.

40. Romano and Leib, "Rastafari Voices," 1979.

41. Rex M. Nettleford, *Caribbean Cultural Identity: The Case of Jamaica, An Essay in Cultural Dynamics* (Kingston: Institute of Jamaica, 1978), 8.

42. Joseph Beaumont, *The New Slavery: An Account of the Indians and Chinese Immigrants in British Guiana* (London: W. Ridgway, 1871), 14.

43. Writing in the 1970s, for example, Joseph Owens stated that the Rastafari used the term "Babylon" for "the whole complex of institutions which conspire to keep the black man enslaved in the western world and which attempt to subjugate coloured peoples throughout the world" (Owens, *Dread,* 70).

44. Homiak, interviewed by author, 2015.

45. "Leonard Howell, On Trial," 1934, 20.

46. Lennox, interviewed by Romano and Leib, 1983.

47. Joseph Franklin Rutherford, "Birth of the Nation," *The Watch Tower and Herald of Christ's Presence,* March 1, 1925, 67. Also see International Bible Students' Association, *The Watch Tower,* April 2, 1910, 119, 120.

48. Fitz Balintine Pettersburgh, *The Royal Parchment Scroll of Black Supremacy* (Kingston: Frontline Books and Miguel Lorne Publishers, 2003 [orig.1926]), 31.

49. Howell, *The Promised Key,* 27, 29, 7, 25, 20, 21.

50. Prince Emmanuel Edwards, "Love in Black Supremacy Internationally Through all Human Rights in Righteousness of Salvation," Rastafari Movement Pamphlet, Kingston, 1979, University of the West Indies Library, Mona, Jamaica, 9, 11.

51. John Africa, "Black Woman," *Rasta Voice* 86 (1979): 21.

52. Samuel Elisha Brown, "Treatise on the Rastafarian Movement," *Caribbean Studies* 6, no. 1 (1966): 39.

53. Lennox, interviewed by Romano and Leib, 1983.

54. Colin Kidd, *The Forging of Races: Race and Scripture in the Protestant Atlantic World, 1600-2000* (Cambridge: Cambridge University Press, 2006), 41, 43; Numbers 12.1, Holy Bible, New King James Version, 1987 printing.

55. Kidd, *The Forging,* 41; Numbers 12.1, Holy Bible.

56. Number 12.15, Holy Bible.

57. Lennox, interviewed by Romano and Leib, 1983.

58. Imani M. Tafari-Ama, "An Historical Analysis of Grassroots Resistance in

Jamaica: A Participatory Research on Gender Relations in Rastafari," MA thesis, Institute of Social Studies, The Hague, Netherlands, 1989, 114; Tafari-Ama, "Rastawoman as Rebel: Case Studies in Jamaica," in *Chanting Down Babylon: The Rastafari Reader*, eds. Nathaniel S. Murrell, William D. Spencer, and Adrian A. McFarlane (Kingston: Ian Randle Publishers, 1998), 105.

59. Ray, "Standing," 150-51.

60. Lennox, interviewed by Romano and Leib, 1983.

61. Galawdewos, *The Life of Walatta-Petros: A Seventeenth-Century Biography of an African Woman*, trans. Wendy L. Belcher and Michael Kleiner (Princeton: Princeton University Press, 2018), ix.

62. Sister Farcia, "Forward Up Daughters," *Rasta Voice* 86 (1979): 16.

63. Ray, "Standing," 151.

64. Empress Yuajah, *How to Become a Rasta: Rastafari, Rasta Beliefs, Rastafarian Culture* (North Charleston: CreateSpace Independent Publishing Platform, 2012), 18, 26.

65. Lennox, interviewed by Romano and Leib, 1983.

66. Ibid.

67. Tracye A. Matthews, "'No One Ever Asks What a Man's Role in the Revolution Is': Gender Politics and Leadership in the Black Panther Party, 1966–71," in *Sisters in the Struggle: African American Women in the Civil Rights-Black Power Movement*, ed. Bettye Collier-Thomas and V. P. Franklin (New York: New York University Press, 2001), 233.

68. Lennox, interviewed by Romano and Leib, 1983.

69. Ibid.

70. Ibid.

71. Ibid.

72. Ibid.; Jeanne Christensen, *Rastafari Reasoning and the RastaWoman: Gender Constructions in the Shaping of Rastafari Livity* (Lanham, MD: Lexington Books, 2014), 69.

73. John [Jake] P. Homiak, "Dub History: Soundings on Rastafari Livity and Language," in *Rastafari and Other African-Caribbean Worldviews*, ed. Barry Chevannes (New Brunswick, NJ: Rutgers University Press, 1998), 133–34.

74. Lennox, interviewed by Romano and Leib, 1983.

75. Frank Loris Peterson, *The Hope of the Race* (Nashville: Southern Publishing Association, 1934), 281–83, 286. Emphasis in original. For more information on Peterson, see F. L. Bland, "Life Sketch of Frank Loris Peterson," *Review and Herald: General Church Paper of the Seventh Day Adventists* 146, no. 46 (1969): 8.

76. Lennox, interviewed by Romano and Leib, 1983.

77. Miriam Lennox, August 18, 1915–September 19, 1995, Half Way Tree, Saint Andrew, Jamaica, Death Registration Form, Registrar General's Department, St. Catherine, Jamaica, no. BA 580.

CHAPTER 5.

Women and the "Holy Herb" Dilemma

1. "Disturbances by Followers of the Ras Tafari Cult," *Daily Gleaner,* July 20, 1934, 6.

2. Ibid.; "Daniel of Ras Tafari Cult Is Put in New Den," *Daily Gleaner,* July 25, 1934, 3.

3. "Disturbances by Followers of the Ras Tafari Cult," 1934, 6.

4. "Man Gets Four Months for Ganja: Women Fined," *Daily Gleaner,* October 24, 1939, 15.

5. Nikolaas J. Van der Merwe, "Cannabis Smoking in 13th–14th Century Ethiopia: Chemical Evidence," in *Cannabis and Culture,* ed. Vera Rubin (The Hague: Mouton Publishers, 1975), 78; Chris S. Duvall, "Cannabis and Tobacco in Precolonial and Colonial Africa," in *Oxford Research Encyclopedia of African History,* ed. Thomas Spear (Oxford: University of Oxford Press, 2018), 8.

6. Brian M. Du Toit, "Dagga: The History and Ethnographic Setting of Cannabis," in *Cannabis and Culture,* ed. Vera Rubin (The Hague: Mouton Publishers, 1975), 88; John Edward Philips, "African Smoking and Pipes," *Journal of African History* 24, no. 3 (1983): 303.

7. John W. Commissiong, *Ganja (Marihuana)* (Kingston: Cultural Studies Initiative and Caribbean Quarterly, University of the West Indies, 1997), 6; Vera Rubin and Lambros Comitas, *Ganja in Jamaica: The Effects of Marijuana Use* (Garden City, NY: Anchor, 1976), 11, 12.

8. Dennis Forsythe, *Rastafari: For the Healing of the Nations* (New York: One Drop Book, 1999), 135.

9. Brian M. Du Toit, "Man and Cannabis in Africa: A Study of Diffusion," *African Economic History* 1 (1976), 26.

10. Charles Price, "Cleave to the Black: Expressions of Ethiopianism in Jamaica," *New West Indian Guide* 77, nos. 1–2 (2003): 38; Barrett, *The Rastafarians,* 2.

11. Du Toit, "Man and Cannabis," 18.

12. J. Edward Chamberlin and Barry Chevannes, "Ganja in Jamaica," in *Smoke: A Global History of Smoking,* ed. Sander L. Gilman and Zhou Xun (London: Reaktion Books, 2004), 147; Elisa Janine Sobo, *One Blood: The Jamaican Body* (Albany: State University of New York Press, 1993), 18.

13. Mukesh Kumar and Rajani Kumari, "Indian Culture in Jamaica—Past and Present," *Proceedings of the Indian History Congress* 60 (1999), 1028.

14. Jamaica, *Eighth Census,* XLIX.

15. *Report of the Indian Hemp Drugs Commission, 1893–94,* vol. IV (Simla: The Government Central Printing Office, 1894), 11.

16. Robert A. Hill, *Dread History: Leonard P. Howell and Millenarian Visions in the Early Rastafarian Religion in Jamaica* (Kingston and Chicago: Frontline Distribution International, 2001), 42. Hill noted that William Powell, a Howellite, recalled

in an interview that an East Indian man known as "Laloo" was also considered "one of Howell's direct bodyguards." He was probably related to Albertha Lalloo.

17. Rastafari embraced attitudes toward cannabis also found in Hinduism, such as the reference to the smoking of cannabis as *sadhana,* that is, the ability to communicate with God, and the reference to the high from smoking as *prasad,* or that which is sanctified. Ajai Mansingh and Laxmi Mansingh argue that the term used by Rastafari for the most "potent" form of cannabis was "kali, after the black, terrifying earth mother of Indian mythology." See Ajai Mansingh and Laxmi Mansingh, "Hindu Influences on Rastafarianism," in *Rastafari,* ed. Rex Nettleford and Veronica Salter (Kingston: Caribbean Quarterly, 2008), 111, 106.

18. Forsythe, *Rastafari,* 132.

19. Casey J. Roulette and Barry S. Hewlett, "Patterns of Cannabis Use among Congo Basin Hunter-Gatherers," *Journal of Ethnography* 38, no. 4 (2018): 521.

20. Forsythe, *Rastafari,* 134.

21. In a general study of cannabis use done in 1978, Commissiong asserted, for example, that "marihuana abuse in the West Indies is predominantly a male affair," and the "small percentage" of women who "smoke" cannabis do so mainly "as a sign of urban sophistication," since "women as yet," he added, "do not abuse marihuana nearly as much as men." See Commissiong, *Ganja,* 12–13.

22. Stewart, interviewed by author, 2016.

23. Sasha Turner, *Contested Bodies: Pregnancy, Childrearing, and Slavery in Jamaica* (Philadelphia: University of Pennsylvania Press, 2017), 129, 157.

24. Judith Carney and Richard N. Rosomoff, *In the Shadow of Slavery: Africa's Botanical Legacy in the Atlantic World* (Berkeley: University of California Press, 2009), 124. Emphasis in original. Also see Pablo F. Gómez, *The Experiential Caribbean: Creating Knowledge and Healing in the Early Modern Atlantic* (Chapel Hill: University of North Carolina Press, 2017), 120.

25. Londa Schiebinger, *Secret Cures of Slaves: People, Plants, and Medicine in the Eighteenth-Century Atlantic World* (Stanford: Stanford University Press, 2017), 62.

26. Carney and Rosomoff, *In the Shadow of Slavery,* 2, 81.

27. Barbara Bush, "Towards Emancipation: Slave Women and Resistance to Coercive Labour Regimes in the British West Indian Colonies, 1790–1838," *Slavery & Abolition* 5, no. 3 (2008): 49; Affette McCaw-Binns and C. O. Moody, "The Development of Primary Health Care in Jamaica," *West Indian Medical Journal* 50, no. 4 (2001): 7–8.

28. Montinol A. Howell, personal communication, February 13, 2020.

29. William "Bill" Howell, interviewed by Hélène Lee, May 1998.

30. Commissiong, *Ganja,* 5.

31. Obiagele Lake, *Rastafari Women: Subordination in the Midst of Liberation Theology* (Durham, NC: Carolina Academic Press, 1998), 76.

32. Barrett, *The Rastafarians,* 123.

33. Owens, *Dread,* 157.

34. Lake, *Rastafari Women,* 77.

35. Barrett, *The Rastafarians,* 92.

36. Christensen, *Rastafari Reasoning,* 61.

37. Mack, *From Babylon to Rastafari,* 82.

38. Barrett, *The Rastafarians,* 123.

39. Christensen, *Rastafari Reasoning,* 68.

40. Owens, *Dread,* 160.

41. Barrett, *The Rastafarians,* 129.

42. Anne E. Cudd, *Analyzing Oppression* (Oxford: Oxford University Press, 2006), 199.

43. Dennis Forsythe, *The Law Against Ganja in Jamaica* (Kingston: Zaika Publications, 1993), 2.

44. Forsythe, *Rastafari,* 133.

45. Carradine, "The Ras Tafarites Retreat," 1940, 54.

46. Yasus Afari, *Overstanding Rastafari: "Jamaica's Gift to the World"* (Kingston: Senya-Cum, 2007), 48.

47. "Victims Tell of Ras Tafarians' Reign of Terror in St. Catherine," *Jamaica Times,* July 12,
1941, page unknown. Also see, Christensen, *Rastafari Reasoning,* 59, n. 13.

48. Homiak, interviewed by author, 2015.

49. Chevannes, *Rastafari,* 219.

50. Barrett, *The Rastafarians,* 17.

51. "Ganja Smoking as a Danger to the Natives of This Colony," *Daily Gleaner,* June 10, 1913, 8, 9; Forsythe, *The Law,* 8.

52. Rubin and Comitas, *Ganja in Jamaica,* 177; "Purchasing Power of British Pounds."

53. "Pleas Taken Yesterday. Trial to take Place Monday and Tuesday," *Daily Gleaner,* July 23, 1941, 9; "Ras Tafari Movement Rose from the Dungle," *Daily Gleaner,* August 4, 1960, 12.

54. Rubin and Comitas, *Ganja in Jamaica,* 177, 178.

55. Audrey Elizabeth Lewis, interviewed by author, Salt River, Clarendon, Jamaica, May 5, 2013.

56. Barbara Bush-Slimani, "Hard Labour: Women, Childbirth and Resistance in British Caribbean Slave Societies," *History Workshop* 36 (1993): 89.

57. Ibid., 92.

58. Lewis, interviewed by author, 2013.

59. Mack, *From Babylon to Rastafari,* 61.

60. William "Bill" Howell, personal communication, June 14, 2013.

61. Lewis, interviewed by author, 2013.

62. Mack, *From Babylon to Rastafari,* 70.

63. "Pleas Taken Yesterday," 1941, 9.

64. "Pinnacle Case: Woman, 70, Among 32 More Sentenced," *Daily Gleaner*, June 17, 1954, 5.

65. "Pinnacle Case: 21 Guilty Pleas," *Daily Gleaner*, June 18, 1954, 5.

66. Ibid.

67. See Peter Tosh, "Legalize It," from the album *Legalize It*, Treasure Isle and Randy's, Kingston, 1976; Bob Marley, "Kaya," from the album *Kaya*, Island Studios, London, 1978.

68. Rita Marley, "One Draw," from the album *Harambe: Working Together for Freedom*, Shanachie Records, United States, 1982.

69. Dionne Jackson Miller, "Jamaican Marijuana Reform, Rastas and Rights," *OxHRH Blog*, March 18, 2015, http://humanrights.dev3.0neltd.eu/jamaican-marijuana-reform-rastas-and-rights/.

70. Barry Chevannes, Webster Edwards, Anthony Freckleton, Norma Linton, DiMario McDowell, Aileen Standard-Goldson, and Barbara Smith, "A Report of the National Commission on Ganja," Office of the Prime Minister of Jamaica, Kingston, August 7, 2001, http://addictionstudies.dec.uwi.edu/Documents/generic%20drug%20information/.

71. Jiachuan Wu and Daniella Silva, "Map: See the States Where Marijuana Is Legal," *NBC News*, November 4, 2020, https://www.nbcnews.com/news/us-news/map-see-if-marijuana-legal-your-state-n938426.

72. Madison Margolin, "Now Decriminalized, Could Jamaica Become Destination for Legal Weed," *Rolling Stone*, August 20, 2018, https://www.rollingstone.com/culture/culture-features/jamaica-legal-weed-rastafari-criminalized-711745/.

73. Ibid.

CHAPTER 6.

Audrey Lewis and the History of the
Early Rastafari's Development

1. Nicole N. Aljoe, *Creole Testimonies: Slave Narratives from the British West Indies, 1709-1838* (New York: Palgrave Macmillan, 2011), 95.

2. Monique A. Bedasse, *Jah Kingdom: Rastafarians, Tanzania, and Pan-Africanism in the Age of Decolonization* (Chapel Hill: University of North Carolina Press, 2017), 10.

3. M. G. Smith, "The Plural Framework of Jamaican Society," *British Journal of Sociology* 12, no. 3 (1961): 249, 257.

4. Edward Brathwaite, *The Development of Creole Society in Jamaica* (London: Oxford University Press, 1971), 306, 307; Viranjini Munasinghe, "Theorizing World Culture through the New World: East Indians and Creolization," *American Ethnologist* 33, no. 4 (2006): 549.

5. Lee, *The First Rasta*, 127.

6. "Ras Tafarites Won't Quit Famed 'Pinnacle,'" 11; Register Book, Office of Titles, Registrar General's Department, Twinkenham Park, Jamaica, vol. 277, folio 52.

7. Dianne M. Stewart, "Womanist Theology in the Caribbean Context: Critiquing Culture, Rethinking Doctrine, and Expanding Boundaries," *Journal of Feminist Studies in Religion* 20, no. 1 (2004): 64; Kenneth Bilby and Elliott Leib, "Kumina, the Howellite Church and the Emergence of Rastafarian Traditional Music in Jamaica," *Jamaica Journal* 19, no. 3 (1986): 22, 26; Christensen, *Rastafari Reasoning*, 60.

8. Stewart, "Womanist Theology," 64, 73.

9. Lucie Pradel, *African Beliefs in the New World: Popular Literary Traditions of the Caribbean* (Trenton, NJ: Africa World Press, 2000), 112.

10. Olive Lewin, *Rock It Come Over: The Folk Music of Jamaica* (Kingston: The University of the West Indies Press, 2000), 307.

11. Stewart, interviewed by author, 2016.

12. Clinton A. Hutton, "Leonard Howell Announcing God: The Conditions that Gave Birth to Rastafari in Jamaica," in *Leonard Percival Howell and the Genesis of Rastafari*, ed. Clinton A. Hutton, Michael A. Barnett, D. A. Dunkley, and Jahlani A. H. Niaah (Kingston: University of the West Indies Press, 2015), 34.

13. Lewin, *Rock It Come Over*, 298, 310.

14. Bilby and Leib, "Kumina," 23.

15. Homiak, interviewed by author, 2015.

16. E. S. P. McPherson, *Honoring Our Original Ancestors: A Royal Ethiopic Salute to 'The Gong'/The Howellites. An Introduction to Kulungu . . . Vols. 1–4*, Ethio-Rastaology Audio Series No. 1, May 1995, 6.

17. Holy Bible, New King James Version, 1987 printing.

18. McPherson, *Honoring Our Original Ancestors*, 6, 7.

19. Erin C. MacLeod, *Visions of Zion: Ethiopians and Rastafari in the Search for the Promised Land* (New York: New York University Press, 2014), 8.

20. Lennox, interviewed by Romano and Leib, 1983.

21. Obiagele Lake, "The Many Voices of Rastafarian Women: Sexual Subordination in the Midst of Liberation," *New West Indian Guide* 68, nos. 3–4 (1994): 244.

22. Lewis, interviewed by author, 2013.

23. Barrett, *The Rastafarians*, xiii.

24. Ennis B. Edmonds, *Rastafari: A Very Short Introduction* (Oxford: Oxford University Press, 2012), 53.

25. Lewis, interviewed by author, 2013.

26. Carradine, "The Ras Tafarites Retreat," 1940, 54; U.D.S., "Plight of Ras Tafarians at Camp Pinnacle in Saint Catherine," *Daily Gleaner*, December 22, 1940, page unknown.

27. Lewis, interviewed by author, 2013.

28. Gertrude Campbell, interviewed by Jahlani Niaah and Ishmahil Blagrove for

"Roaring Lion, The Rise of Rastafari: A Documentary," Kingston and Brampton, Front-line Productions and Knowledge Bookstore, 2001, 8.

29. Ibid. For the initial estimate of 700 people, see Carradine, "The Ras Tafarites Retreat," 1940, 54.

30. Stewart, interviewed by author, 2016.

31. Reports of Medical Officer F. W. Aris, St. Catherine, Copy of Reports, M.O.H., JA 5073/34.

32. Ibid.

33. Copy of Reports, M.O.H., Report of December 31, 1940, JA 5073/34, 2.

34. Ibid.

35. Copy of Reports, M.O.H., Report of January 11, 1941, JA 5073/34, 2.

36. J. Hall, Assistant Director of Medical Services, to Colonial Secretary, January 16, 1941, Minutes, JA 5073/34. Hall based his conclusions on Aris's reports.

37. "The Raid Didn't Seem to Bother These Juvenile Ras Tafarians," *Jamaica Times*, July 19, 1941, 1.

38. Post Office Telegraph (Inland), Hon. McNeill, 5 Portland Road, Kingston, to Hon. Colonial Secretary, December 23, 1940, JA 5073/34, 1–3. For the 1948 amendment to the Dangerous Drugs Act, see Suzette A. Haughton, *Drugged Out: Globalization and Jamaica's Resilience to Drug Trafficking* (Lanham, MD: University Press of America, 2011), 48; Forsythe, *Rastafari*, 140; and Rubin and Comitas, *Ganja in Jamaica*, 177, 178.

39. Colonial Secretary to A.C.S., January 17, 1941, Minutes, JA 5073/34, 10.

40. Letter to the Hon. Colonial Secretary, April 15, 1941, Minutes, JA 5073/34, 13–14.

41. Attorney General to the Colonial Secretary, July 2, 1941, JA 5073/34 Minutes.

42. James Robertson, "'That Vagabond George Stewart of England': Leonard Howell's Seditious Sermons, 1933–1941," in *Leonard Percival Howell and the Genesis of Rastafari*, ed. Clinton A. Hutton, Michael A. Barnett, D. A. Dunkley, and Jahlani A. H. Niaah (Kingston: University of the West Indies Press, 2015), 105. Also see "£50 Fine for Ganja," *Daily Gleaner*, September 1, 1938, 10. The *Gleaner* report stated, "James Nelson of Duckensfield was fined £50 or six months' hard labour for having ganja in his possession. He made a very impressive plea for time to pay but it was found that he failed to pay a fine of 8/ [shillings] in the lower Court a few months before. He was offered time with a surety which he could not find."

43. "110 Dead as Hurricane Hits South Coast," *Daily Gleaner*, August 26, 1951, 1.

44. Lewis, interviewed by author, 2013.

45. Ibid.

46. Ibid. Lewis said, "a killer for black," which I have changed to "a killer [of] black" for clarity.

47. A. Bustamante, Duke Street, Kingston, Jamaica, to the Colonial Secretary, July 6, 1939, JA 1B/5/79/735.

48. Lewis, interviewed by author, 2013.

49. Ibid.

50. Woodville K. Marshall, "The Emergence and Survival of the Peasantry," in *General History of the Caribbean, Vol. IV, The Long Nineteenth Century: Nineteenth-Century Transformations*, ed. K. O. Laurence (Paris and London: UNESCO, and Macmillan Education, 2011), 173.

51. Ibid., 176, 177.

52. Veront M. Satchell, *From Plots to Plantations: Land Transactions in Jamaica* (Kingston: Institute of Social and Economic Research, 1990), 119.

53. Jay R. Mandle, "Review of *From Plots to Plantations: Land Transactions in Jamaica, 1866–1900*, by Veront M. Satchell," *Journal of Economic History* 51, no. 2 (1991): 503.

54. Altamont Reid, Philip Walker, and R. N. White to Governor Edward Brandis Denham, circa January 1937, JA 5073/34, 1; Commander R. N., Private Secretary, to Mr. Altamont Reid, February 3, 1937, JA 5073/34.

55. Yvonne McLean, interviewed by author, Miami, Florida, July 28, 2018.

56. D. A. Dunkley, "Occupy Pinnacle and the Rastafari's Struggle for Land in Jamaica," *Jamaica Journal* 35, nos. 1–2 (2014): 42. In 2017, the Rastafari organization known as the Millennium Council objected to the Jamaican government's attempt to declare the other five plots at Pinnacle as a protected National Monument. The Council has argued that the declaration should be as a protected National Heritage site, as was done in the case of the plot that was declared as protected in 2013. So far, only one plot has been designated as a protected site.

CHAPTER 7.

A Prototype of Pinnacle: Edna Fisher and the African Reform Church

1. "The Rastafarite Cult," Headquarters, Jamaica Constabulary, Kingston, January 13, 1959, Appendix 1, TNA C01031/2767.

2. Gallimore, interviewed by author, 2016.

3. "Judge's Summing Up," 1960, 9.

4. "The Rastafarite Cult," Appendix 1 & 2, TNA C01031/2767.

5. Barrett, *The Rastafarians*, 92. Note that the Rastafari organization known as Youth Black Faith was formed in the 1940s, and the Nyahbinghi and Bobo Shanti organizations were established in the 1950s, followed by the Ethiopian Zion Coptic Church, formed in Mountain View, Kingston, in 1960, which was described as "deracialized." Its leadership "prophesied the unification of black and white." See Michael Barnett, "Differences and Similarities Between the Rastafari Movement and the Nation of Islam," *Journal of Black Studies* 36, no. 6 (2006): 876; and Walter Wells, "History

of the Ethiopian Zion Coptic Church," *Ethiopian Zion Coptic Church,* 2017, http://www.ethiopianzioncopticchurch.org/Home/History. In 1968, the Twelve Tribes of Israel was formed and continued the trend to deracialize Rastafari organizations with branches formed even in Britain, Europe, United States, Australia, New Zealand, and other countries. See Monique Bedasse, "Rasta Evolution: The Theology of the Twelve Tribes of Israel," *Journal of Black Studies* 40, no. 5 (2010): 961–62.

6. Paulette Sweeney, interviewed in "Omega Rising: Woman of Rastafari," filmed in Jamaica and Britain, directed by D. Elmina Davis and produced by Imruh Bakari for Ceddo Film and Video Workshop, London, 1988.

7. "Current Items," *Daily Gleaner,* February 26, 1970, 4.

8. "Sentences of 3 to 10 Years on Treason Felony Accused," *Daily Gleaner,* October 31, 1960, 4.

9. Frank Jan van Dijk, "Sociological Means: Colonial Reactions to the Radicalization of Rastafari in Jamaica, 1956–1959," *New West Indian Guide* 69, nos. 1–2 (1995): 67; Brian Meeks, "Obscure Revolt, Profound Effects: The Henry Rebellion, Counter-Hegemony and Jamaican Society" *Small Axe* 2 (1997): 39.

10. Anthony Bogues, *Black Heretics, Black Prophets: Radical Political Intellectuals* (New York: Routledge, 2003), 166, 170. Other studies with very little or no information on Fisher include, for example, Orlando Patterson, "Rastafari: The Cult of Outcasts," *New Society* 12 (1964): 15–17; Barry Chevannes, "The Repairer of the Breach: Reverend Claudius Henry and Jamaican Society," in *Ethnicity in the Americas,* ed. Frances Henry (The Hague: Mouton, 1976), 263–90; and Terry Lacey, *Violence and Politics in Jamaica, 1960–1970: Internal Security in a Developing Country* (Manchester: Manchester University Press, 1977).

11. "Treason Felony Trial," *Daily Gleaner,* October 25, 1960, 4.

12. "Judge's Summing Up," 1960, 9.

13. Kathryn Wirtenberger, "The Jesuits in Jamaica," MA thesis, Loyola University, Chicago, Illinois, December 1942, 125.

14. "Sought-After Primary Schools Top Grade 4 Literacy, Numeracy," *Jamaica Observer,* January 14, 2018, http://www.jamaicaobserver.com/career-education/sought-after-primary-schools_122274?profile=1270.

15. "Judge's Summing Up," 1960, 9.

16. Frank Jan van Dijk, *Jahmaica: Rastafari and Jamaican Society* (Utrecht: ISOR, 1993), 128; Van Dijk, "Sociological Means," 85; Giulia Bonacci, "The Ethiopian World Federation: A Pan-African Organization Among Rastafari in Jamaica," *Caribbean Quarterly* 59, no. 2 (2013): 78, 80; Giulia Bonacci, *Exodus!: Heirs and Pioneers, Rastafari Return to Ethiopia* (Kingston: University of the West Indies Press, 2015), 159, 163.

17. Smith, Nettleford, and Augier, *The Ras Tafari Movement,* 13.

18. Hill, *Dread History,* 20.

19. "Accused: No Subscription Was Taken from Members of the Church" *Daily Gleaner,* October 22, 1960, 4.

20. Meeks, "Obscure Revolt," 41.

21. Bogues, *Black Heretics,* 166; "Judge's Summing Up," 1960.

22. Besentie Thompson, interviewed by author, Green Bottom, Clarendon, Jamaica, December 16, 2017.

23. "Claudius Henry Tells the Court," *Daily Gleaner,* October 25, 1960, 4.

24. "Judge's Summing Up," 1960, 9.

25. Johnathan Reid, interviewed by author, Green Bottom, Sandy Bay, Clarendon, Jamaica, December 16, 2017.

26. Robyn C. Spencer, *The Revolution Has Come: Black Power, Gender, and the Black Panther Party in Oakland* (Durham: Duke University Press, 2016), 45. Also see Matthews, "'No One Ever Asks," 233.

27. "Accused: No Subscription," 1960, 4.

28. R. A. Leevy, "Ras Tafarianism: Haile Selassie, Emperor of Abyssinia, Inspired a New Religion in Jamaica," *Public Opinion,* February 20, 1943, 3.

29. "Accused: No Subscription," 1960, 4.

30. Douglas McKay, interviewed by author, Green Bottom, Sandy Bay, Clarendon, Jamaica, December 16, 2017.

31. Honor Ford-Smith, "Women and the Garvey Movement in Jamaica," in *Garvey: His Work and Impact,* eds. Rupert Lewis and Patrick Bryan (Trenton, NJ: Africa World Press, 1994), 77.

32. Ibid., 75, 79.

33. Tony Martin, "Women in the Garvey Movement," in *Garvey: His Work and Impact,* 70.

34. Stanley Haughton, interviewed by author, Green Bottom, Sandy Bay, Clarendon, Jamaica, December 16, 2017.

35. "Treason-Felony Trial: Keeping of Sabbath," *Daily Gleaner,* October 25, 1960, 4.

36. Hugh Foot to M. Phillips, November 19, 1956, TNA CO1031/1958, 3.

37. Monthly Intelligence Report, April 1960, TNA CO1031/3994, 16.

38. Ibid.

39. Norman Girvan, "Assessing Westminster in the Caribbean: Then and Now," *Commonwealth & Comparative Politics* 53, no. 1 (2015): 97.

40. Extract from Personal Intelligence Report of the Governor of Jamaica for August–September 1960, TNA CO1031/3995, 82.

41. King's House, Jamaica, H. L. Lindo, Governor's Deputy [Drafted by the Governor], to J. E. Marnham, Colonial Office, April 12, 1960, TNA CO1031/3998, 7.

42. Ibid.

43. Carradine, "The Ras Tafarites Retreat," 1940, 54.

44. Extract from Local Standing Intelligence Committee Report March, 1960, TNA CO1031/3994, 9. Emphasis in original.

45. Inward Telegram, To the Secretary of State for the Colonies, from Jamaica (Sir K. Blackburne), April 14/15, 1960, TNA CO1031/3998, 5.

46. May 17, 1960, TNA C01031/3998, 8. Handwritten notes, author unclear.

47. Sylvia Wynter, "A Dream Deferred: Will the Condemned Rasta Fari ever Return to Africa?" TNA C01031/3995, 51.

48. O. Nigel Bolland, *The Politics of Labour in the British Caribbean: The Social Origins of Authoritarianism and Democracy in the Labour Movement* (Kingston, Oxford, and Princeton: Ian Randle, James Currey, and Markus Wiener Publishers, 2001), 307. In the 1950s, Richard Hart, Ken Hill, Frank Hill, and Arthur Henry were expelled from the PNP on the grounds of constituting a Marxist threat to the party. This incident is referred to as the ouster of the 4Hs. They went on to form the PFM, whose involvement with Rastafari was also noted by Jamaican anthropologist M. G. Smith. Smith was a member of a "rehabilitation" committee authorized by Manley's cabinet in 1960 to address the Rastafari problem. But Smith quickly abandoned this committee to lead his own research on the Rastafari movement after the arrests of Fisher, Henry, and other key members of the ARC on treason-felony charges. Historian Robert Hill has argued that Smith was interested in the Rastafari movement because he was secretly working for the Manley government to undermine the spread of communism in Jamaica. See Robert A. Hill and Annie Paul, "Our Man in Mona: A Conversation between Robert A. Hill and Annie Paul," September 27, 2013, https://anniepaul.net/our-man-in-mona-an-interview-by-robert-a-hill-with-annie-paul/.

49. Extract from Report of Local Standing Intelligence Committee Jamaica for June, 1960, TNA C01031/3994, 70.

50. Extract from Report of Local Standing Intelligence Committee Jamaica for July, 1960, TNA C01031/3994, 75; Rupert Lewis, via Christopher Charles, personal communication, April 10, 2018; M. G. Smith, "Robotham's Ideology and Pluralism: A Reply," *Social and Economic Studies* 32, no. 2 (1983): 112.

51. Extract from Local Standing Intelligence Committee Report March, 1960, TNA C01031/3994, 8.

52. "Letter to Castro Put in Evidence," *Daily Gleaner*, May 6, 1960, 16.

53. "Accused: No Subscription," 1960, 4.

54. "Treason-Felony Trial: Keeping of Sabbath," 1960.

55. "Sentences of 3 to 10 Years," 1960, 4.

56. Thompson, interviewed by author, 2017.

57. "Treason Felony Trial," 1960, 4.

58. Ibid.

59. "Accused: No Subscription," 1960, 4.

60. Extract from Report of Local Standing Intelligence Committee Jamaica for April, 1960, TNA C01031/3994, 17.

61. "Letter to Castro in Court," *Daily Gleaner*, May 6, 1960, 1.

62. "Letter to Castro Put in Evidence," 1960, 16.

63. Ibid.

64. Ibid.

65. Ibid.; "Accused: No Subscription," 1960, 4.

66. "Accused: No Subscription," 1960, 4.

67. Uncataloged-CID Exhibit Stores, Kingston, Statement of Eldred Morgan, August 5, 1960, JA Ex. No. 93, 1; "Reynold Henry, Gabbidon, Morgan, Jetter to Hang," *Daily Gleaner,* October 1, 1960, 1.

68. Rupert Charles Lewis, *Walter Rodney's Intellectual and Political Thought* (Kingston and Detroit: The Press University of the West Indies and Wayne State University Press, 1998), 96.

69. Ibid.

70. Thompson, interviewed by author, 2017.

71. Lewis, *Walter Rodney's Intellectual,* 97.

72. Ibid.

73. Reid, interviewed by author, 2017.

74. McKay, interviewed by author, 2017.

75. Ibid.

76. Reid, interviewed by author, 2017.

77. Burnett Hall, interviewed by author, Green Bottom, Sandy Bay, Clarendon, Jamaica, December 16, 2017.

78. "Henry and 15 Committed," *Daily Gleaner,* May 11, 1960, 16. Emphasis in original.

79. Ibid., 1.

80. Ibid., 16.

81. Hill and Paul, "Our Man in Mona."

82. See Smith, Augier, and Nettleford, *Report on the Ras Tafari.*

83. Thompson, interviewed by author, 2017.

84. Filmore Alvaranga and Douglas Mack to Harold Macmillan, Prime Minister of Britain, April 4, 1961, TNA C01031/3995, 142/E1.

85. Brother Mortimo Togo Desta Planno, "Maniaphopia of the Invisible Establishment," Unpublished Lecture, given to the Black Community Movement, York University, Toronto, November 1973, 25.

86. Claudius V. Henry, "The New Creation International Peacemaker's Association: Violence in Jamaica," Kemps Hill District, International Peacemakers Association, Jamaica, April 28, 1969, 1. Emphasis in original.

87. Yvette Clarke, interviewed in "Omega Rising: Woman of Rastafari."

Conclusion: Disrupting the Status Quo

1. Shepherd, *Maharani's Misery,* xiii.

2. Owen F. Wright to Alexander W. G. H. Grantham, January 15, 1940, JA 1B/5/79, 35.

3. Taylor, *The Promise of Patriarchy,* 122, 123, 124.

4. Jacquelyn Grant, "Black Theology and the Black Woman," in *The Black Studies*

Reader, ed. Jacqueline Bobo, Cynthia Hudley, and Claudine Michel (New York: Routledge, 2004), 423.

5. Taylor, "'Negro Women,'" 105.

6. "Jamaica's Great Ras Tafarite Kingdom Comes to an End," *Daily Gleaner,* October 14, 1945, 8.

7. Lennox, interviewed by Romano and Leib, 1983.

BIBLIOGRAPHY

ARCHIVAL DOCUMENTATION

Most of the archival files used in this book can be found at the Jamaica Archives, Spanish Town, St. Catherine. They contain handwritten and typed documents that cover the period of 1932–58 and include government minute papers, police reports, health department reports, court rulings, letters from the public, and petitions from church leaders and Rastafari members. The Jamaica Archives also has uncataloged police and court files on Rastafari members in 1960. Documents covering the activities of the Rastafari movement from 1954 through 1960 can be found at the National Archives at Kew in Great Britain and contain information about police surveillance of the movement. The National Library of Jamaica, Kingston, and the University of the West Indies Library, Mona, house files relating to the Rastafari movement and cannabis that cover the 1930s through the present. The International Rastafari Archives Project at the National Anthropological Archives, Smithsonian Institution, has a large collection of anthropological research and records created by the Rastafari movement from the 1950s through the present that were also used in this book. Weston Library, Oxford University, houses the papers of former governors of Jamaica and colonial secretaries in the 1930s and 1940s, which contain occasional remarks on the Rastafari movement. In addition, Rastafari members and other individuals associated with the movement granted me access to their personal archives of letters, fliers, pamphlets, essays, and photographs from the colonial period.

ARTICLES (JOURNALS AND MAGAZINES)

Africa, John. "Black Woman," *Rasta Voice* 86 (1979): 21.

Alexander, Jack. "The Role of the Male in the Middle-Class Jamaican Family: A Comparative Perspective," *Journal of Comparative Family Studies* 8, no. 3 (1977): 369–89.

Bandele, Ramla. "Understanding African Diaspora Political Activism: The Rise and Fall of the Black Star Line," *Journal of Black Studies* 40, no. 4 (2010): 745–61.

Barnett, Michael. "Differences and Similarities Between the Rastafari Movement and the Nation of Islam," *Journal of Black Studies* 36, no. 6 (2006): 873–93.

Bedasse, Monique. "Rasta Evolution: The Theology of the Twelve Tribes of Israel," *Journal of Black Studies* 40, no. 5 (2010): 960–73.

Benard, Akeia A. "The Material Roots of Rastafarian Marijuana Symbolism," *History and Anthropology* 18, no. 1 (2007): 89–99.

Bilby, Kenneth, and Elliott Leib. "Kumina, the Howellite Church and the Emergence of Rastafarian Traditional Music in Jamaica," *Jamaica Journal* 19, no. 3 (1986): 22–28.

Bland, F. L. "Life Sketch of Frank Loris Peterson," *Review and Herald: General Church Paper of the Seventh Day Adventists* 146, no. 46 (1969): 8.

Bonacci, Giulia. "The Ethiopian World Federation: A Pan-African Organization Among Rastafari in Jamaica," *Caribbean Quarterly* 59, no. 2 (2013): 73–95.

Brereton, Bridget. "Women and Gender in Caribbean (English-speaking) Historiography: Sources and Methods," *Caribbean Review of Gender Studies* 7 (2013): 1–18.

Brown, Samuel Elisha. "Treatise on the Rastafarian Movement," *Caribbean Studies* 6, no. 1 (1966): 39–40.

Burke, Kelsey C. "Women's Agency in Gender-Traditional Religions: A Review of Four Approaches," *Sociology Compass* 6, no. 2 (2012): 122–33.

Burrows, Rufus J., Jr. "Development of Womanist Theology: Some Chief Characteristics," *Ashbury Theological Journal* 54, no. 1 (1999): 41–57.

Bush, Barbara. "Defiance or Submission? The Role of the Slave Woman in Slave Resistance in the British Caribbean," *Immigrants & Minorities: Historical Studies in Ethnicity, Migration, and Diaspora* 1, no. 1 (1982): 16–38.

———. "Towards Emancipation: Slave Women and Resistance to Coercive Labour Regimes in the British West Indian Colonies, 1790–1838," *Slavery and Abolition* 5, no. 3 (2008): 27–54.

Dadzie, Stella. "Searching for the Invisible Woman: Slavery and Resistance in Jamaica," *Race and Class* 32, no. 2 (1990): 21–38.

Doyle, Connor. "Rastafarianism and Michael Manley," *Caribbean Quilt* 2 (2012): 107–23.

Drescher, Seymour. "Civil Society and Paths to Abolition," *História (São Paulo)* 34, no. 2 (2015): 29–57.

Duncan, Graham A. "Ethiopianism in Pan-African Perspective, 1880–1920," *Studia Historiae Ecclesiasticae* 41, no. 2 (2015): 198–218.

Dunkley, D. A. "Hegemony in Post-Independence Jamaica," *Caribbean Quarterly* 57, no. 2 (2011): 1–23.

———. "Leonard P. Howell's Leadership of the Rastafari Movement and His 'Missing Years,'" *Caribbean Quarterly* 58, no. 4 (2012): 1–24.

———. "Occupy Pinnacle and the Rastafari's Struggle for Land in Jamaica," *Jamaica Journal* 35, nos. 1–2 (2014): 36–43.

Dwyer, Asheda. "Left Waiting in Vain for Y/our Love: Situating the (In) Visibility of Black Women of Rastafari as Lovers, Partners and Revolutionaries in Brooklyn Babylon and One Love," *Caribbean Quarterly*, Special Issue 59, no. 2 (2013): 25–38.

Erickson, Arvel B. "Empire of Anarchy: The Jamaica Rebellion of 1865," *Journal of Negro History* 44, no. 2 (1959): 99–122.

Evans, William McKee. "From the Land of Canaan to the Land of Guinea: The Strange Odyssey of the 'Sons of Ham,'" *American Historical Review* 85, no. 1 (1980): 15–43.

Farcia, Sister. "Forward Up Daughters," *Rasta Voice* 86 (1979): 16.

Girvan, Norman. "Assessing Westminster in the Caribbean: Then and Now," *Commonwealth & Comparative Politics* 53, no. 1 (2015): 95–107.

Handler, Jerome S., and Matthew C. Reilly. "Contesting 'White Slavery' in the Caribbean," *New West Indian Guide* 91 (2017): 30–55.

Hogg, Donald W. "II. Documents: Statements of a Ras Tafari Leader," *Caribbean Studies* 6, no. 1 (1966): 37–38.

Hunting, P. "The Royal Society of Medicine," *Postgraduate Medical Journal* 81 (2005): 45–48.

Ilaloo, Sister. "Rastawoman as Equal," *Yard Roots* 1, no. 1 (1981): 5–7.

"International Bible Students' Association," *The Watch Tower* (April 2, 1910): 119–20.

Kandiyoti, Deniz. "Bargaining with Patriarchy," *Gender and Society* 2, no. 3 (1988): 274–90.

Kumar, Mukesh, and Rajani Kumari. "Indian Culture in Jamaica—Past and Present," *Proceedings of the Indian History Congress* 60 (1999): 1027–33.

Lake, Obiagele. "The Culturalization of African Female Pollution: Rastafari Adaptations," *Caribbean Quarterly Monograph* (2008): 150–71.

———. "The Many Voices of Rastafarian Women: Sexual Subordination in the Midst of Liberation," *New West Indian Guide* 68, nos. 3–4 (1994): 235–57.

Mathews, K. "Africa and Non-Alignment," *India Quarterly* 43, no. 1 (1987): 40–51.

McCaw-Binns, Affette, and C. O. Moody. "The Development of Primary Health Care in Jamaica," *West Indian Medical Journal* 50, no. 4 (2001): 6–10.

Meeks, Brian. "Cuba from Due South: An Anglo-Caribbean Perspective," *Caribbean Quarterly* 58, no. 1 (2012): 87–98.

———. "Obscure Revolt, Profound Effects: The Henry Rebellion, Counter-Hegemony and Jamaican Society," *Small Axe* 2 (1997): 39–62.

Munasinghe, Viranjini. "Theorizing World Culture through the New World: East Indians and Creolization," *American Ethnologist* 33, no. 4 (2006), 549–62.

Niaah, Jahlani A. H. "'I'd Rather See a Sermon than Hear One . . .': Africa/Heaven and Women of the Diaspora in Creating Global Futures and Transformation," *Africa Development* 41, no. 3 (2016): 1–24

Nicholson, Linda J. "'The Personal Is Political': An Analysis in Retrospect," *Social Theory and Practice* 7, no. 1 (1981): 85–98.

Padmore, George. "Hands Off the Colonies!" *New Leader* (February 25, 1938): 5.

Patterson, Orlando. "Rastafari: The Cult of Outcasts," *New Society* 12 (1964): 15–17.

Philips, John Edward. "African Smoking and Pipes," *Journal of African History* 24, no. 3 (1983): 303–19.

Pretorius, Stephan. "The Significance of the Use of Ganja as a Religious Ritual in the Rastafari Movement," *Verbum et Ecclesia* 27, no. 3 (2006): 1012–30.

Reddock, Rhoda. "Diversity, Difference and Caribbean Feminism: The Challenge of Anti-Racism," *Caribbean Review of Gender Studies* 1 (2007): 1–24.

Roulette, Casey J., and Barry S. Hewlett. "Patterns of Cannabis Use among Congo Basin Hunter-Gatherers," *Journal of Ethnography* 38, no. 4 (2018): 517–32.

Rowe, Maureen. "The Woman in Rastafari," *Caribbean Quarterly* 26, no. 4 (1980): 13–21.

Rutherford, Joseph Franklin. "Birth of the Nation," *The Watch Tower and Herald of Christ's Presence* (March 1, 1925): 67–74.

Schlesinger, Benjamin. "Family Patterns in Jamaica: Review and Commentary," *Journal of Marriage and Family* 30, no. 1 (1968): 136–48.

Semaj, Leachim. "Race and Identity and Children of the African Diaspora: Contributions of Rastafari," *Caribe* 4, no. 4 (1980): 14–18.

Silvera, Makeda. "An Open Letter to Rastafarian Sistren," *Fireweed* (Spring 1983): 115–20.

Smith, M. G. "Robotham's Ideology and Pluralism: A Reply," *Social and Economic Studies* 32, no. 2 (1983): 103-39.

———. "The Plural Framework of Jamaican Society," *British Journal of Sociology* 12, no. 3 (1961): 249-62.

Spitzer, Leo, and LaRay Denzer. "I.T.A. Wallace-Johnson and the West African Youth League," *International Journal of African Historical Studies* 6, no. 3 (1973): 413-52.

Stewart, Dianne M. "Womanist Theology in the Caribbean Context: Critiquing Culture, Rethinking Doctrine, and Expanding Boundaries," *Journal of Feminist Studies in Religion* 20, no. 1 (2004): 61-82.

Stubbs, Jean. "Political Idealism and Commodity Production: Cuban Tobacco in Jamaica, 1870-1930," *Cuban Studies* 25 (1995): 51-81.

Taylor, Ula Y. "'Negro Women Are Great Thinkers as well as Doers': Amy Jacques-Garvey and Community Feminism in the United States, 1924-1927," *Journal of Women's History* 12, no. 2 (2000): 104-26.

Thompson, E. P. "The Moral Economy of the English Crowd in the Eighteenth Century," *Past & Present* 50 (1971): 76-136.

Van Dijk, Frank Jan. "Sociological Means: Colonial Reactions to the Radicalization of the Rastafari in Jamaica, 1956-1959," *New West Indian Guide* 69 (1995): 67-101.

Watson, G. Llewellyn. "Patterns of Black Protest in Jamaica: The Case of the Ras-Tafarians," *Journal of Black Studies* 4, no. 3 (1974): 329-43.

Carole D. Yawney, "Review of *Women, Race and Class in a Cultural Context, Many Voices, One Chant—Black Feminist Perspectives*, and *Rastafari: Conversations Concerning Woman*," *Canadian Woman Studies* 7, nos. 1-2 (1984): 207-9.

Zeidenfelt, Alex. "Political and Constitutional Developments in Jamaica," *Journal of Politics* 14, no. 3 (1952): 512-40.

BOOKS

Accounts and Papers of the House of Commons, Colonies: Jamaica, Volume 51. London: House of Commons, 1866.

Afari, Yasus. *Overstanding Rastafari: "Jamaica's Gift to the World."* Kingston: Senya-Cum, 2007.

Aljoe, Nicole N. *Creole Testimonies: Slave Narratives from the British West Indies, 1709-1838.* New York: Palgrave Macmillan, 2011.

Alleyne, Mervyn C. *The Construction and Representation of Race and Ethnicity in the Caribbean and the World.* Kingston: University of the West Indies Press, 2002.

Barrett, Leonard E. *The Rastafarians.* Boston: Beacon Press, 1997.

Beckles, Hilary McD. Centering Woman: *Gender Discourses in Caribbean Slave Society.* Kingston: Ian Randle, 1998.

——. *Natural Rebels: A Social History of Enslaved Women in Barbados.* New Brunswick, NJ: Rutgers University Press, 1989.

Bedasse, Monique A. *Jah Kingdom: Rastafarians, Tanzania, and Pan-Africanism in the Age of Decolonization.* Chapel Hill: University of North Carolina Press, 2017.

Bell, Beverly. *Walking on Fire: Haitian Women's Stories of Survival and Resistance.* Ithaca, NY: Cornell University Press, 2013.

Blake-Hannah, Barbara Makeda. *Rastafari: The New Creation.* Kingston: Jamaica Media Productions, 2011.

Bogues, Anthony. *Black Heretics, Black Prophets: Radical Political Intellectuals.* New York: Routledge, 2003.

Bolland, O. Nigel. *The Politics of Labour in the British Caribbean: The Social Origins of Authoritarianism and Democracy in the Labour Movement.* Kingston: Ian Randle/ Oxford: James Currey/ Princeton: Markus Wiener Publishers, 2001.

Bonacci, Giulia. *Exodus!: Heirs and Pioneers, Rastafari Return to Ethiopia.* Kingston: University of the West Indies Press, 2015.

Brathwaite, Edward [Kamau]. *The Development of Creole Society in Jamaica.* London: Oxford University Press, 1971.

Bush, Barbara. Slave Women in Caribbean Society, *1650–1838.* Bloomington: University of Indiana Press, 1990.

Camp, Stephanie M. H. *Closer to Freedom: Enslaved Women and Everyday Resistance in the Plantation South.* Chapel Hill: University of North Carolina Press, 2004.

Campbell, Horace. *Rasta and Resistance: From Marcus Garvey to Walter Rodney.* Trenton, NJ: Africa World Press, 1994.

Carney, Judith, and Richard N. Rosomoff. *In the Shadow of Slavery: Africa's Botanical Legacy in the Atlantic World.* Berkeley: University of California Press, 2009.

Chevannes, Barry. *Rastafari: Roots and Ideology.* New York: Syracuse University Press, 1994.

Christensen, Jeanne. *Rastafari Reasoning and the RastaWoman: Gender*

Constructions in the Shaping of Rastafari Livity. Lanham, MD: Lexington Books, 2014.

Clarke, Peter Bernard. *Black Paradise: The Rastafarian Movement.* San Bernardino, CA: The Bargo Press, 1994.

Commissiong, John W. *Ganja (Marihuana).* Kingston: Cultural Studies Initiative and Caribbean Quarterly, University of the West Indies, 1997.

Cudd, Anne E. *Analyzing Oppression.* Oxford: Oxford University Press, 2006.

Cundall, Frank. *Jamaica in 1922.* Kingston: Institute of Jamaica, 1922.

Dayfoot, Arthur Charles. *The Shaping of the West Indian Church, 1492–1962.* Gainesville: University Press of Florida, 1999.

Dodd, Kathlyn, ed. *A Sylvia Pankhurst Reader.* Manchester: Manchester University Press, 1993.

Dunkley, D. A. *Agency of the Enslaved: Jamaica and the Culture of Freedom in the Atlantic World.* Lanham, MD: Lexington Books, 2013.

Dunn, Richard S. *Sugar and Slaves: The Rise of the Planter Class in the English West Indies, 1624–1713.* Chapel Hill: University of North Carolina Press / Kingston: The University of the West Indies Press, 1972.

Edmonds, Ennis B. *Rastafari: A Very Short Introduction.* New York: Oxford University Press, 2012.

———. *Rastafari: From Outcasts to Culture Bearers.* New York: Oxford University Press, 2003.

Erskine, Noel Leo. *From Garvey to Marley: Rastafari Theology.* Gainesville: University Press of Florida, 2004.

Evans, Sarah. *Personal Politics: The Roots of Women's Liberation in the Civil Rights Movement and the New Left.* New York: Vintage Books, 1979.

Ferrer, Ada. *Insurgent Cuba: Race, Nation, and Revolution, 1868–1898.* Chapel Hill: University of North Carolina Press, 1999.

Forsythe, Dennis. *Rastafari: For the Healing of the Nations.* New York: One Drop Book, 1999.

———. *The Law Against Ganja in Jamaica.* Kingston: Zaika Publications, 1993.

Francis, O. C. *The People of Modern Jamaica.* Kingston: Department of Statistics, Jamaica, 1963.

Gilligan, Carol. *In a Different Voice: Psychological Theory and Women's Development.* Cambridge, MA: Harvard University Press, 1993.

Gómez, Pablo F. *The Experiential Caribbean: Creating Knowledge and Healing in the Early Modern Atlantic.* Chapel Hill: University of North Carolina Press, 2017.

Government of Jamaica. *Census of Population and Housing—Jamaica.* Kingston: Statistical Institute of Jamaica, 2011.

———. *Eighth Census of Jamaica and Its Dependencies, 1943: Population, Housing and Agriculture*. Kingston: Central Bureau of Statistics, formerly Census Office, 1945.

Hansing, Katrin. *Rasta, Race and Revolution: The Emergence and Development of the Rastafari Movement in Socialist Cuba*. Berlin: Lit Verlag, 2006.

Hart, Richard. *Labour Rebellions of the 1930s in the British Caribbean Region Colonies*. London: Caribbean Labour Solidarity and the Socialist History Society, 2002.

Haughton, Suzette A. *Drugged Out: Globalization and Jamaica's Resilience to Drug Trafficking*. Lanham, MD: University Press of America, 2011.

Hill, Robert A. *Dread History: Leonard P. Howell and Millenarian Visions in the Early Rastafarian Religion in Jamaica*. Kingston and Chicago: Frontline Distribution International, 2001.

Hooker, James R. *Black Revolutionary; George Padmore's Path from Communism to Pan-Africanism*. New York: Praeger, 1967.

Howe, Stephen. *Afrocentrism: Mythical Pasts and Imagined Homes*. London: Verso, 1998.

Howell, Leonard P. *The Promised Key*. Kingston: Headstart Books and Craft/ Frontline Distribution Int., 1995 [Orig.1935].

Kidd, Colin. *The Forging of Races: Race and Scripture in the Protestant Atlantic World, 1600–2000*. Cambridge: Cambridge University Press, 2006.

Lacey, Terry. *Violence and Politics in Jamaica, 1960–1970: Internal Security in a Developing Country*. Manchester: Manchester University Press, 1977.

Lake, Obiagele. *Rastafarl Women: Subordination in the Midst of Liberation Theology*. Durham, NC: Carolina Academic Press, 1998.

Lawless, Elaine J. *Holy Women, Wholly Women: Sharing Ministries of Wholeness Through Life Stories and Reciprocal Ethnography*. Eugene, OR: Wipf and Stock Publishers, 1993.

Lee, Hélène. *The First Rasta: Leonard Howell and the Rise of Rastafarianism*, translated by Lily Davis. Chicago: Lawrence Hill Books, 2003.

Lewin, Olive. *Rock It Come Over: The Folk Music of Jamaica*. Kingston: University of the West Indies Press, 2000.

Lewis, Rupert Charles. *Walter Rodney: 1968 Revisited*. Kingston: Canoe Press, University of the West Indies, 1998.

———. *Walter Rodney's Intellectual and Political Thought*. Kingston: University of the West Indies Press / Detroit: Wayne State University Press, 1998.

Machado Tobacco Company Ltd. *The Machado Story: A Pioneer Industry in*

Jamaica, 1874–1962. Kingston: B. & J. B. Machado Tobacco Company Ltd., 1962.

Mack, Douglas. *From Babylon to Rastafari: Origin and History of the Rastafarian Movement*. Kingston: Frontline Distribution International, 1999.

Mahmood, Saba. *Politics of Piety: The Islamic Revival and the Feminist Subject*. Princeton, NJ: Princeton University Press, 2005.

Marsala, Vincent John. *Sir John Peter Grant, Governor of Jamaica, 1866–1874*. Kingston: Institute of Jamaica, 1972.

Mathurin-Mair, Lucille. *A Historical Study of Women in Jamaica, 1655–1844*. Edited by Hilary McD. Beckles and Verene A. Shepherd. Kingston: University of the West Indies Press, 2006.

McPherson, E. S. P. *Honoring Our Original Ancestors: A Royal Ethiopic Salute to 'The Gong'/The Howellites. An Introduction to Kulungu . . . Vols. 1–4*. Ethio-Rastaology Audio Series no. 1, May 1995.

Moore, Bryan L., and Michelle A. Johnson. *"They do as they please": The Jamaican Struggle for Cultural Freedom after Morant Bay*. Kingston: University of the West Indies Press, 2011.

Murrell, Nathaniel Samuel. *Afro-Caribbean Religions: An Introduction to Their Historical, Cultural, and Scared Traditions*. Philadelphia, PA: Temple University Press, 2010.

Nettleford, Rex M. *Caribbean Cultural Identity: The Case of Jamaica, An Essay in Cultural Dynamics*. Kingston: Institute of Jamaica, 1978.

———. *Mirror, Mirror: Identity, Race and Protest in Jamaica*. Kingston: LMH Publishing Ltd., 2001.

New King James Version of the Bible, 1987 printing.

Owens, Joseph. *Dread: The Rastafarians of Jamaica*. Kingston: Sangster, 1976.

Palmer, Colin A. *Eric Williams and the Making of the Modern Caribbean*. Chapel Hill: University of North Carolina Press, 2006.

Petley, Christer. *White Fury: A Jamaican Slaveholder and the Age of Revolution*. Oxford: Oxford University Press, 2018.

Perry, Kennetta Hammond. *London Is the Place for Me: Black Britons, Citizenship, and the Politics of Race*. Oxford: Oxford University Press, 2015.

Peterson, Frank Loris. *The Hope of the Race*. Nashville, TN: Southern Publishing Association, 1934.

Pettersburgh, Fitz Balintine. *The Royal Parchment Scroll of Black Supremacy*. Kingston: Frontline Books and Miguel Lorne Publishers, 2003 [orig.1926].

Pollard, Velma. *Dread Talk: The Language of Rastafari*. Kingston: Canoe

Press, 2000.

Pradel, Lucie. *African Beliefs in the New World: Popular Literary Traditions of the Caribbean*. Trenton, NJ: Africa World Press, 2000.

Price, Charles. *Becoming Rasta: Origins of Rastafari Identity in Jamaica*. New York: New York University Press, 2009.

Ransby, Barbara. *Ella Baker and the Black Freedom Movement: A Radical Democratic Vision*. Chapel Hill: University of North Carolina Press, 2003.

Report of the Indian Hemp Drugs Commission, 1893–94, vol. IV. Simla: Government Central Printing Office, 1894.

Rodney, Walter. *How Europe Underdeveloped Africa*. London: Bogle-L'Ouverture Publications; Dar-es-Salaam: Tanzanian Publishing House, 1973.

Rubin, Vera, and Lambros Comitas. *Ganja in Jamaica: The Effects of Marijuana Use*. Garden City, NY: Anchor, 1976.

Shepherd, Verene A. *Maharani's Misery: Narratives of a Passage from India to the Caribbean*. Kingston: University of the West Indies Press, 2002.

———. *Women in Caribbean History*. Kingston: Ian Randle, 2012.

Schiebinger, Londa. *Secret Cures of Slaves: People, Plants, and Medicine in the Eighteenth-Century Atlantic World*. Stanford, CA: Stanford University Press, 2017.

Smith, M. G., Roy Augier, and Rex Nettleford. *Report on the Ras Tafari Movement in Kingston, Jamaica*. Kingston: Institute of Social and Economic Research, University College of the West Indies, 1960.

Spencer, Robyn C. *The Revolution Has Come: Black Power, Gender, and the Black Panther Party in Oakland*. Durham, NC: Duke University Press, 2016.

Spencer, William David. *Dread Jesus*. London: Society for Promoting Christian Knowledge, 1998.

Sautter, Cia. *The Merriam Tradition: Teaching Embodied Torah*. Urbana: University of Illinois Press, 2010.

Scott, James C. *Weapons of the Weak: Everyday Forms of Peasant Resistance*. New Haven, CT: Yale University Press, 1985.

Stephens, Evelyne Huber, and John D. Stephens. *Democratic Socialism in Jamaica: The Political Movement and Social Transformation in Dependent Capitalism*. Princeton, NJ: Princeton University Press, 1986.

Taylor, Ula Y. *The Promise of Patriarchy: Women and the Nation of Islam*. Chapel Hill: University of North Carolina Press, 2017.

———. *The Veiled Garvey: The Life and Times of Amy Jacques Garvey*. Chapel Hill: University of North Carolina Press, 2002.

Turner, Sasha. *Contested Bodies: Pregnancy, Childrearing, and Slavery in*

Jamaica. Philadelphia: University of Pennsylvania Press, 2017.

Van Dijk, Frank Jan. *Jahmaica: Rastafari and Jamaican Society*. Utrecht: ISOR, 1993.

Vaughan, Alden T. *Roots of American Racism: Essays on the Colonial Experience*. New York: Oxford University Press, 1995.

Walker, Alice. *In Search of Our Mothers' Gardens: Womanist Prose*. New York: Harcourt Brace Jovanovich, 1983.

Waters, Anita. *Race, Class, and Political Symbols: Rastafari and Reggae in Jamaican Politics*. New Brunswick, NJ: Transaction Books, 1985.

White, Deborah Gray. Aren't I a Woman? Female Slaves in the Plantation South. New York: W. W. Norton & Company, 1999.

Williams, Eric. *Capitalism and Slavery*. Chapel Hill: University of North Carolina Press, 1944.

Wingerden, Sophia A. van. *The Women's Suffrage Movement in Britain, 1866–1928*. Houndmills: Palgrave Macmillan, 1999.

Yuajah, Empress. *How to Become a Rasta: Rastafari, Rasta Beliefs, Rastafarian Culture*. North Charleston: CreateSpace Independent Publishing Platform, 2012.

———. *Life as a Rasta Woman: 20 Rules & Principles for Living as a Rastafari Empress*. North Charleston: CreateSpace Independent Publishing Platform, 2015.

———. *Rasta Way of Life: Rastafari Livity Book*. North Charleston: CreateSpace Publishing Company, 2014.

CHAPTERS AND ESSAYS

Bilby, Kenneth. "The Holy Herb: Notes on the Background of Cannabis in Jamaica." In *Rastafari*, edited by Rex Nettleford and Veronica Salter, 135–51. Kingston: Caribbean Quarterly, 2008.

Cannon, Katie Geneva. "The Emergence of Black Feminist Consciousness." In *Feminist Interpretation of the Bible*, edited by Letty M. Russell, 30–40. Philadelphia: Westminster Press, 1985.

Chevannes, Barry. "The Repairer of the Breach: Reverend Claudius Henry and Jamaican Society." In *Ethnicity in the Americas*, edited by Frances Henry, 263–90. The Hague: Mouton, 1976.

Dance, Daryl Cumber. "Black Eve or Madonna? A Study of the Antithetical Views of the Mother in Black American Literature." In *Sturdy Black Bridges: Visions of Black Women in Literature*, edited by Roseann P. Bell,

Bettye J. Parker, and Beverly Guy-Sheftall, 123–32. Garden City, NY: Anchor Press/Doubleday, 1979.

Du Toit, Brian M. "Dagga: The History and Ethnographic Setting of Cannabis." In *Cannabis and Culture*, edited by Vera Rubin, 81–116. The Hague: Mouton Publishers, 1975.

Dunkley, D. A. "Cudjoe (c. 1690–1744)." In *Dictionary of Caribbean and Afro-Latin American Biography*, vol. 1, edited by Franklin W. Wright and Henry Louis Gates Jr., 265–67. Oxford: Oxford University Press, 2016.

Duvall, Chris S. "Cannabis and Tobacco in Precolonial and Colonial Africa." In *Oxford Research Encyclopedia of African History*, edited by Thomas Spear, 1–38. Oxford: University of Oxford Press, 2018.

Ford-Smith, Honor. "Women and the Garvey Movement in Jamaica." In *Garvey: His Work and Impact*, edited by Rupert Lewis and Patrick Bryan, 73–83. Trenton, NJ: Africa World Press, 1994.

Grant, Jacquelyn. "Black Theology and the Black Woman." In *The Black Studies Reader*, edited by Jacqueline Bobo, Cynthia Hudley, and Claudine Michel, 421–34. New York: Routledge, 2004.

Hepner, Tricia Redeker, and Randal L. Hepner. "Gender, Community, and Change among the Rastafari of New York City." In *New York Glory: Religions in the City*, edited by Tony Carnes and Anna Karpathakis, 333–54. New York: New York University Press, 2001.

Higman, B. W. "Population and Labor in the British Caribbean in the Early Nineteenth Century." In *Long-term Factors in American Economic Growth, Studies in Income and Wealth*, vol. 51, edited by Stanley L. Engerman and Robert E. Gallman, 605–39. Chicago: University of Chicago Press, 1986.

Homiak, John [Jake] P. "Dub History: Soundings on Rastafari Livity and Language." In *Rastafari and Other African-Caribbean Worldviews*, edited by Barry Chevannes, 127–81. New Brunswick, NJ: Rutgers University Press, 1998.

Hutton, Clinton A. "Leonard Howell Announcing God: The Conditions That Gave Birth to Rastafari in Jamaica." In *Leonard Percival Howell and the Genesis of Rastafari*, edited by Clinton A. Hutton, Michael A. Barnett, D. A. Dunkley, and Jahlani A. H. Niaah, 9–52. Kingston: University of the West Indies Press, 2015.

Kelley, Robin D. G. "How the West Was One: On the Uses and Limitations of Diaspora." In *The Black Studies Reader*, edited by Jacqueline Bobo, Cynthia Hudley, and Claudine Michel, 41–46. New York: Routledge, 2004.

Mair, Lucille. "Recollections of a Journey into a Rebel Past." In *Caribbean

Women Writers: Essays from the First International Conference, edited by Selwyn R. Cudjoe, 51–60.Wellesley, MA: Calaloux Publications, 1990.

Mansingh, Ajai, and Laxmi Mansingh. "Hindu Influences on Rastafarianism." In *Rastafari*, edited by Rex Nettleford and Veronica Salter, 105–33. Kingston: Caribbean Quarterly, 2008.

Martin, Tony. "Women in the Garvey Movement." In *Garvey: His Work and Impact*, edited by Rupert Lewis and Patrick Bryan, 67–72. Trenton, NJ: Africa World Press, 1994.

Matthews, Tracye A. "'No One Ever Asks What a Man's Role in the Revolution Is': Gender Politics and Leadership in the Black Panther Party, 1966–71." In *Sisters in the Struggle: African American Women in the Civil Rights-Black Power Movement*, edited by Bettye Collier-Thomas and V. P. Franklin, 230–56. New York: New York University Press, 2001.

Niaah, Jahlani, and Ijahnya Christian. "Introduction: What Is Rastafari." In *Rastafari: A National Museum Jamaica Exhibition*, edited by Jonathan Greenland, 14–61. Kingston: Institute of Jamaica, 2013.

Post, Ken. "The Bible as Ideology: Ethiopianism in Jamaica, 1930–38." In *African Perspectives: Papers in the History, Politics and Economics of Africa Presented to Thomas Hodgkin*, edited by Christopher Allen and R. W. Johnson, 185–207. London: Cambridge University Press, 1970.

Robertson, James. "'That Vagabond George Stewart of England': Leonard Howell's Seditious Sermons, 1933–1941." In *Leonard Percival Howell and the Genesis of Rastafari*, edited by Clinton A. Hutton, Michael A. Barnett, D. A. Dunkley, and Jahlani A. H. Niaah, 69–106. Kingston: University of the West Indies Press, 2015.

Smith, Raymond T. "The Family in the Caribbean." In *Caribbean Studies: A Symposium*, edited by Vera Rubin, 67–75. Kingston: University College of the West Indies, 1957.

Tafari-Ama, Imani M. "Rastawoman as Rebel: Case Studies in Jamaica." In *Chanting Down Babylon: The Rastafari Reader*, edited by Nathaniel S. Murrell, William D. Spencer, and Adrian A. McFarlane, 89–106. Kingston: Ian Randle Publishers, 1998.

Van der Merwe, Nikolaas J. "Cannabis Smoking in 13th–14th Century Ethiopia: Chemical Evidence." In *Cannabis and Culture*, edited by Vera Rubin, 77–80. The Hague: Mouton Publishers, 1975.

Williams, Delores S. "Womanist Theology: Black Women's Voices." In *The Womanist Reader*, edited by Layli Phillips, 117–25. New York: Routledge, 2006.

Winslow, Barbara. "The First White Rastafarian: Sylvia Pankhurst, Haile

Selassie, and Ethiopia." In *At Home and Abroad in the Empire: British Women Write the 1930s*, edited by Robin Hackett, Freda Hauser, and Gay Wachman, 171–86. Newark: University of Delaware Press, 2009.

Yawney, Carole D. "To Grow a Daughter: Cultural Liberation and the Dynamics of Oppression in Jamaica." In *Feminism: From Pressure to Politics*, edited by A. Miller and G. Finn, 119–44. Montreal: Black Rose Books, 1983.

INTERNET SOURCES

Altink, Henrice. "'Marrying Light': Skin Colour, Gender and Marriage in Jamaica, c. 1918–1980." *The History of the Family* (2019): 1–21. https://doi.org/10.1080/1081602X.2019.1582433.

Bishton, Derek. "Meeting Joseph Nathaniel Hibbert, July 23, 1983," March 11, 2013. https://derekbishton.wordpress.com/2013/03/11/meeting-joseph-nathaniel-hibbert-july-23-1983/.

Chevannes, Barry, et al. "A Report of the National Commission on Ganja." Office of the Prime Minister of Jamaica, Kingston, August 7, 2001. http://addictionstudies.dec.uwi.edu/Documents/generic%20drug%20information/.

"EarthLight Ises to Queen Mother of the Rastafari Movement Tenet Bent Howell." March 7, 2015. http://lphfoundation.org/earthlight-ises-to-queen-mother-of-the-rastafari-movement-tenet-bent-howell/.

Government of Jamaica. "Judicature (Resident Magistrates) Act." February 22, 1928. GJ LN146/1999. http://moj.gov.jm/sites/default/files/laws/The%20Judicature%20%28Resident%20Magistrates%29%20Act.pdf.

"Hampton School." Jamaica National Heritage Trust, 2011. http://www.jnht.com/site_hampton_school.php.

"Jamaica's First Treason/Felony Trial Featuring the Rev. Claudius Henry." *Jamaica Observer*, December 10, 2014. http://www.jamaicaobserver.com/news/Jamaica-s-first-treason-felony-trial-featuring-the-Rev-Claudius-Henry_15610651.

Miller, Dionne Jackson. "Jamaican Marijuana Reform, Rastas and Rights." *OxHRH Blog*, March 18, 2015. http://humanrights.dev3.oneltd.eu/jamaican-marijuana-reform-rastas-and-rights/.

New York Academy of Medicine. *The La Guardia Committee Report: The Marijuana Problem in the City of New York*. New York: Mayor's Committee on Marihuana, City of New York, 1944. http://www.druglibrary.org/schaffer/library/studies/lag/lagmenu.htm.

"New York Smokers Get Bolder." *The O'Shaughnessy's Reader Online*,

2015–16. http://www.beyondthc.com/new-york-smokers-get-bolder/.

"The 1912 Hague International Opium Convention." *United Nations Office on Drugs and Crime*, 2008. https://www.unodc.org/unodc/en/frontpage/the-1912-hague-international-opium-convention.html.

O'Gilvie, Diana. "Tug of War: Traditional Rastafarian Women in Modern Jamaican Society." *Griots Republic*, February 6, 2018. http://www.griotsrepublic.com/tug-war-traditional-rastafarian-women-modern-jamaican-society/.

Paton, Diana. "Enslaved Women and Slavery Before and After 1807." *History in Focus*, Issue 12: Slavery (Spring 2007). https://www.history.ac.uk/ihr/Focus/Slavery/articles/paton.html.

"Popular Rastafarian Words and Phrases." *Jamaican Patwah: Patois and Slang Dictionary*, 2014. http://jamaicanpatwah.com/b/popular-rastafarian-words-and-phrases#.W1Tv1y2ZPUo.

"Purchasing Power of British Pounds from 1270 to Present." *MeasuringWorth*, 2020. www.measuringworth.com/ppoweruk/.

"Rastafari." *International Encyclopedia of the Social Sciences*, 2008. http://www.encyclopedia.com/doc/1G2-3045302184.html.

"Rastafari Millennium Council Press Release on Pinnacle," February 14, 2014. https://www.facebook.com/notes/wesley-priest-kelly/rastafari-millennium-council-press-release-on-pinnacle/10151891189430598/.

"Read Across Jamaica at Mayfield All Age." *Jamaica Observer*, June 5, 2017. http://www.jamaicaobserver.com/news/read-across-jamaica-at-mayfield-all-age_100895.

Sheller, Mimi. "Quasheba, Mother, Queen: Black Women's Public Leadership and Political Protest in Postemancipation Jamaica." Published by the Department of Sociology, Lancaster University, Lancaster, UK, 2003. http://www.comp.lancs.ac.uk/sociology/papers/Sheller-Quasheba-Mother-Queen.pdf.

Smart, Carol. "Divorce in England 1950–2000: A Moral Tale." CAVA Workshop Paper 2. Prepared for Workshop One: Frameworks for Understanding Policy Change and Culture. Leeds University, October 29, 1999. https://www.leeds.ac.uk/cava/papers/wsp2.pdf.

"Sought-After Primary Schools Top Grade 4 Literacy, Numeracy." *Jamaica Observer*, January 14, 2018. http://www.jamaicaobserver.com/career-education/sought-after-primary-schools_122274?profile=1270.

Steckles, Garry, Mark Meredith, and Nazma Muller. "The World of Rastafari." *Caribbean Beat Magazine* 31 (1998). MEP Publishers. http://caribbean-beat.com/issue-31/world-rastafari#axzz4u71DTJpf.

Torres-Bennett, Aileen. "Jamaica Mulls Legal Pot." *USA Today*, June 9, 2014.

https://www.usatoday.com/story/travel/destinations/2014/06/08/
jamaica-marijuana-ganja/9992405/.

Walters, Basil. "The Story of the Rasta Woman." *Jamaica Observer*, March 19,
2012. http://www.jamaicaobserver.com/news/The-story-of-the-
Rasta-woman_10997495.

Wells, Walter. "History of the Ethiopian Zion Coptic Church." *Ethiopian Zion
Coptic Church*, 2017. http://www.ethiopianzioncopticchurch.org/Home/
History.

Wu, Jiachuan, and Daniella Silva. "Map: See the States Where Marijuana Is
Legal." *NBC News*, November 4, 2020. https://www.nbcnews.com/news/
us-news/map-see-if-marijuana-legal-your-state-n938426.

INTERVIEWS

Campbell, Gertrude. Interviewed by Jahlani Niaah and Ishmahil Blagrove for
"Roaring Lion, The Rise of Rastafari: A Documentary." Kingston: Frontline Productions; and Brampton, Ontario: Knowledge Bookstore, 2001.

Downer, Gerald Lloyd. Interviewed by author, Tredegar Park, St. Catherine,
Jamaica, August 24, 2011.

Dunkley, Henry Archibald. Interviewed by Robert Hill, Kingston, Jamaica,
1976. Published as Robert Hill and Boris Lutanie, "Le Troi-sième Homme:
Interview de Henry Archibald Dunkley, par Robert Hill (1976)." *Reggae
Vibes* 22 (2012): 68–73.

Fong, Geraldine E. Personal communication to author, October 14, 2014.

Gallimore, Alphonso. Interviewed by author, Tredegar Park, St. Catherine,
Jamaica, April 24, 2011.

Hall, Burnett. Interviewed by author, Green Bottom, Sandy Bay, Clarendon,
Jamaica, December 16, 2017.

Haughton, Stanley. Interviewed by author, Green Bottom, Clarendon, Jamaica,
December 16, 2017.

Hill, Robert A., and Annie Paul. "Our Man in Mona: A Conversation
between Robert A. Hill and Annie Paul," September 27, 2013.
https://anniepaul.net/our-man-in-mona-an-interview-by-robert-a-hill-
with-annie-paul/.

Homiak, Jake. Interviewed by author, Smithsonian Institution, Suitland,
Maryland, June 23, 2015.

Howell, Montinol A. Personal communication to author, February 13, 2020.

——. Personal communication to author, June 9, 2018.

——. Personal communication to author, November 27, 2013.

Howell, William "Bill." Interviewed by Hélène Lee, May 1998.

———. Personal communication to author, June 14, 2013.

Lee, Hélène. Personal communication to author, January 4, 2021.

Lennox, Merriam. Interviewed by Renee Romano and Elliott Leib, Old Harbour, St. Catherine, Jamaica, 1983.

Lewis, Audrey Elizabeth. Interviewed by author, Salt River, Clarendon, Jamaica, May 5, 2013.

McKay, Douglas. Interviewed by author, Green Bottom, Clarendon, Jamaica, December 16, 2017.

McLean, Yvonne. Interviewed by author, Miami, Florida, July 28, 2018.

Reid, Jonathan. Interviewed by author, Green Bottom, Clarendon, Jamaica, December 16, 2017.

Romano, Renee, and Elliott Leib. "Rastafari: Conversations Concerning Woman." Filmed in Jamaica, Eye In I Filmworks. New Haven, CT: 1983.

———. "Rastafari Voices." Filmed in Jamaica, Eye In I Filmworks. New Haven, CT: 1979.

Stewart, Florence. Interviewed by author, Pinnacle and Tredegar Park, St. Catherine, Jamaica, July 19, 2016.

Stewart, Florence, and Delrieta Simpson. Interviewed by author, Tredegar Park, St. Catherine, Jamaica, August 24, 2011.

Swaby, Canute. Interviewed by author and Yvonne McLean, Tredegar Park, St. Catherine, Jamaica, October 22, 2015.

Sweeney, Paulette. Interviewed in "Omega Rising: Woman of Rastafari." Filmed in Jamaica and Britain. Directed by D. Elmina Davis and produced by Imruh Bakari for Ceddo Film and Video Workshop. London: 1988.

Thompson, Besentie. Interviewed by author, Green Bottom, Clarendon, Jamaica, December 16, 2017.

LECTURES, PAMPHLETS, AND THESES

Burke, Tarana. "Black History Month Keynote Lecture." Tate Hall, University of Missouri, Columbia, February 20, 2018.

Certificate of Membership. The Lepers Government. African Reform Church, March 2, 1959.

Edwards, Prince Emmanuel. "Love in Black Supremacy Internationally Through all Human Rights in Rightousness [sic] of Salvation." Rastafari Movement Pamphlet. University of the West Indies Library. Kingston: Publisher Unknown, 1979.

Henry, Claudius V. "The New Creation International Peacemaker's Association: Violence in Jamaica." Kemps Hill District, International Peacemakers Association, Jamaica, April 28, 1969.

Montlouis, Nathalie. "Lords and Empresses in and out of Babylon: The EABIC Community and the Dialectic of Female Subordination." PhD diss., Department of the Languages and Cultures of Africa, School of Oriental and African Studies, University of London, 2013.

Planno, Brother Mortimo Togo Desta. "Maniaphopia of the Invisible Establishment." Unpublished Lecture. Black Community Movement, York University, Toronto, November 1973.

Porter, Binghi Glen. "The Watch Lion Roars." Unpublished Communication, October 2015. Listserv.

Standing in the Gap with Unquestionable Truth. African Reform Church, International Peacemakers Association, Jamaica, May 11, 1959.

Standing in the Gap with Unquestionable Truth. Pioneering Israel Back Home to Africa. African Reform Church, International Peacemakers Association, Jamaica, March 25, 1959.

Tafari-Ama, Imani M. "An Historical Analysis of Grassroots Resistance in Jamaica: A Participatory Research on Gender Relations in Rastafari," MA thesis, Institute of Social Studies, The Hague, Netherlands, 1989.

Wirtenberger, Kathryn. "The Jesuits in Jamaica," MA thesis, Loyola University, Chicago, Illinois, December 1942.

MUSICAL RECORDINGS

Marley, Bob. "Kaya," from the album *Kaya.* Island Studios, London, 1978.

Marley, Rita. "One Draw," from the album *Harambe: Working Together for Freedom.* Shanachie Records, United States, 1982.

Tosh, Peter. "Legalize It," from the album *Legalize It.* Treasure Isle and Randy's, Kingston, 1976.

NEWSPAPER ARTICLES

"11 Sentenced to Prison as Pinnacle Case Trial Opens." *Daily Gleaner.* June 12, 1954.

"110 Dead as Hurricane Hits South Coast." *Daily Gleaner.* August 26, 1951.

"Accused: No Subscription Was Taken from Members of the Church." *Daily Gleaner.* October 22, 1960.

"Appearance of Armed Policemen Caused Dungle Squatters to Flee." *Daily*

Gleaner. February 24, 1939.

"Back to Africa Petition Presented at King's House." *Daily Gleaner*. September 21, 1948.

Bailey, Amy. "Our Women—Their Status." *Public Opinion*. December 28, 1940.

Bailey, F. E. "I Would Not Work for a Woman." *Daily* Gleaner. November 2, 1935.

"Canadian 'Undesirable' Here." *Daily Gleaner*. July 16, 1960.

Carradine, John. "The Ras Tafarites Retreat to Mountain Fastness of St. Catherine." *Daily Gleaner*. November 23, 1940.

"Chief Justice Denounces Howell as a Fraud." *Daily Gleaner*. March 17, 1934.

"Claudius Henry Tells the Court." *Daily Gleaner*. October 25, 1960.

"Council Shows Concern in Respect to Audit of the Colony's Accounts." *Daily Gleaner*. April 3, 1935.

"Cultist Sent to Prison for Assaulting Policeman." *Daily Gleaner*. January 19, 1953.

"Current Items." *Daily Gleaner*. February 26, 1970.

"Dangerous Cults." *Daily Gleaner*. January 19, 1937.

"Daniel of Ras Tafari Cult is Put in New Den." *Daily Gleaner*. July 25, 1934.

DeLeon, Beryl. "Are We Rearing Trained Seals in Our Schools and Homes?" *Daily Gleaner*. November 2, 1935.

"Detained in Connection with Woman's Death." *Daily Gleaner*. December 24, 1943.

"Disturbances by Followers of the Ras Tafari Cult." *Daily Gleaner*. July 20, 1934.

Esserman, Rabbi Rachel. "Defrosting Judaism: A Look at the Ritualwell Web Site." *The Reporter*. September 1, 2006.

"Fooling the Masses." *Daily Gleaner*. August 6, 1934.

Frater, Adrian. "Rastas Remember Massacre: 1963 Coral Gardens Riot Brings Back Bitter Memories." *Daily Gleaner*. April 17, 2003.

"Ganja." *Daily Gleaner*. January 11, 1961.

"Ganja Smoking as a Danger to the Natives of This Colony." *Daily Gleaner*. June 10, 1913.

"Governor Puts Ban on Rastafari Meeting." *Daily Gleaner*. February 9, 1940.

"Harm Rastafari Advocates Are Doing in Eastern Parish." *Daily Gleaner*. May 23, 1935.

"Henry and 15 Committed." *Daily Gleaner*. May 11, 1960.

"Howell Remanded." *Daily Gleaner*, January 14, 1944.

"Is Ganja Really a Dangerous Drug?" *Sunday Gleaner*. November 16, 1958.

"Jamaican Proverbs You Should Know." *Daily Gleaner*. November 2, 1935.

"Jamaica's Great Ras Tafarite Kingdom Comes to an End." *Daily Gleaner*. October 14, 1945.

"Judge's Summing Up at Treason Felony Trial." *Daily Gleaner*. October 31, 1960.

Leevy, R. A. "Ras Tafarianism: Haile Selassie, Emperor of Abyssinia, Inspired a New Religion in Jamaica." *Public Opinion*. February 20, 1943.

"Leonard Howell Being Tried for Sedition in Saint Thomas." *Daily Gleaner*. March 14, 1934.

"Leonard Howell, on Trial says Ras Tafari is Messiah Returned to Earth." *Daily Gleaner*. March 15, 1934.

"Leonard Howell, Two Others Sent to Prison." *Daily Gleaner*. March 2, 1951.

"Letter to Castro in Court." *Daily Gleaner*. May 6, 1960.

"Letter to Castro Put in Evidence." *Daily Gleaner*. May 6, 1960.

"Man Gets Four Months for Ganja: Women Fined." *Daily Gleaner*. October 24, 1939.

"Menace." *Daily Gleaner*. January 11, 1947.

"Mr. Abendana Strongly Urges That Court of Appeal Be Not Set Up Now." *Daily Gleaner*. May 16, 1934.

"Mr. Edward Bent Dies at 79." *Daily Gleaner*. July 18, 1950.

Nembhard, Len. S. "Mrs. Howell Believes Only in One Man." *Jamaica Times*. July 19, 1941.

"News of the Ethiopian World Federation, Inc." *The Voice of Ethiopia*. December 31, 1938.

Peat, R. A. "Operation Rescue." *Daily Gleaner*. June 4, 1962.

"Pinnacle Case: 21 Guilty Pleas." *Daily Gleaner*. June 18, 1954.

"Pinnacle Case: Woman, 70, Among 32 More Sentenced." *Daily Gleaner*. June 17, 1954.

"Pinnacle Property Erstwhile Lair of Lost Men is Silent Now." *The Jamaica Times*. July 19, 1941.

"Pleas Taken Yesterday. Trial To Take Place Monday and Tuesday." *Daily Gleaner*. July 23, 1941.

"Police Hold Chief of Pinnacle Ras Tafarians." *Jamaica Times*. July 26, 1941.

"Police Raid Pinnacle Again." *Daily* Gleaner. May 25, 1954.

"'Ras Tafari' Disciple Found Guilty of Sedition." *Daily Gleaner*. March 16, 1934.

"Ras Tafari Movement Rose from the Dungle." *Daily Gleaner*. August 4, 1960.

"Ras Tafari Priest Gets Nine Months: Found Guilty of Slugging Man with Iron;

Appeals." *Daily Gleaner.* December 30, 1938.

"Reynold Henry, Gabbidon, Morgan, Jetter to Hang." *Daily Gleaner.* October 1, 1960.

"Robber Leaves Pearls Behind: Lucky Woman Still Has Jewellery Valued £100." *Daily Gleaner.* August 27, 1938, p. 23.

"Sentences of 3 to 10 Years on Treason Felony Accused." *Daily Gleaner.* October 31, 1960.

Silvera, Janet. "Cindy on Trial: Marley Relationship Goes Public." *Daily Gleaner.* February 20, 2014.

"Sixaola in Yesterday from New York with Mails and Passengers." *Daily Gleaner.* November 18, 1932.

"St. Thomas Wars on the Ras Tafari Cult." *Daily Gleaner.* January 18, 1937.

"The Women's Federation of the Baptists." *Daily Gleaner.* March 20, 1934.

"Three Freed in Pinnacle Camp Cases." *Daily Gleaner.* July 23, 1941.

"Treason Felony Trial." *Daily Gleaner.* October 25, 1960.

U.D.S. "Plight of Ras Tafarians At Camp Pinnacle in Saint Catherine." *Daily Gleaner.* December 22, 1940.

"Women's Work." *Daily Gleaner.* April 15, 1944.

INDEX